Gender and Entrepreneurship in Iran

Gender and Entrepreneurship in Iran

Microenterprise and the Informal Sector

Roksana Bahramitash

palgrave
macmillan

GENDER AND ENTREPRENEURSHIP IN IRAN

First published in 2013 by PALGRAVE MACMILLAN® in the United States—a division of St. Martin's Press LLC, 175 Fifth Avenue, New York, NY 10010.

Where this book is distributed in the UK, Europe and the rest of the world, this is by Palgrave Macmillan, a division of Macmillan Publishers Limited, registered in England, company number 785998, of Houndmills, Basingstoke, Hampshire RG21 6XS.

Palgrave Macmillan is the global academic imprint of the above companies and has companies and representatives throughout the world.

ISBN: 978-1-137-34286-7

Library of Congress Cataloging-in-Publication Data

Bahramitash, Roksana, 1956–
Gender and entrepreneurship in Iran : microenterprise and the informal sector / by Roksana Bahramitash.
pages cm
ISBN 978-1-137-34286-7 (alk. paper)
1. Self-employed women—Iran. 2. Women—Iran—Employment. 3. Informal sector (Economics)—Iran. 4. Small business—Iran. 5. Entrepreneurship—Iran. I. Title.

HD6072.6.I7B34 2013
331.40955—dc23 2013019244

A catalogue record of the book is available from the British Library.

Design by Scribe Inc.

First edition: October 2013

10 9 8 7 6 5 4 3 2 1

This book is dedicated to my dear brother, Mr. Ramin Bahramitash,
with my love and admiration for endurance.

Contents

Acknowledgments ix

Introduction: Tehran 1

1 The Other Women and the Other Economy 21

2 Gender, Micro-Entrepreneurship, and the Informal Economy 43

3 Women's Employment in Iran: Entering the Formal Sector 73

4 Low-Income Female Workers, Micro-Entrepreneurs, and the Informal Sector 101

5 Low-Income Male Workers and Micro-Entrepreneurs: Comparing the Male and Female Samples 149

Conclusion: Some Insight for Forward-Looking Initiatives 171

Appendix 189

Notes 197

References 203

Index 221

Acknowledgments

This project started in 2008, after I finished my two recent books on Iran: *Veiled Employment: Islamism and the Political Economy of Women's Employment in Iran* and *Gender in Contemporary Iran*. The idea for the book originated in fieldwork I carried out for my earlier books, when I saw that working mainly on the formal sector overlooks an important part of the story. And the value of firsthand data, especially on Iran, in my view, remains extremely critical to the field of sociology of development in the Middle East and North Africa (MENA) region.

The book has been a labor of love and has gone through several redrafts. As many of us who work on the MENA region and especially on Iran are aware, data on Iran become quickly outdated, and every single draft had to be updated. Even this current version ended up having data from before the recent round of sanctions with their massive crippling impact, the worst of which occurred in November 2012. It led to the devaluation of rials by nearly a quarter, though more recently some of its value has been regained.

One of my major challenges in writing this book has been the fact that literature on poverty, gender, and microenterprise in MENA is extremely lean, and I have had to spend a great deal of time trying to digest the rich literature on Latin America and South Asia in order to apply it to Iran.

In this rather difficult path I have been assisted by top academics such as Eric Hooglund, who read numerous redrafts and has been the strongest critic of the work but at the same time my greatest source of real support.

There have been other scholars, such as my colleagues Jennifer Olmsted and Hadi Salehi-Esfahani, and scholarly associations, such as the International Association for Feminist Economics (IAFFE), whose academic support has been indispensable. On the topic of Islam, my book has benefited from the support of a dear friend and a unique scholar, Patric Brodeur. His support has been truly important, as he has provided me with an intellectual home, and I have been affiliated with his Canada Research Chair at University of Montreal. Shahram

Nahidi has been another scholar whose immense knowledge on Iran has been very important. The book has benefited from Dr. Haleh Esfandiari's intellectual insight and support, and I wish to thank her as well.

There have been supportive research assistants; I wish to thank Ashleigh Delaye, who has been a highly responsible research assistant and onboard from the time this work started, and others—namely, Mojtaba Tabatabi in Montreal and Freshteh Farahani and Mehdi Meshkat (my male interviewer) in Iran.

But perhaps the most important support for this project has come from men and women in Iran, who were not paid for their interviews. For the most part, they cooperated out of the goodness of their hearts after I explained for what reason the data were being gathered, and some have insisted on keeping their names with their interviews. Their hope has been that the information they shared would help policy makers to bring better policies. In cases where the permission to disclose information was not granted, names have been changed.

Some of my friends and colleagues in Iran have provided a great deal of assistance: to name a few, Hossien Nori, Nahid Farasat, Shahla Kazemipour, Mostafa Azkia, and especially Greta Gregorian, who helped gather data and assisted with the indexing of the book.

On a different note, I wish to thank my friends Farkhondeh Aghani, Lynda Clark, Margaret Guest, Parvin Zarsav, and Forough Kafai. Various community centers in Montreal have provided space and opportunities to share my work at a community level; Zagros Cultural Center and MEKIK Gallery have been among them.

Last but not least, I wish to express my deep gratitude toward my wonderful children, Mahsana, Arash, Iman, and Atena Sadegh, who have been the pillars of my life and anchorage in an otherwise fairly chaotic working schedule. I thank my other family members in Canada, Mathieu Roy, Jean-Pierre Roy, and Andrèe Pelletier, who were wonderful to have around. In Iran, my cousin Zohreh Bahramast, my uncle Behzad Farrahi, and my mother Fatmeh Haghigh should be mentioned. I also wish to thank my brother, Ramin Bahramitash, to whom this book has been dedicated, for his love and support.

Introduction

Tehran

Spring 2008

It was a warm spring afternoon when two research assistants and I arrived at a focus group being held in the Molavi neighborhood of Tehran, close to Darvazeh Ghar. Molavi is a part of old Tehran, close to the main bazaar. It is a place with well established, if checkered, social networks, and since the time of the last shah (r. 1941–79), it has been a favorite haunt of drug traffickers and prostitutes. The neighborhood is dominated by migrants from Iranian Azerbaijan, who settled there as entire extended families or even several families from the same villages. They are proud of their heritage, and by living in the vicinity of kin and friends from Azerbaijan, they continue to maintain the strong ties of their premigration pasts. Women play a major role in maintaining these social networks—in fact, they have a vested interest in maintaining them. There are traditional sources of female power—a topic that will be discussed later in relation to female-sphere theory.

Our host received me with great hospitality and she was generous with her time. One of the more exceptional invitees was Fatimah, a woman in her early forties. Fatimah had never married, and she worked out of her house as a hairdresser, a skill that she learned through apprenticeship. She was the eldest daughter of a highly religious and traditional family. She kept her *hejab* on throughout the meeting even though we were all women. Fatimah had been working in the neighborhood since she was 15 years old and over time had become the sole income earner in the family. With her elderly parents ailing, Fatimah is the only breadwinner and has had to take responsibility for the care of her younger brothers and sister. She financed her brothers' weddings. She prepared her sister's *jahizieh*, the household furniture that each bride takes to her new home, the value of which depends on the wealth of her natal family. Fatimah's current responsibilities include making sure her siblings are handling their finances properly by helping them apply for mortgages and providing emergency loans in times of need.

Fatimah is not only the pillar of her family; she is also, according to the other women at the focus group, a major pillar of the community. Many female members of the community expressed their deepest respect for Fatimah for having turned her hair salon into a place where women could come together. Women in crisis with family or personal problems come to Fatimah's salon to find consolation and support. Fatimah's house is where a woman can flee from an abusive husband even late at night. Her house is not just a hair salon but also a shelter. Fatimah has also organized a whole array of community activities. She is in charge of group pilgrimages to Mashhad and Qom. Her reputation as a highly trustworthy, female community leader, despite her relatively young age, has helped many women to persuade their husbands to allow them to go on these pilgrimages. For those familiar with organized female pilgrimages in Iran, it is no secret that they are a great deal of fun, with a lot of shopping, festivities, and bonding away from the daily domestic chores. The women doubtlessly engage in many religious and spiritual activities, but they also exercise a great deal of freedom in an all-female space where they pray, sing, tell jokes, dance, or cry together, and above all build solidarity.

Fatimah, similar to many other women whom I met in my research, raises charity funds through her neighborhood network. These funds act as an emergency resource for members of the community in need; cases range from funds to enable young couples to marry to funds to help those who suddenly find themselves unemployed, injured, or ill. Fatimah's salon, similar to many other salons I observed (this includes both formal as well as informal salons), is a place where many women engage in a highly sophisticated network. These networks operate extremely efficiently and serve as gatekeepers of highly important economic functions. This simple research observation and focus group inspired my research for many years to come, part of which is included in this book.

One method of research was, as a participant-observer, to drop questions while pretending to be a single woman in need of a rental apartment. A simple question about rentals, irrespective of the neighborhood, would receive a huge response from those in attendance (although in lower-income neighborhoods women were far more engaged in these types of networks than in high- and middle-income neighborhoods). Research in low-income neighborhoods has been a joy, as women were very generous with their time. For example, their welcoming help, regardless of the neighborhood, when I said I was searching for a rental, operated through their powerful networks often by just going to a hairdressing salon. In some cases, the available rental would be in return for a monetary reward, while in other instances it simply would be found as women offering help to a fellow woman. These networks operated both as part of social safety nets and as part of an invisible, parallel, or shadow economy—effectively an informal economy run by women for women. This book is part of a larger project to shed light on this invisible economy that is spreading a massive social safety net among low-income women by way of mutual help and community development/sustainment.

****

The central aim of this book is to shed light on this invisible economy and to examine whether low-income women who operate in the informal sector as micro-entrepreneurs are in fact empowered (primarily monetarily) or, as the majority of the literature on the topic tends to suggest, are exploited. It has been difficult to write this book, because much of the written research on the topic primarily has been, and continues to be, done in South Asia, Latin America, and Africa (in the context of the developing world). It is indeed important to shed light on the intellectual lacuna of gender and the informal sector in Iran and to relate the topic to the literature in the field. One could argue that the topic is underresearched not just in the case of Iran but also in the Middle East and North Africa (MENA) region. To examine why the topic has become an academic blind spot, we need to overcome many degrees of separation. The first degree of separation feeds on the way discourses about economic development in Third World countries are born and articulated. The second degree of separation is the domination of mainstream economics and how development prescriptions are formulated and imposed by international development actors. Third is implicit and explicit Orientalism (to be elaborated in Chapter 1) and a tendency to overlook the Muslim world when it comes to issues related to economic development. Fourth are some of the shortcomings of how gender and development discourse have been formulated. The fifth degree of separation involves how one can actually examine the issue of gender among the low income without the distortion of academic bias of Western-educated researchers. And the last degree of separation involves how to overcome the challenges of carrying out fieldwork in Iran.

My use of six degrees of separation is not accidental but refers to an important empirical work on the structure of social networks by Michael Gurevich published in 1961. My book, as we shall see later, utilizes some of Gurevich's discussion of social network theories based on his research at Harvard University. His theory later became relevant for the notion of social capital, which also will be discussed later in this book. Interestingly, the theory initially argued, based on study results, that all people in the United Stated seemed to be connected by approximately three friendship links. Stanley Milgram later popularized the idea of links in an article published in *Psychology Today*. Milgram conducted an experiment that may be considered as the origin of the notion of six degrees: that everyone is separated from one another by only six other people (1967). This book will later discuss theories of social networks and social capital and their relationship to the social safety net and poverty alleviation.

This introductory chapter will deal with issues related to development and how it has been criticized as well as the implicit and explicit Orientalism of the discourse, especially with regard to the Muslim world. Other topics such as gender and development, as well as the problem of academic bias in Western-educated research, will be discussed. Following this theoretical background, Chapter 1 provides readers with contextualization for theories of social capital (social network), micro-entrepreneurship, and microcredit as they relate to gender. Chapter 2 examines gender and micro-entrepreneurship and the informal sector. It could be argued that an essential part of the book has been to bring to Iran specifically, and the broader MENA region generally, some of the theoretical discussion around the topic of gender and micro-entrepreneurship, which is very rich for other regions of the world. Chapter 3 focuses on women's employment in Iran. Chapters 4 and 5 are based on fieldwork and present the results of 180 interviews with men and women from low-income households in Tehran as well as material from my participant observation.

Mainstream Development Discourse and Its Critique

The concept of development can be traced to the rise of industrial society, itself a social transformation of unprecedented increases in productive capacity leading to urban migration, impoverishment, and unemployment (Polanyi 1957; Wallerstein 1974; Braudel 1975; Hobsbawm 1999; and Arrighi 2007). In the first phase of development theory, the topic is concerned with understanding the origins of capitalism, an upheaval that was painful for European societies and created momentous social disruption and chaos (Edelman and Haugerud 2005). On the one hand, it brought wealth, prosperity, and improved standards of living for the rich and powerful in European countries, who depended on the ideological underpinnings of the Enlightenment. The ideas of the Enlightenment itself were found only among academics and a small minority of the elite educated intellectuals in the eighteenth and nineteenth centuries. Furthermore, Orientalism glorified the heritage of the West to justify colonialism. On the other hand, in Europe by the nineteenth century the situation of the masses was deplorable, and it led to more than 25 million poor Europeans immigrating to North America between 1880 and 1914. This mass migration was very important socially, for it reduced surplus cheap labor and finally empowered workers through unions in Western Europe. It also led to the intellectual countermovement of Marxism, an ideology drawn from the same principles of the Enlightenment.

The origins of today's development literature are rooted in the history of intellectual thought in Britain, France, Holland, and other European countries. It began as an attempt to increase productivity in the colonies to levels prevailing in Europe as the ability to keep colonies became more difficult in the early twentieth century. Although the terms *developed* and *underdeveloped* were coined before the Second World War, it was in 1944 with the establishment of the Bretton Woods institutions[1] that the modern "Three Worlds" era began. Postwar development was no longer a European colonial domination crisis, but an American concern. It was President Harry Truman in his 1949 inaugural speech that announced that his mission, as the most powerful man in the most powerful nation, was to bring growth and improved standards of living to "underdeveloped areas." The issue of newly decolonized countries and their economic fate became central to American and Western European policy. As the Cold War unfolded, the United States in particular became preoccupied with economic development as a means to prevent the emergence of revolutionary movements, such as the ones in Cuba and Vietnam, and to prevent countries from falling under the political influence of their ideological rivals: the Soviet Union and its allies. The developed world, together with international aid agencies, aimed to address "underdevelopment" defined in purely economic terms such as gross national product (GNP).

The goal of development became transformation of the economy from "traditional" to "modern." Among academics, the issue of development was rooted in the Enlightenment notion of progress. It dominated the work of sociologists such as Max Weber, who saw the rise of modern society as a development characterized by individualism, rationality, and economic progress, whereas he viewed traditional society as based on community, religion, and nonindustrial modes of production. Modernization theory as a normative discourse relies on several assumptions, such as economic progress being ideal, unidirectional, and only possible if the Western path is replicated. To be or to become modern, modernization theory argues that the path is transformation from a traditional society, meaning non-Western, to one that is similar to those of Western countries. A modern society/country is one that has freed itself from its own cultural heritage and has adapted one resembling those of Western Europe. In effect, Max Weber's pioneering work on the "Protestant Ethic and the Spirit of Capitalism" has dominated development discourse. Weber argues that the rise of modern capitalism was because of ethnics embedded in Protestant Christianity and that the modern world characterized by rationalization and intellectualization is a world of disenchantment.

The rise of the new industrial society as being unidirectional has been criticized by famous anthropologists such as James Ferguson in *Expectations of Modernity*, where he argues that such assumptions about urbanization and industrialization in academia and popular understandings of modernization are misleading (Ferguson 1999). The process of industrialization caused upheaval in Europe and created even more traumatic conditions for the colonized world. It was in the work of John Hobson that the notion of imperialism was elaborated. In Latin America, Raul Prebisch founded the United Nations' Economic Commission for Latin America and the Caribbean by the late 1940s and developed the "center/core-periphery" framework. Fernando Cardoso, who later would become Brazilian president, wrote about the dependency of the ex-colonies on the developed world. Two theories critical of post–World War II development were formulated: dependency and world systems theory, particularly after the 1973 Chilean coup (Wallerstein 1974; Frank 1971). These critiques argued that developed countries continued to dominate "underdeveloped" countries economically through unequal terms of trade and various social and political mechanisms that ensure subservience of the underdeveloped/periphery to the developed/core countries.

The lack of economic progress in "undeveloped" countries has been explained away in mainstream literature, by scholars such as Talcott Parsons (Moss and Savchenko 2006), Marion Levy (1972), and Alex Inkeles (1969), along the same lines as Kipling's "white man's burden." In essence, the problem of underdevelopment is ascribed to backward behavior. In order to develop, underdeveloped countries have to adapt Western values and practices to achieve greater material prosperity (Woolcock 1998, p. 153). In the context of Official Development Assistance and the Bretton Woods institutions, funds first began to flow into developing-state coffers to be distributed in line with a Keynesian model of full employment, which at that time was prevalent in the West. Mainstream development, which is based on modernization, was articulated in the work of W. W. Rostow,[2] who argued that there are four stages of development, starting from predevelopment and traditional, where through aid an underdeveloped country could be assisted and reach a take-off stage from which it would drive to maturity and, finally, high levels of consumption. This was a linear model based on Western experience and was adopted by US foreign policy as well as the Bretton Woods institutions.

However, the postwar developed world faced its first major economic crisis in the early 1970s. This has been blamed variously on the OPEC price spike, the US abandonment of the gold standard, the post-Fordist industrial landscape, and the declining profitability of capital in the face of strong labor. This crisis led to a rightward shift away from Keynesianism, especially among politicians such as Margaret Thatcher, who became Prime Minister of the United Kingdom in 1979, and Ronald Reagan, who became President of the United States in 1981.

Neoliberalism became mainstream economics; it was critical of Keynes, thus seeking to limit the role of the state in the economy, freeing transnational capital flows, and prescribing a reduction of the size of the welfare state. Its proponents argued that in countries where economic growth and development had happened—defined as the Newly Industrialized Countries (NICs) of Taiwan, South Korea, Singapore, and Hong Kong—free markets and free trade were the driving force. At this point discourse transformed from development to globalization.

Neoliberal economics has been criticized by a variety of developmental state theorists such as Alice Amsden (1985); Theda Skocpol (1985); Peter Evans, Dietrich Rueschemeyer, and Theda Skocpol (1985); Robert Wade (1988); Manuel Castells (1992); and R. P. Appelbaum and J. Henderson (1992). They argued that, rather than the invisible hand, increases in the GNPs of NICs were due to the role of the state. They argued that prosperity was the result of the heavy hand of a developmentalist state and that embracing liberalized markets and deregulation is anathema to development. Indeed the financial crisis of 2007 can be taken as Exhibit A that economic deregulation can lead to economic meltdown. Those working in the area of women and development also have argued against mainstream economists. In my first book, I documented how NICs prospered not only because of the role of a developmentalist state but also because of the way women were used as a flexible source of cheap labor for making cheap consumer export goods (Bahramitash 2005). This idea will be explored later in this section.

The turmoil of the 1970s also led to ideological shifts within international development organizations. In the initial post–World War II era, there was a concerted effort on the part of Western countries and the local elite to bring about industrialization and modernization (after the late 1970s, this term began to be used interchangeably with *globalization*). Gross domestic product (GDP) per capita levels for ex-colonies and much of the "underdeveloped" world did not rise as quickly as anticipated, and in some cases massive abject poverty became a glaring fact. The previously simple interpretation of development (solely in economic terms) was replaced under the guidance of Amaryta Sen as the United Nations Development Programme (UNDP) instituted a Human Development Index incorporating indictors related to health, education, political participation, and, more recently, the position of women in society. However, Sen would prove unable to halt the changing tide of development practices; as with sub-Saharan Africa in the mid-1970s and Latin America's debt crises and lost decade of the 1980s, no country in the Muslim world became economically prosperous. On the contrary, urbanization and industrialization led to a rise in poverty and income inequality. It should be noted that the 1970s was not just a decade of crisis for Western countries; the Soviet bloc was also beginning to crumble. As socialism failed to become a real alternative ideology to Westernization/modernization, liberation theology replaced socialism in the case of Latin America. In the Muslim world, disappointment with Westernization/modernization led to a quest for an alternative based on indigenous cultural specificities. It was this quest that led to a surge in popularity of political Islam, a point that will be explored further in a later section.

It must be noted that since World War II successive mainstream economic models have succeeded in some respects, not least of which is in terms of global GNP growing from $1.3 trillion in 1960 to $30 trillion by the late 1990s. "Nonetheless, at the end of the 20th century, over 840 million people were undernourished, and close to 1.3 billion people [lived] on less than a dollar a day" (FAO 2003, 6; UNDP 2006, 22). There has been improvement in the lives of many when measured by health and education, but perhaps the worst problem is economic inequality; in 1960 the wealthiest 20 percent had an income thirty times that of the poorest 20 percent, but by the end of the twentieth century, "the world's 200 wealthiest individuals had assets equal to more than the combined income of 41 percent of the world's population" (UNDP 2006, 38). Furthermore, the current economic model created the world's worst crisis in generations, and it is unclear to what extent debt-laden economies such as those prevailing in the United States and the Eurozone will be able to recover. Worse, contemporary economic growth models come at a massive environmental cost, as the Gulf of Mexico oil spill of April 2011 bears witness to. In addition, in a recent article in *The Economist*, Robert Zoellick, president of the World Bank, argued that the Third World is no more. *The Economist* states that, according to International Monetary Fund forecasts, public debt in rich countries will rise from 75 percent of GDP at the time of the crisis in 2007 to 110 percent by 2015 (*Economist* 2010).[3]

In closing this section, in the context of Iran's post-2009 presidential election, many arguments of neoliberal economists indeed may be relevant; the state has clamped down on civil rights, has become highly bureaucratic—making it prone to corruption—and much of the economy is in the hands of the state and parasitical organizations (Krueger 1974; Bauer, Meier, and Seers 1984). Those in favor of market liberalization, as opponents of state intervention, argue that empowered state bureaucracies are more interested in corruption and rent-seeking behavior than in promoting economic development (Krueger 1974, p. 302). Others who are critical of state intervention include Jagdish Bhagwati and Anne Krueger, Harry Johnson, Deepak La, and Bela Belassa. Nevertheless, it does not necessarily follow that a market-driven economy would be the solution.

Anthropological Critique: Spelling Out the Third Degree of Separation

Development/modernization/Westernization has been criticized by some of the most highly respected sociologists and anthropologists. Chief among its opponents is Arturo Escobar, who was one of the first to argue that mainstream literature on development—and its dialogue—is ethnocentric and based on Western experiences and perspectives (Batterbury and Fernando 2004). Escobar asserts that development as a linear, universal model of economic and social development that can be applied objectively to diverse local cultures and societies grouped together as a Third World is culturally biased: "To sum up, I propose to speak of development as historically singular experience, the creation of a domain of thought and action, by analyzing the characteristics and interrelations of the three aces that define it; the forms of knowledge that refer to it and through which it comes into being and is elaborated into objects, concepts, theories, and the like; the system of power that regulates its practice, theories, and the forms of subjectivity fostered by this discourse, those through which people come to recognize themselves as developed and underdevelopment" (Escobar 1995, p. 10). Escobar cites Edward Said in his argument that development as a discourse shares much with other colonizing discourses such as Orientalism. According to Said, Orientalism "can be discussed and analyzed as the corporate institution for dealing with the Orient—dealing with it by making statements about it, by teaching it, settling it, ruling over it, in short, Orientalism as a Western style for domination, restructuring and having authority over the Orient" (Said 1979, p. 3). Development likewise defined abnormalities (the poor, the malnourished, the illiterate, the landless) and sought to address these problems by using the West as the point of reference.

Indeed, establishing a domain outside of the discourse is difficult, given the fact that the critique of development is within the very framework of development, and thus "[development's] opponents [are] obliged to phrase their critiques in development terms: another development, participatory development, socialist development, and so on" (Peet and Hartwick 1999). Escobar contends that critical thought can raise social awareness about the power that discourse shapes and can assist communities to move away from development into a different domain, and he argues for alternatives to development and a rejection of the paradigm, preferring social movements as a place where alternative spaces can be formulated. Calderon, Piscitelli, and Reyna (1992), following Escobar, argue that collective action is nourished by the daily production of alternative frameworks for meaning, on which the networks themselves are founded and live from day to day. This line of argument has been taken further, and it has been argued that this is the space in which social movements seek democracy and have the potential of becoming counter hegemonic (St. Martin 2009).

Given development's dependence on Western modernity and historicity, Escobar asks if the hegemonic discourse of development can be modified significantly (Escobar 1995, p. 343). In this book, a critique of mainstream development is based on Said's *Orientalism*

(1979). Said famously argued that during the colonial period Europeans viewed the Orient as justifiably dominated and in need of civilizing, explaining how the Orient is constructed as a homogenous cultural entity based on irrational religiosity and mysticism, emotional and promiscuous yet feminine, and therefore penetrable, and as the place of corrupt despotism. The Orient is backward and undeveloped in contrast with the Occident, which is modern, civilized, rational, and secular, and where progress has occurred.

Said's *Orientalism* in turn was influenced by Michel Foucault, particularly the latter's *L'Archeologie du Savoir* (1969). Foucault unpacked Western knowledge as a discourse reflecting the power of the West over the rest of the world—how European and American economic and political power has been translated into debates that implicitly reflect the superiority of the West. Although this type of discursive Othering has dominated studies of (and development efforts in) Africa, Asia, and Latin America, Said largely limits his discussion to the Middle East. One can—and many have—criticize the Othering of what is considered to be the "undeveloped" world, and in this book the focus will be on the Other of the Muslim world.

As Karen Armstrong eloquently writes, the experience of the Muslim world with modernity has been one of great difficulty: "The Islamic world has been convulsed by the modernization process. Instead of being one of the leaders of the world civilization, Islam was quickly and permanently reduced to a dependent bloc by the European process" (2000, p. 146). The introduction of modernization/development to the Muslim world began in earnest with colonization of much of the Middle East, North Africa, Indonesia, and India, whose large Muslim minority population would form the independent states of Pakistan and Bangladesh during the decolonization process. Worse yet, during the decolonization of the postwar glory years of development in the 1950s and 1960s was when some leaders in the Muslim world came to power through political repression and fostered extreme income inequality. The most prominent examples are Iran and Indonesia, whose governments were overthrown after US-engineered coups.

The Fourth Degree of Separation: Gender and Development

Implicit in the mainstream view of the development/modernization project, and in line with colonial thinking, was the idea that the situation of women would automatically improve (Tinker 1997; Moser

1993; Sen and Grown 1987). It was assumed that with development/modernization/Westernization, women in Third World countries would be "liberated" like Western women and could achieve equality. As a result, policy prescriptions for the Third World were gender blind. It was later realized that development did not improve the lives of all women and, indeed, had in some cases led to greater inequality. In the 1970s, the publication of Ester Boserup's book *Women and Development* documented that economic development had an inverse impact, as it changed the division of labor within the family and increased the burden on women (Boserup 1970).

In the aftermath of the 1970s crisis and the shift in development to favor free market economies, the impact of development continued to attract the attention of academics and social advocates of women's rights. As the development effort continued to fail women, increasing numbers of feminists documented the negative aspect of development from a gender perspective (Afshar 1991; Brydon and Chant 1989; Afshar and Dennis 1992). They argued the free market and minimalist state policies of deregulation left those most vulnerable and most in need of state intervention—namely, women, deprived of aid (Çağatay, Elson, and Grown 1995; Elson 1993; Palmer 1992). Moreover, the debt crises during the 1980s and parts of the 1990s led to the imposition of structural adjustment policies (SAPs), which translated into social spending cuts that disproportionately affect women. As government spending on health and education decreased, women's reproductive work as primary care givers in their families increased. Many feminist economists have documented how erosion of public services has meant that women have had to spend more time looking after those who rely on them for care. Moreover, as public services are privatized, many more women have to work outside the home to make up for the loss of public services (Moser 1989; Çağatay, Elson, and Grown 1995; Palmer 1992).

In response to these criticisms, some economists argued that the long-run impact of development would be positive, following a U-shape whereby the position of women would deteriorate initially but would improve as certain levels of development were achieved (Goldin 1994; Oppenheimer 1970). Whether this may have been true in some individual cases, overall there is scant evidence that poverty has been eradicated globally or that there has been a major improvement in women's lives in the past half-century since the development effort started. There is no major literature to indicate that (1) economic development has transformed many parts of the Third World or (2) women have improved their lives on a global scale. Indeed there is evidence to the contrary, which will be discussed in the following chapter.

In fact, it may be that where the impact of development on women has been positive, there have been steps backward with respect to the conditions of men. Recently, feminists have argued that any gender analysis that separates the experiences of women from that of men can be misleading.[4] Moreover, it is argued that female entry into the labor market and their educational attainments have led to shifts in the balance of power within the household. This shift has led to rising violence and crime. Further, it is argued that a decline in men's traditional role as breadwinners has led to an identity crisis and marginalization as they feel less capable and responsible to provide for their families (Chant and Gutmann 2001; Safa 2005, p. 241).

This is of high importance in planning programs that target women, such as those that provide microcredit to help female entrepreneurship, because they sometimes create male backlash and lead to economic marginalization of men.[5] It is unknown to what extent the change in male status and patriarchal power has brought fear and insecurity, and has transformed men's roles in women's lives (Chant and Gutmann 2001), but it is interesting that some of the fieldwork does capture male resistance and hostility toward rising female employment in the context of Iran.

How to Overcome Separation: Feminist Postcolonial Theory and Subaltern Studies

Although much of the data gathered for this book were in the form of survey (standardized closed) questionnaires, the process of questionnaire formulation took place through several focus-group discussions. The final questionnaires had open-ended questions as well. As critical as one may be of the mainstream discourse of development and feminist research, one is still rooted deeply in the epistemological discourse generated in the West.

Essentially, social science as we know it is based on fundamental questions of knowledge: What do we know? How do we know? Its epistemology is largely transferable to any number of other disciplines. Feminist philosophers, including Helen Longino and Sandra Harding, observe the highly uniform race, ethnicity, and sex of communities of knowers—that is, authorities in a given subject area tend to be white, Western men. In this respect, mainstream development theory and practice, dominated as it is by Western intergovernmental institutions, universities, and nongovernmental organizations, can be viewed as a construct reinforcing Eurocentric, patriarchal norms. Indeed Harding, in talking about the purported rationality and objectivity of science, notes its "rude and brutal cultural intrusion" (1986, p. 61) on non-Western cultures.

Because rationality and objectivity often are ascribed to the market-oriented and secular developmental ideologies of the West, the indictment would not be out of place there either. Development has come under criticism from feminists, who argue that the distinction between private and public stems from modernist thinking (Haraway 1991; Harding 1986; Longino 1990). Longino, in reference to science—but also easily applicable to the field of development—recommends that those oppressed adopt an "oppositional stance" against "background assumptions, language models and arguments and theories" (1990, p. 117). Feminist theorists like Donna Haraway (1991, p. 163) note that the very fundamentals of thought and communication are affected by prevailing culture: "At the level of ideology, we see translations of racism and colonialism into languages of development and under-development, rates and constraints of modernization" (1991, p. 117).

When examining development issues related to women, it is important to incorporate the work of postcolonial feminist theorists, who are critical of the type of discourses that are described by Gayatri Spivak as the tendency "to liberate brown women [in this case Muslim women] from brown men [Muslim men]" (quoted in Alloula 1986). Historically, saving brown women from brown men has been reflected in the way the French in Algeria disenfranchised Arabs because of the "backwardness" of Muslim men's treatment of women. European men had to civilize them. In the case of Algeria as well as with the French and the British in Egypt, the same European men were lobbying domestically against giving their women the right to vote. More recently, George W. Bush evoked a parallel position—that is, saving Afghani women from the Taliban, while, as a born-again Christian, he supported antiabortion laws in the United States as well as a whole array of antifeminist efforts from shutting down women's organizations to opposing global women's rights treaties (Finlay 2006).

Within Iranian studies, Minoo Moallem has elaborated on the ways in which Iranians have been portrayed as barbarians because of the way women have been treated. For instance, Moallem quotes a popular book published in England in 1890: "Persia is an almost barbarous country . . . I have heard that in the case of ladies being wrecked, the young and pretty are sold to great chiefs . . . and the old and Ugly? . . . They are made into slaves or killed outright" (*Alice, the Adventure of an English girl in Persia*, 1890, p. 10, as quoted in Moallem 2005). The treatment of Muslim women falls within the dichotomy of East and West, whereby the latter is the place of women's liberation where a process of secularization and modernization/development has led to improvements for women.

Yet, since most documentation on the adverse impacts of modernization/development on women come from Africa, Asia, Latin America, and the Caribbean rather than the Middle East and North Africa, the MENA region remains obscure. Furthermore, it often is argued that a woman's status in the MENA region is primarily—if not exclusively—related to the Islamic religion. However, the relationship between religion and, say, women's employment in the Muslim world is complex, as Naila Kabeer (1994) argues in her work on Bangladeshi women. In *Reversed Realities*, Kabeer illustrates that the globalization of production has created a situation where Bangladeshi women are brought into the job market as cheap labor, but those who have migrated to Britain are forced to work in the home. The idea of sexual segregation has been turned upside down as the forces of the global economy seek cheap labor (Kabeer 1994). In fact, the idea that modern life will lead to a situation of personal autonomy and liberation of women, celebrated by the modernist agenda, does not automatically occur to all women.

The literature on women in the Muslim world has been enriched by the work of postcolonial feminist theory, starting with the groundbreaking work of Chandra Mohanty, who warned academics of the dangers of using the same framework that exists in development/modernization literature for Western feminist discourse. She argues that women and development literature are not necessarily free from subjective assumptions and tend to reproduce the dominant discourse of mainstream development and to view non-Western countries as backward (Mohanty 2003, p. 50). She further argues that the notion of the Third World woman as a victim can be erroneous and leads to the familiar notion that brown women must be saved by white men. The same "savior" role has been reproduced in some Western feminist writing by replacing *white men* with *white women*. Academics of postcolonial feminist theory have questioned the depiction of Third World women and Muslim women as a homogeneous and powerless group who need to be rescued (Minh-Ha 1989; Yegenoglu 1998; Olmsted 2005; Lewis 1996; Hasso 2005; Lewis and Mills 2003). In the case of Iran, Paidar argues that the interpretation of women as categorical victims is highly problematic, and she calls into question their perceived lack of agency (Paidar 1995).

It can be suggested that as a way of overcoming some of the Western biases, one can draw on subaltern studies and the existence of a subaltern domain where alternatives to development can be found (Escobar 1995, p. 347). In this research, this attempt has manifested itself by looking into the possible ways in which women of low-income households see themselves as victims or agents. Choosing to document and record daily networks as a form of resistance to the parallel networks of power, alternatives to development can be sought in social movements, not just in relation to the state, but also (drawing from Foucault) in relation to knowledge and other forms of power at the level of the family and society. This book explores resistance to an array of knowledge centers, from the state to the family.

Can the Subaltern Be Spoken About?

In addition to postcolonial and feminist studies, as mentioned before, another body of literature relevant to this discussion is subaltern studies. This literature originates in the argument that elite Indian narratives that omit the subaltern have dominated assessments of the anticolonization movement in India. Scholars thus sought to look past the elites and instead to the subalterns by writing them into history and presenting them as the agents of political and social change. There is a tendency for the discourse on women in the Muslim world to be dominated by the elite women of these societies, not just because they have access to academic publications and by definition are in the elite, but also because they represent the perspective of the elite.

This is true to some extent in the case of literature on Iranian women. What is certainly true is that issues relating to civil rights dominate a great deal of the debate on women in the Muslim world in general—and in Iran in particular. While there is no doubt that civil rights such as freedom of expression and freedom from imposed dress codes are important, especially from a modernist position, it does not follow that such issues are primary matters of concern to the poor. For instance, those who come from low-income households have never been unveiled (they remained veiled during the shah's era), and therefore they may not think of the veil as a pressing issue, and some in fact may feel that it is part of their everyday lives. Nor would one expect that freedom of expression and being able to publish or speak freely is a matter of immediate concern. For low-income women, community and communal values may be of higher value than personal ones.

Yet rarely if ever do we hear about matters that relate to women's economic status as it relate to concerns of women from low-income households. Instead there is a tendency to concentrate on what matters to nonreligious, urban middle-class women, and in many cases, the tendency to focus on one social group of middle-class women goes hand in hand with the brown-women-as-victims argument. It should be noted, however, that the middle-class women cannot be homogenized, because some did and still do in fact valorize *hejab* (the covering of women's hair in public). It has been argued that there is no single social group called the middle class (Blumin 1989), but there are diverse social groups that are similar by income and economically fit a definition of middle class. The diversity is broad and not exclusive to Iran, as I have found in conducting more than eight years of field work that members of the middle class have diverse political opinions.

This is illustrated by the fact that, although the literature on women in Iran is rich and growing, it tends to omit poverty despite the fact that female unemployment in Iran is among the worst in the region (Haghighat-Sordellini 2011; Moghadam 2011; Bahramitash and Salehi-Esfahani 2011). However, it is imperative to look into the topic, particularly as sanctions on Iran are having a devastating impact on low-income households (Bahramitash 2013a). Given all the valid criticism against falling into mainstream development discourse, one must look at those whose concerns are rarely a topic of research, as it is necessary to go beyond the elite narratives of women in Muslim countries and include the subaltern. Scholars and policy makers will surely gain insights and understanding from such an approach.

While many scholars have been critical of the mainstream literature that treats women in the Global South as victims (Spivak 1988; Abu-Lughod 2001; Hasso 2005), it remains a challenge to speak of women from low-income households—the subalterns—and avoid treating them as categorical victims since, as Chandra Mohanty argues, Muslim/Third World women are portrayed as ignorant, irrational, poor, uneducated, traditional, and passive (Mohanty 2003, p. 56). There is a now a growing school of academics demonstrating that, in the context of Iran, this depiction is false, including academics such as Minoo Moalem, Neyreh Tohidi, Parvin Paydar, and Val Moghadam (the list is long). Nevertheless, when it comes to subaltern women from low-income households, there seems to be less discussion, and it remains an underresearched area.

To move away from Third World/Iranian women as victims is not to romanticize women of low-income households and to view them as agents who wish—and can—press to enact social transformation. However, in viewing them as victims, one falls into the same mainstream development discourse and is unable to see that in some cases this may be true but in other cases may not. The question, therefore, for an academic engaged in research on the subaltern woman in Iran is, How can one best conduct research on the subalterns? It has been a preoccupation of the author of this book; the aim is, on the one hand, to avoid falling into the fallacy of the dominant Western discourse, which tends to view Iranian women as victims, but on the other hand, to also be realistic in one's research and attempt to be accurate in the type of methodology one chooses.

For this reason, the author wishes to return to an old dilemma Weber elaborated and articulated concerning value-free sociology (in this case mixed with social anthropology): Can a sociologist conduct research free from values? The goal, no doubt, is to conduct scientific research based on objectivity. Yet one cannot step outside to a scientific discourse within a subject of such great controversy. Does this mean one has to abandon research on women from low-income households because it is impossible to step outside the discourse? I. Kapoor echoes Spivak's trepidation of an elite global professional class (to which all authors and academics belong), including both First and Third Worlders, who work on marginalized groups and are prone to project developmentalism/ethnocentrism onto the subaltern (Kapoor 2004). The problem of being a native informant, either from the Third World or in the Third World diaspora living in the West (to which, like Spivak, I belong), is that "it is dangerous to assume that one can encounter the Third World, and especially the Third World subaltern, on a level playing field. Our interaction with, and representations of, the subaltern are inevitably loaded" (Kapoor 2004, p. 631). In her critique of Robert Chambers and his Participatory Rural Appraisal, which is critical of top-down approaches, Spivak warns us about viewing the subaltern as "poor, weak, vulnerable and exploited" (Chambers 1994). Kapoor questions the participatory space because, even when the subalterns speak, they may be influenced by their own communities and what a development project's funders expect them to say; indeed, in the eyes of the subaltern, the role of researcher could be confused with that of a project administrator who is in the field to implement a predefined project. This means that depending on how people perceive the role of the researcher, they may or may not give real answers. Spivak criticizes Escobar and Shiva, as they may have "essentialized the oppressed" (Spivak 1988, p. 293). In line with Spivak, Kapoor argues,

> It is possible to work within the belly of the beast and still engage in persistent critique of hegemonic representations. Development may indeed have become a shady business, but this does not mean one cannot retrieve from within it an ethico-political orientation to the Third World and the subaltern. Thus, for instance, the World Bank and IMF may well be "imperialistic" organizations, but they are too important and powerful to turn our backs on; instead, we can engage them unrelentingly from all sides to try to make them accountable to the subaltern. (Kapoor 2004, p. 641)

She continues by elucidating some of the ways one can be engaged in subaltern research through what she calls the concept of "Hyper-Reflexive Self." Here the researchers acknowledge their complicity, as there is no way of stepping outside and unlearning one's privilege. Rather, one must learn to learn from below and refrain from wanting to teach, mobilize, lecture, or enlighten, as these are the building blocks of a desire for mastery and domination.

To end this section, I wish to return to Max Weber and draw on his work as a sociologist who sought to understand another's values but believed that one can still engage in scientific research and seek objectivity. What's more, with all the valuable literature provided by the critique of mainstream development/modernization, Orientalism, postcolonial, and subaltern studies, one can learn to engage in legitimate research. It may be that feminist theorists, such as Donna Haraway (1991), have provided us with an interesting way of conducting social research. Haraway (1991) argues that in order to procure alternative epistemologies, a feminist perspective calls for subjects to discuss with, not objects to study. Longino has delineated six feminist virtues (1986, 1995a, b, 1997), all of which can be viewed through a developmental as well as scientific lens to assist theorists and practitioners in becoming more representative of reality: (1) empirical accuracy, the value of testable theories with corresponding results; (2) novelty, the value of new theories; (3) ontological heterogeneity, the value of parity between—and recognition of—different natures, processes, and beings; (4) mutuality of interaction, the value of theories that admit to—and account for—complex relationships and interactions between different natures, processes, and beings; (5) applicability to human needs, the value of theories that are centered on the human being and its total welfare; and (6) diffusion of power, the value of theories that can be spread to an ever-wider "community of knowers."

When discussing the "Other" women, this book seeks to document ways in which the invisible subaltern women exercise agency or lack of it (this has been attempted by bringing in the voices of some of the respondents), particularly through social networks, social capital, and the informal economy. Drawing on social relationships formed within networks enables many women to engage in income-generating activities, mostly in the informal sector (Ruwanpura 2008, p. 418). It can be argued that social capital indirectly fights poverty, because it provides connections and opportunities for women to be able to draw from one another's resources. "Feminists and postcolonial scholars have appropriately uncovered the power dynamics persisting in our stratified social space, disclosing that people's embodied negotiation of the social world is far more diverse, complex, and nuanced than a simple public/private binary" (Ruwanpura 2008, p. 421).

In terms of methodology, the topic of this book has been the main research preoccupation of the author for the past seven years and is a continuation of previous publications on Iran. Other than literature review, several trips to Iran in the past five years along with trips within the country have provided a rich background. The research has benefited from previous publications as well as focus groups, which helped first to prepare the questionnaires and then to test and adjust each before it was used for a semisurvey method (here *semisurvey* refers to a mix of closed and open-ended questions). The questionnaires have been complemented with participant observations and interviews with academics and policy makers throughout the past few years while the ideas about the book had been simmering.

Although this introductory chapter ends here, the anxiety about how one's background as an academic trained in the Western academic tradition and rooted in the critique of development discourses can affect findings remains always present. The critique of the discourse around development itself is influenced by the framing of what it comes to criticize, and one always struggles to move away from academic bias, which is deeply imbedded in one's training in the Western academic milieu. The anxiety about how accurately one has been able to produce/reproduce knowledge and for whom has been part and parcel of carrying out research as well as writing its results.

CHAPTER 1

THE OTHER WOMEN AND THE OTHER ECONOMY

The introductory chapter ended with a discussion on the importance of the concept of Other/subaltern women—women of low-income households. In this chapter, I will introduce the concept of social capital (social networks) before discussing the major theme of the book. The aim is to create a space within which to view the critique of the discourses around mainstream development, gender, and development/gender and the informal sector in ways other than portraying women as victims. There are two main questions: How can women of low-income households exercise agency? And how can the Other women operate through the Other economy (as an alternative to the market-led formal economy) in ways that can contest social and economic power structures, rather than reproducing and reinforcing them?

Here I wish to share with my readers a point about the reason for placing this chapter before the main focus of the book: It is in part my attempt to create a dialogue between my training as an academic with preformulated ideas and my findings in the field. I started this project first by reading the relevant literature. However, once the fieldwork was completed, I realized that more ideas were essential in order to contextualize the focus of the book. This chapter came together after the data gathering and data processing was completed.

In some ways, it became imperative at the final stage of writing the book to incorporate a discussion of such concepts as social network and social capital, some reflection on social economy, and some analysis of informal and microfinance to provide a framework for discussion of micro-entrepreneurship and the informal sector. Microfinance in particular proved to be an important part of the findings due to its prevalence among women throughout many parts of Iran. Moreover, microfinance becomes an important concept when social economy, also known as the third sector, is reviewed. The social economy/third sector is an interesting economic space, because it is in neither the hands of the state nor those of the private sector, and it has potential for social transformation (or some degree of personal or at least economic empowerment and access to resources) as it is not necessarily geared to pure profit-making and market-led growth.

SOCIAL CAPITAL AND SOCIAL NETWORK

One of the ways the Other women can earn access to economic resources and become part of the social economy is through their social networks. This became evident as the research uncovered layer after layer of how individual women found survival strategies both personally as well as through/for their community. The latter is highly related to their role as part of social safety nets, on which I have conducted further research (Bahramitash forthcoming).

Social capital as a political notion has been articulated in the work of Robert Putnam (1993) as a way of creating civic engagement through social networks. It enhances social values both individually and collectively (when collectively it is a building block of democracy). Alejandro Portes defines social capital as "the capacity of individuals to command scarce resources by virtue of their membership in networks or broader social structures" (1998, p. 12). Michael Woolcock defines social capital in broader terms as "the norms and networks facilitating collective action for mutual benefit" (Woolcock 1998, p. 155).

According to the World Bank, "social capital is the institutions, the relationships, the attitudes and values that govern interactions among people and contribute to economic and social development."(Grootaert and van Bastelaer 2001, p. 18) In effect, social capital through social networks facilitates individual or collective actions and enhances relationships, reciprocity, and trust. The latter is an important component of microcredit (Grootaert and van Bastelaer 2001), something that will be discussed in more detail later in this chapter and is vital to the Other/shadow/informal economy. Elsewhere the World Bank argues that social capital is the glue that holds society together. It has been treated as the missing link of development, yet critics argue that the way it has been used in development literature is as a stopgap to replace the state and thus facilitate neoliberal economic policies and globalization (Schuurman 2003).

Although the idea of social capital can be seen in the works of Durkheim, Weber, and Marx in the field of economic sociology, during recent times it has been elaborated in two different schools: the mainstream and conservative, and its critique.[1] The mainstream has been endorsed by free market advocates and conservatives who see it as based on a long tradition of volunteer organizations, such as churches, clubs, and private business organizations, all of which act as a buffer between the state and individuals (Fukuyama 1995). The significance of social capital for development is cultural, and its significance for economic development is in the form of voluntary groups/organizations that attempt to fill the gap that is left behind when a state becomes minimalist; in a neoliberal state, civil society is expected to deal with the human cost of market adjustments and failures.

A different approach is taken up in the work of Alejandro Portes and Julia Sensenbrenner, who view social capital as "those expectations for action within a collectively that affect the economic goals and goal-seeking behaviour of its members, even if these expectations are not oriented toward the economic sphere" (Portes and Sensenbrenner 1993). They emphasize the noneconomic aspect of social capital, which can be traced back to the work of Marx and Engles and their notion of "bounded solidarity." This is nearly synonymous with Simmel's "reciprocity transactionism"—that is, the norms and obligations that emerge through personalized networks of exchange, or simply favors between neighbors (Woolcock 1998).

Some academics have been critical of social capital at the level of the state and the market. For instance, in the work of Bourdieu, in agreement with that of Coleman, social capital and social networks are viewed as producers or reproducers of inequality. In an elaborate discussion, Bourdieu argues that capital is the expression of social forces present in the habitus of social actors.[2] The habitus is the internalization of objective social and material conditions available in an individual's daily reality, and thus within the habitus, the individual manipulates and uses capital that enables the actor to carry out actions in the social world, although the relationship between objective structural conditions, the habitus, and action is not one that is deterministic in nature. However, the habitus does predispose individual actors to a general understanding of the immediate social universe and hence creates only a circumscribed range of actions within this social universe. That is, social capital can reinforce existing social inequalities—for example, male-female inequalities or age inequalities within a community of low-income women (Bourdieu 1977).

Bourdieu distinguishes three forms of capital: economic capital, cultural capital, and social capital (1986).[3] Habitus encompasses the predisposition and transmission of embodied cultural capital. When contrasted to other forms of capital, social capital is not entirely contained or possessed by the actor. Instead, social capital is embedded in the network of relations among actors. Social relationships that are part of ethnicity, family, friendship, and other façades of networks become an important source of *nonphysical* capital to people. The forms and nature of the networks in which people are situated determines the total amount of social capital available to them. It allows actions and reward-seeking activities to occur. Its existence is unrelated to individual perceptions, interpretations, or even usage. Social capital has been widely used to examine community dynamics (Putnam 1993, 1995) and opportunities (Portes 1998; Portes and Sensenbrenner 1993; and Sanders, Nee, and Sernau 2002). Bourdieu argues that economic capital facilitates the accumulation of cultural and social capital, but at the same time, lack of one form of capital can translate into lack of access to other forms (1977, 1986).

Bourdieu emphasizes the role of trust based on informal networks in countries where there are insufficient formal institutions and there are no agents to safeguard rights and honor contracts. Trust in informal networks (i.e., social capital), according to such authors as A. Fox (1974) and Edwards and Foley (1998), is a second-best alternative where there is an absence of rule of law and there are no safeguards against those who fail to fulfill their social contract (Schuurman 2003, p. 1003). Grootaert et al. emphasize the importance of trust when social norms are failing. On the positive side, however, social capital in the world of public policy emanates from the basis of *gemeinschaft*, a type of society where there are mutual bonds among its members and a feeling of togetherness, and it is rooted in communitarian ways of dealing with the rupture that modernity has brought; as an institution, it can facilitate transformation. Here I wish to extend the analysis of social capital to women of low-income households who have to face the challenge of being women and survive economic hardship in a society that revolves around men; these challenges will be explored when the results of my fieldwork are presented.

On the critical side, some argue that social capital can reinforce existing norms and values, and the type of communitarianism discussed here can be used against women's rights. This I found to be true among women of low-income households who endorse a strict code of religious interpretation (Bahramitash and Olmsted 2012a, b) and are against the personal and autonomous women's rights celebrated in the modernist literature. Incidentally, it should be clear that the tone of much of this book is within the modernist/modernization frame as well, though one can argue that community and communal lives are also important, especially when it comes to women of low-income households. Nonetheless, we need to be aware that there is an undertone implicit in reproducing modernist views of women's rights that emphasize personal autonomy/freedom over and above that of the community. This complicates the results, as we shall see, because sometimes the Other women prefer communal and sometime traditional values over their personal autonomy/freedom, thus making it difficult to make categorical statements about the findings and implications of research.

To make it even more complex, Portes and Sensenbrenner argue that since social capital works on the basis of social inclusion, it also can mean social exclusion, which can recreate inequality; males in groups versus women, more affluent women versus those of low income, older women versus younger women. Some of this inequality comes through in the chapter wherein my fieldwork is discussed. Here women complain about the shame they feel, that working in low-paid and low-status jobs is the source of this negative feeling, and that clearly social networking is a liability rather than an asset. But as we shall see, some women are extremely happy having their own income, and it gives them bargaining power at home.

At the level of public policy, there have been critiques of the use of social capital in neoliberal economic policies, which as mentioned earlier call for a minimalist state—that is, a state withdrawing from the provision of public services. In the debate over development, feminists have criticized neoliberalism due to its assumption that by reducing social services the need for those services will disappear. Their academic research has documented how the reduction of the welfare state and its transformation into a workfare state has increased women's unpaid labor. For example, reductions of social services, especially under the banner of structural adjustment policies as part of debt repayment, and cutbacks in health care and education have been absorbed by women's reproductive roles. These developments have been documented, and there is a vast literature on the topic (Benería 1992; Sparr 1994; and Tsikata and Kerr 2001).

Some academics have argued against the minimalist state and neoliberalism from a developmental state perspective. They argue that, far from reducing the role of state, to achieve economic development and promote social welfare requires a more active role for the state. From a public policy point of view, they argue that the state must be engaged with civil society, but as a representative entity responsive and responsible to civil society. Amsden, Wade, and Evans advocate that state-led development, as opposed to market-led development, at the macro level can utilize social capital in a way that works in synergy with the civil society and uses social capital as a means to alleviate poverty (Amsden 1985; Wade 1990; Evans 1995), and the work of Portes argues similarly at the micro level (Portes 1998).

Woolcock argues, with respect to development initiatives in poor societies, "where there are so many obstacles to forging mutually beneficial complementarities between the state and society," that social capital is important (1998, p. 158). In a synergy between the state and civil society and in the work of state-led development advocates, Rankin argues that when the state is highly cooperative, accountable, and flexible, social capital can be used successfully and for the advancement of the country (Rankin 2002, p. 5).

In addition, social capital in the form of social networks and associational activities is effective in dealing with poverty and social disintegration and delivering effective social welfare (Molyneux 2002, p. 185). As we will see in the fieldwork, some women find employment through their network of friends and extended family. Schuurman (2003) discusses the concept of community social capital and argues that it is constructed and maintained especially by women who have shifted their frame of reference from the family and the neighborhood toward career perspectives. Molyneux produces vast documentation on the ways in which women have been mobilized for poverty-relief and community-development programs: "The evidence shows across a range of countries that women among low-income groups are frequently those with the strongest community and kin ties; many such women do network, they do engage in reciprocal supportive relations, they are those who support church activities and participate in local forms of associational life. They are to be found too, at the heart of voluntary self-help schemes whether in health, education or neighbourhood food and housing programmes" (2002, p. 177). These concepts will be explored further when I discuss fieldwork from Iran concerning ways in which volunteer work and self-help groups are formed (especially in the form of rotating credit and saving associations).

Much like Molyneux, this book emphasizes the importance of social capital and its potential to enrich the development debate from a policy point of view. Research on networks, community ties, and kinship are important ways in which to address poverty. This is especially important, because in formulating development projects, the local social fabric and the importance of social solidarity and cooperation (negative or positive) are vital. When formulating projects, it is important to take note of such existing reposes (Molyneux 2002). Unfortunately there is not a great deal of debate at the level of public policy. Although the World Bank heavily endorses social capital, there is no reference to it in *Engendering Development* (Mason and King 2001). Molyneux mentions that social capital in the name of participation has been articulated in participatory development, and it has had a long history in the Catholic Church and the Left in the context of Latin America. Social capital, or networks in the forms of associational activity, has been operationalized in the form of bottom-up development, particularly when it is decentralized. There will be forthcoming documentation on the role of women of low-income households through Islamic charitable efforts in the context of Iran (Bahramitash forthcoming).

For Catholic mothers, taking care of the community is part of their role as good Christians, and self-help relies on low-paid or unpaid women's labor as part of their care for the community. Women help and provide in times of economic crisis, just as was the case in Peru during the 1980s and 1990s, and this is evidence of social capital at work, because if they were not providing such care, there would be social crisis as well (Pearson 1997). In Iran, all women's religious rituals, such as Qur'anic reading groups and mourning for Shi'a Saint Imam Hussein during the month of Muharam, bring women of low-income households together. These occasions go hand in hand with networking, where information about the needs of particular members of their community can be exchanged and assistance in cash and kind is delivered (Bahramitash and Olmsted 2012a, b).

Generally, there exists a tendency to overlook female-run networks, and this is the case with the literature on the Middle East and North Africa, especially from a policy perspective. However, social capital among men in the Middle East and North Africa has long been researched. For instance, the work of R. Cunningham reveals that the traditional market or *souq* provides a location for exchange and distribution of goods and services with political implications and influence (Cunningham 1992). In the context of Iran, Arang Keshavarzian has documented how the bazaar and social networks within it played a key role in the mobilization of political forces against the shah during 1978. He writes that the "Tehran Bazaar maintained its cooperative hierarchies which created a sense of community" (2007, p. 127). Relevant to Keshavarzian's work is the concept of *etebar*—honor as guarantee for credit (2007, p. 83). Where women are concerned,

Diane Singerman examines informal networks and the family network and how they tend to be absent from debates on poverty and women's rights (2006, p. 2). In part this is because the family is in the private sphere, where power is believed to be absent. Singerman argues that "there is a rupture between innovative theory and empirical research when the focus turns toward the Middle East. Instead, family, tribe and informal networks are dismissed as pre-political forms (Zubida, 1998), vestiges of traditional societies or primordial attachments that will wither away with modernity" (2006, p. 7). It is true that family can reinforce hierarchy and domination (Bayat 1994), but equally it can be a source through which women empower themselves. As Schuurman and Singerman emphasize, the family network and civil society, and the potential within them for resistance, can be catalysts of emancipation. Katherine Rankin argues that in feminist literature a much more complex analysis of resistance has been developed than what is found in the work of Bourdieu's typology of "Doxa," "Habitus," and "Political consciousness" (2002). In fact, some academics have argued that women in the Middle East and Asia lean toward male-dominant ideology in a strategic way to secure their lives and that of their children.[4]

Singerman argues that informal networks operate to transcend bureaucracies, religious institutions, civil society organizations, the market, the extended family, and the neighborhood in order to fulfill individual and collective needs. Such networks are pervasive, flexible, and efficient (2006, p. 17). She argues that informal networks in Egypt create a wider public sphere and bring power to the private as a "buffer" between citizens and the state. This reiterates a theme that developmentalist state theorists have articulated but also leads us to a different sphere—that of the third sector—which I will discuss later in this chapter after reviewing the notion of microcredit. This next section will examine microcredit as a way of operationalizing social capital in development planning.

MICROENTERPRISE, MICROCREDIT, AND SOCIAL ECONOMY

By and large, women as micro-entrepreneurs have been researched in the context of the critique of neoclassical economics and its results on employment—in this case, the lack of it for women. Neoliberalism has led, it has been argued, to a decline of well-paid, full-time jobs and further has led to the rise of low-wage jobs as self-employed homeworkers/microenterprise owners due to market-oriented types of employment (Castells and Portes 1989; Sassen 1997; Bahramitash and Olmsted 2012a, b). Increasingly in developing countries, many women are working as vendors, hawkers, small-store saleswomen, peddlers, as well as domestic caregivers (although the latter can hardly be called entrepreneurship), and they work without the protection of labor laws (ILO 2002a, b; Kapoor 2007). This concept will be discussed further in Chapter 2, where the issue of microenterprise is reviewed with regard to its connection with the informal economy.

As a matter of fact, social capital in the world of development has been operationalized in the form of microcredit as a means to address poverty. This links our discussion of social capital to microcredit first, before we read more about microenterprise in relation to the informal economy of low-income households. Microcredit has become an extremely popular development strategy in the past few decades. Microcredit is model through which small loans are granted (in this example) to women of low-income households based on community trust and community networks. The donor provides small loans to women who form a group and receive these loans on the basis of collective collateral. In other words, women are encouraged to apply as a group and then are held responsible for repayment as a collective. The model, as Rankin argues, operates on the basis of "social collateral," which is provided by membership in the borrower groups (2002, p. 12). C. Leigh Anderson and Laura Locker argue that group-based microfinance enhances social capital and solidarity by bringing members together for a common goal, and it strengthens the groups' understanding, incentive, and trust while promoting cooperation due to its anticipated pay offs (Anderson, Locker, and Nugent 2002). As Naila Kabeer argues, the institution has proven to have a high repayment rate and a low rate of default (1994). A. M. Goetz and Rina Sen Gupta have argued that microcredit has given more power to women due to an increase in their access to income, which in turn has translated into better health and education for their children (Goetz and Gupta 1996).

The model has proven to be effective in both poverty alleviation and community building and is a preferred model to what Linda Mayoux calls the financial self-sustainability paradigm with its emphasis on charitable approaches to saving and credit delivery in programs sponsored by nongovernmental organizations (NGOs) or governmental initiatives (2001). The model has become especially popular after the success of the Grameen Bank, which started in the 1970s by lending to the poor, especially poor women. Muhammad Yunus pioneered the initiative, and in 2006 he won a Nobel Peace Prize. Banks lending only to women have been taken up by organizations such as Bangladesh Rural Advancement Committee (BRAC) and NGOs such as Pro Mojer. The popularity of the model to some extent is due to the fact that it has provided benefits not only to those from low-income households but also to those who invest in development initiatives, since a low default rate has made the model viable and sustainable. It also has been argued that the model has provided many women who do not possess collateral access to credit and has enhanced group solidarity.

In cases (which constitute the majority) where microcredit relies on social capital, similar criticisms of social capital theory have been raised. Like theories of social capital, the model is criticized for its inherent market-driven ideology (Mayoux 1995; Rankin 2002). Despite these criticisms, by and large the aim of microcredit is to alleviate poverty within a market-led economy. These critiques take us back to the Introduction and the critique of development initiatives by Foucault and Escobar, but such critiques also can be found in the work of Antonio Gramsci, Jürgen Habermas, and Paulo Freire, as well as Helen Longino and Sandra Harding. In essence, market-led poverty alleviation is synonymous with mainstream and Western-led development, and it has been criticized to a greater degree in the Introduction. In sum, the primary problem with such initiatives is that these efforts are not necessarily aimed at bringing about change in the social structure; rather, they aim to maintain it. In effect, the sustainability of a market-led economy, in line with mainstream economic development practice, relies on ensuring that the poor can survive without having to alter society.

Some of the critiques of the model emanate from the fact that it is influenced by neoliberalism. It has been argued that the microcredit model often charges high interest rates to the benefit of the bankers, when the donors are banks. There are cases where development agencies and national NGOs have entered into microcredit lending and have earned huge profits, and these have not necessarily been for the borrowers. The Mexican Compartamentos is a clear example of an NGO that received foreign aid and made major profit on the basis of giving high-interest loans to the poor and making a huge profit that was not shared with the poor. Yunus has condemned Compartamentos, and while some argue that it has empowered women economically, especially those with no collateral, the fact that it has made major profit shows the limitations of microcredit organizations that turn into financial profit-making institutions aiming to maximize profits rather than help their clientele.

Moreover, the market-led model provides little or no incentives for fostering collective consciousness raising, as noted by Brooke Ackerly (Goetz and Gupta 1996; Rankin 2002; Ackerly 1997). It is a win-win situation for market-led growth, where the donors cut down on administrative costs by transforming them into group pressure to make sure their repayments are secure. This lending does not necessarily empower women, for at the core the objectives are alleviation of poverty and sustainability of microcredit, not social transformation.

In addition, similarly to critiques of social capital, the issue of gender inequality remains pertinent. For instance, the household may not be (in many cases it is not) a site of gender equality, and men are seen to have power over women. This is what A. Sen has articulated in his work as "co-operative conflict" (Sen 1990). Interestingly, as others have documented in studies related to the Grameen Bank, the benefits of microcredit may be brought not to women but to men as the heads of the households. Here it must be noted that in some cases where men are poor and powerless, women giving loans to women may create a backlash and lead to domestic violence. It should also be noted that the evidence regarding male violence is mixed. Some argue, conversely, that because women earn cash, there is a tendency to transform their relationships and reduce women's vulnerability to men's violence by strengthening their economic roles and making their lives more public (Schuler, Hashemi, and Badal 1998).

Perhaps when women challenge gender norms, some men tend to respond with increased violence. Male violence against women is serious, widespread, and often an ignored problem. It is therefore critical to examine how and under what conditions microcredit tends to decrease or exacerbate violence against women. This examination is imperative on the part of any microcredit-lending institution. It may be true that when microcredit revolves around a fundamental change in social structure and gender norms that leads to social transformation, it has a tendency to provoke a backlash.

In the case of Iran, there are some microcredit programs sponsored by the state. In my last book on women's employment in Iran, an international and national initiative of microcredit (which started and finished during Khatami's presidency, 1997–2005) yielded some interesting results that resonate with some of the general findings in the literature (Bahramitash 2011). The microcredit initiative was based on participatory development and was implemented in Shirabad, a shanty town on the edge of Zahedan, the capital Sistan and Baluchistan province, and close to the border with Afghanistan and Pakistan. The area was and is extremely impoverished and has been plagued by several years of drought and a vast refugee population of Afghans, as well as ethnic and religious conflict between Baluchis, Afghans, Shi'as, and Sunnis. In addition, the local economy is based on illicit drug trade and arms smuggling, as well as smuggling gas across the border from Iran and into Afghanistan and Pakistan (this may have changed since the spring of 2011 due to cutbacks on fuel subsidies and cheap gas in Iran).

The initiative was not intended to be an all-women initiative, but men lost interest and withdrew their participation while women continued to join, even as I was gathering data, despite complaints about the limited amount of credit given. On the positive side, the initiative raised consciousness and mobilized women to lobby the city to prevent it from destroying their "illegal housing." It had given them solidarity and self-confidence for collective action against the local authorities (although they had support from UNDP, the wife of the president, and her NGO). The women had managed to bring the city to task and stop authorities' harassment and planned destruction of their homes. There was also some evidence with regard to women's empowerment in the local community and in their households, as some had managed to generate a small income. On the negative side, however, many expressed their frustration about group punishment for default repayment, which had created some intergroup conflict and resentment. Moreover, it excluded those who had no capital, since, like any other microcredit project, it required some initial capital for group membership.

There has been an effort on the part of the government to provide microcredit. Ahmadinejad has attempted to provide microcredit for self-employment and to boost employment opportunities to combat unemployment. These efforts were largely targeted at men as official heads of households, but there have been efforts to target women as well. In August 2010, there were several attempts and announcements about efforts to set up interest-free credit for women. The head of the Business Women's Association announced that she was lobbying for an interest-free microcredit initiative for women. There is evidence that several Chamber of Commerce members welcomed the plan (interview with Ms. H.[5] Tehran 2011). There are similar efforts on the part of elite women. The Association of Women Manager Entrepreneurs has also lobbied for providing low-interest or no-interest loans for women. The government has some targeted microcredit, but it is primarily for female-headed households, and thereby does not contest the male-breadwinner model directly (although it does indirectly, as when women who get a divorce and become heads of households become eligible). For example, the head of the women's section at the Ministry of Cooperatives has been attempting to create microcredit for self-employed women (*Jahan News* 2010). These attempts have been designed to address high unemployment in both urban and rural areas. In effect, the government officially is recognizing that the traditional extended-family system in which the patriarch of the family looks after the widow is no longer necessarily in place.

These types of microcredit are not based on the international development model where groups are formed and they rely on government officials for allocation as well as monitoring, but the officials are not necessarily concerned with repayment. It appears that once women are able to obtain this credit, the monitoring process is fairly loose. However, like other types of microcredit, lending tends to create corruption, and women need to be linked to the right social network—that is, know somebody who knows somebody. Moreover, as with other types of government initiatives, they are subject to major bureaucratic processes. This may be why none of our interviewees reported having received any credit from different sources of credit aimed at targeting women for self-employment purposes or for female heads of households. Microcredit remains primarily a national project since the election of President Ahmadinejad; foreign-funded projects have been stopped even by organizations such as UNDP (fieldwork 2010–11).

Here I wish to introduce a different aspect of microcredit in the context of Iran, which is an especially interesting venue for creating a space in which women in fact can increase their access to economic resources. In the absence of microcredit programs, many women have become engaged in rotating credit and saving associations (ROCSAs). The ROCSAs have become highly prevalent in Iran, perhaps due to the increasing need for women to become economically self-sufficient. My 2012 fieldwork in Iran suggested that ROCSAs are more prevalent among the lower middle class and the poor. Literature on the topic first appeared in the 1950s in Indonesia (Geertz 1956). ROCSAs are not unique to Iran, and there are examples in other countries, especially in Africa as well as Indonesia, as documented by Shirley Ardener and Sandra Burman (1995) and Grant and Allen (2002). Lindsay Gifford found them in Syria, where they are popular among women (Gifford 2011).

ROCSAs operate on the basis of trust and one's social capital, and they have existed for a long time. These associations rely on groups that regularly meet and whose members contribute a fixed amount of funds during a set period of time, and where the total sum rotates, sometimes by taking turns. In my fieldwork, these ROCSAs gave loans mostly on the basis of lottery. The loans are interest free and the rate of default is low because of its community-based nature. ROCSAs are self-sustaining and independent, and therefore they are not vulnerable to an individual donor's decision.

Although ROCSAs are for credit and savings among women, there seems to be silence on their potential for development purposes. As a part of informal finance, they are highly linked to the informal sector and are prevalent in developing countries as well as among immigrant populations in Western countries. Yet, as Rankin argues, they remain outside of the mainstream and are viewed as an interesting facade of "the Other" (2002, p. 2).

ROCSAs have been important to women in low-income households. Linda Mayoux and Shri Anand, in their study of south India, find that women use these group savings as a way of preventing men from misusing household income and gaining control over expenditures (Mayoux 1995). Margaret Niger-Thomas confirms the same finding in Indonesia and in an urban setting and views it as a way for women to preserve control over household disposable income (Niger-Thomas 1995). In an earlier study, V. V. Nguyen noted that in some cases it is really men's income that is used for these rotating credit associations and not that of women (1949). In the same way as with the Grameen Bank, it has been shown that men borrow through their women and use their wives to cover for what is essentially their borrowing. Nevertheless, as we shall see later in the case of Iran, where two ethnographic examples are given, ROCSA lending is primarily done by women, for women, going hand in hand with gender segregation, and is also part of the informal economy. The two ethnographic examples given show that these ROCSAs are not just about finances but go beyond and in some instances act as part of the social safety net by providing economic and also social solidarity/empowerment.

To compare and contrast, ROCSAs are free of some of the negative aspects of microcredit, such as the tension that sometimes arises among members when they are under pressure for group repayment. They are interest free, unlike the microcredit model, which has high interest. ROCSAs can be a source of economic and social solidarity and are less prone to provoke male violence, since they are indigenous organizations, and unlike many cases of microcredit, which are funded by international agencies and where the money comes from outside the family and community resources, ROCSAs are entirely community based and spontaneous. They tend not to provoke male violence, because the likelihood is lessened when the source of funding is within the community itself, and any social transformation stems from resources from within the community and the family rather than outside of it. Moreover, ROCSAs may lead to social transformation, but it is much less drastic and more subtle. It could be that some men (and I did come across them) join these groups through their women, but even there it seems that women were in control.

Like the microcredit model, ROCSAs do not seem to reach the very poor, because it requires some capital to start or join one. In my research I found ROCSAs to be both market led and socially transformative. They were market led because in most cases the credit was channeled into buying consumer goods, but there were cases where women used the funds to invest in their own or their children's education and thereby transform their access into economic and social sources of power. There was no evidence from what I observed for collective action, but a great deal of solidarity building was evident, especially when members were in need. In the case of crisis for one of the members, women came together to help and some gave up their turn for the benefit of the one in crisis. The potential of ROCSAs to act as social safety nets was, in the cases I observed, especially crucial. Additionally, the ROCSA cases I observed were linked to social assistance, as other kinds of charity and self-help efforts for and by women fall into neither state assistance nor private-sector assistance but constitute the third sector, otherwise known as the social economy.

SOCIAL ECONOMY: THE THIRD SECTOR

This is the appropriate place to examine the idea of the social economy. The concept is not new, as it dates back to mid-nineteenth-century France, with sociologist Frédéric Le Play at the vanguard, founding the *Société Internationale des Etudes Pratiques d'Economie Sociale* and the *Revue d'Economie Sociale*, as well as debuting the term to an international audience at the 1867 Universal Exhibition (Bidet 1997, p. 31). It was originally conceived of as the study of the interaction between the working classes and other classes (Topalov 1999, p. 13), at a time of great societal upheaval and experimentation, as the industrial workforce gathered in both numbers and strength (Moulaert and Ailenei 2005, p. 2039).

At the end of the nineteenth and beginning of the twentieth century, prominent French economists Léon Walras and Charles Gide provided studies of the social economy with fully fledged academic recognition. Gide conceived it as a "science of social justice" (Moulaert and Ailenei

2005, p. 2040). Walras, with whom Gide corresponded, viewed the social economy as the "voluntary distribution of wealth, based on the criteria of the 'just' [and] thus differentiating it from the natural production through pure economics" (Demoustier and Rousseliere 2006, p. 116). But far from being an exclusively French phenomenon, social economy has taken on a wide variety of manifestations, of which cooperative enterprises, mutual benefit societies, and nonprofit associations are its pillars (Defourny and Develtere 1999). In contemporary scholarship, Moulaert and Ailenei (2005, p. 2039) argue that many academics continue to write on the topic of social economy, among them Lester M. Salamon and Helmut K. Anheier (1995), and Andrew Leyshon, Roger Lee, and Colin C. Williams (2003). Crystal Tremblay is rather encouraged, stating that the field is maturing with time as governments, academics, and civil society are coming to grips with its importance, leading to "a growing conceptualization of the Social Economy as a distinct framework for socio-economic development." Nevertheless, generally missing from the literature is African and Asian social economy, as well as "the experiences of grass-roots self-help associations with often no status" (Tremblay 2009, p. 44).

A sharper focus on self-help and grassroots movements would be particularly useful given the relationship that generally is believed to exist between social economy and socioeconomic crises (Moulaert and Ailenei 2005, p. 2041). As the institutional or formal aspects of the economy (state and market) breakdown, social and solidarity mechanisms begin to develop to fill the void left behind. For example, Tremblay argues, "There is widespread recognition in the literature that the social economy is a major vehicle for addressing intertwined and interdependent issues of social, economic, environmental and cultural well-being. Alongside this recognition is the growing discourse on the role that the social economy plays in democratic participation and empowerment of women, indigenous people and other excluded groups in society, both in meeting their needs for sustainable livelihoods, and in increasing their power in democratic decision-making" (Tremblay 2009, p. 44). Moulaert and Ailenei contend that "when the economic growth engine starts to stutter, formal distribution mechanisms begin to fail and new social forces develop and give rise to alternative institutions and mechanisms of solidarity and redistribution as a means of addressing the failures of the institutions of the socioeconomic movements to guarantee solidarity among economic agents" (2005, p. 2038).

The social economy as seen in practice, concept, and policy emerges in response to the scarcity of needs usually provided by the public or private sector in periods of socioeconomic crisis. To highlight this phenomenon, Marie Bouchard, Giles L. Bouroue, and Benoît Lévesque (2000, p. 6) distinguished three steps of the "old social economy" in reference to three pre–World War II instances of socioeconomic crisis. Some of the social economy activities seen in the instances discussed by Bouchard, Bouroue, and Lévesque became part of national social institutions during the post–World War II period. For instance, trade unions and mutual aid associations were recognized as partners in France's welfare system. While some significant sections of the social economy became institutionalized, other activities remained at the grassroots level but were explored and utilized in many of the cooperative movements of the 1970s (Moulaert and Ailenei 2005).

The third sector is a term synonymous with others such as the *social* or *solidarity economy*; *nonprofit*, *not-for-profit*, or *nonlucrative sector*; and the *voluntary*, *idealist*, or *alternative sector*. Benoît Lévesque, Marie-Claire Malo, and Jean-Pierre Girard (1999) showed that this third sector coexisted alongside the private and public sector almost everywhere in Western and Eastern Europe and the United States. According to Lévesque, Malo, and Girard, this third sector (in French *troisie`me secteur* or *tiers secteur*) is different from the public and private market sectors at its various structural, productive, and organizational levels. At the organizational level, the third sector combines formal and informal elements, such as utilizing the market, the state, and the domestic economy as well as self-help and volunteerism. Production may be market and nonmarket oriented, and funding may be received in a mix of monetary and nonmonetary methods, such as goods and services.

Although Lévesque, Malo, and Girard find evidence of a European-wide and United States–based social economy, Jeremy Rifkin distinguishes between the North American and European understanding of the term. Rifkin found that American usage of the term *social economy* refers largely to nonprofit organizations that are charitable associations and foundations, whereas the European concept also includes cooperatives and mutual support organizations (Rifkin 1995). However, in 1980s Europe, *the third sector* had a narrower definition and was used, according to Perri and Isabel Vidal (as quoted in Vuorinen 1999), within a context of a work and social crisis. Indeed, the 1980s conception of the third sector had more to do with an ideological rejection of mainstream, capitalist-oriented labor markets than a phenomenon that arises in reaction to socioeconomic crisis. Currently, however, it is studied and applied in efforts to expand the social element of the market. It is supposed that the term now eliminates the duality between social life (first sector) and economic life (second sector) and the market versus state dichotomy (Gaiger 2000). For example, J. Pearce of the Community Business Scotland Network distinguishes two sectors within the greater third sector. Pearce contends that the difference between NGOs and community organizations lies in their size and sources of funding. NGOs, despite the nongovernmental moniker, rely on state funding or contracts and tend to be quite large in scale. Community organizations, however, tend to be very small, independent, and reliant on resources from within the locality they serve (Pearce 1999, p. 2).

The range of third-sector initiatives and institutions that rely solely on state funding and those that rely solely on market funding, and everything in between, is wide. Social economy is not a static or rigid set of fundamentals from which certain other third-sector type initiatives can necessarily be excluded. Social economy is a variety of social mechanisms that mix elements from market exchange, state intervention, reciprocity, and solidarity-driven collectives. Importantly, Frank Moulaert and Oana Ailenei argue that if any definition of the term is to be forged, it "must account for the many forms of social relations that exist and their embeddedness in a specific social, cultural, historical and institutional background" (Moulaert and Ailenei 2005, p. 2050). These thoughts will become particularly significant when this book considers the importance of rotating credit and saving associations in Iran, which have social, cultural, and historical significance in Iran's third sector.

Common to the third sector is a dissatisfaction and frustration felt on the part of the public with both state intervention and the failure of the market to provide necessities. Often what is felt as an alienating paternalism on behalf of the state or the market creates a space for communities to strengthen community social bonds when community takes over in providing those lacking necessities. This community provision for its needs is done in solidarity with one's neighbor and a deeply embedded expectation of reciprocity.

As predicted by Bouchard, Bouroue, and Lévesque, these preexisting social bonds lead to community reciprocity and solidarity in times of socioeconomic crisis and sometimes become more formal in nature. Recent examples of the organization of the social economy can be seen in Europe; the Canadian province of Quebec; in Argentina, Brazil, and Chile (where it is referred to as *solidarity economy*); in Asia as the *people's economy*; and in Senegal and Turkey (where it is referred to as *associative movements*). The term *community economic development* has been adopted to describe a similar level of organization of the third sector in the United States, English-speaking Canada, the United Kingdom, and New Zealand.

However, only recently have these organizations attracted serious attention in policy circles. As a consequence, basic information about these organizations—their numbers, size, activities, economic weight, finances, and role—has been lacking in most places, while deeper understanding of the factors that contribute to their growth and decline has been almost nonexistent. This has hampered the civil society sector's ability to participate in the significant policy debates now under way and limited its potential for contributing to the solution of pressing problems.

Currently, there exists economic activity that embodies social values in every corner of the globe, even if these initiatives do not identify consciously as efforts of a social economy movement. Despite global debates about the theoretical concept of social economy, "its practice is everywhere engaged in and, in important ways, has always been with us" (McMurtry 2009). Formalizing the informal sector and supporting the goal of full employment therefore is being discussed to an increasing degree in economic development literature (Williams 2006; Mansoor 1999; Medina 1997). Integrating the informal sector into community-based and social enterprises, cooperatives, and unions is becoming a widely used approach in Mexico (Medina 2003), Colombia (Moreno-Sanchez, Del Pilar, and Maldonado 2006), and Brazil (Gutberlet 2005).

Community wealth based on social value, known as *social capital*, is well accepted in the literature as an element of the social economy (Neamtan 2005). Ana Maria Peredo and James J. Chrisman highlight social capital and positive social networks as useful concepts in understanding community-based enterprises, which are seen as necessary components for economic development. It is within these networks that "communities are able to build strong relationships, which, over time, allow trust, cooperation, and a sense of collective action to develop among members" (2006, p. 314).

There is some critical analysis of the role that the social economy can play in contributing to further social exclusion and marginalization. John Loxley and Dan Simpson provide some critical concerns with respect to social services that devolve into social economy organizations, as this development actually could reinforce neoliberalism. They argue that this could become a way to reduce public-sector employment and wages and help to create cheap labor pools that don't really influence the overall quality of conditions. There is also a limited literature that presents trade union perspectives and their arguments and concerns for how the social economy can undermine direct-employment benefits and wage rights (see, for example, Loxley and Simpson 2007).

Both the informal economy and ROCSAs fall into the domain of social economy when they are part of the social safety net, and it is important to be keep this in mind. Here the emphasis on the social economy is pertinent, not just to what will be taken up in more detail in the discussion of fieldwork in Iran and the informal sector (as well as ROCSAs), but also for its potential to alleviate poverty in ways that could create social solidarity and perhaps have potential for social transformation. In line with this, one can introduce the concept of social entrepreneurship as a catalyst for change. The emphasis on social entrepreneurship is to move away from market-driven economic activities and in the direction of social responsibility and a quest for bringing social justice.

An interesting caveat of social economy is the topic of social entrepreneurship, which recently has attracted attention. Existing definitions about social entrepreneurship tend to be rather poor and fuzzy (Mair and Marti 2006, p. 36). Here we can define it broadly as an initiative that is brought about by those who are seeking to resolve a particular social problem and utilize social entrepreneurship to organize, create, and manage a venture to bring about change. In contrast to business entrepreneurship, where the objectives are economic and monetary profit, a social entrepreneur concentrates on creating or strengthening social capital in such a way as to facilitate a greater goal. Social entrepreneurship is a part of the social economy, relies on voluntary work, and is not for profit. There are other definitions and interpretations, but for the purpose of this book, this definition is sufficient.

Although the term *social entrepreneurship* is relatively new, the concept is not and has a long history. In recent history, many associate the term with Bill Drayton, the founder of Ashoka: Innovators for the Public. Some academics have argued that social entrepreneurship can be important in successful poverty-alleviation initiatives (Krishna, Uphoff, and Esman 1997; Tendlar 1989).

Sarah L. Alvord, L. David Brown, and Christine W. Letts explore the concept by way of choosing seven examples of social entrepreneurship. Before closing this chapter, it would be helpful to examine a few of the relevant cases that Alvord, Brown, and Letts analyze in order to bring to life the concepts we have explored: Self-Employed Women of Ahmadabad (SEWA), Green Belt Movement (GBM), Bangladesh Rural Advancement Committee (BRAC), and Six S will be discussed. We already have seen some analysis of the Grameen Bank (which is also one of the seven they selected).

SEWA was founded in 1972 by Ela Bhatt for a group of women who were working in the informal sector. SEWA's website describes the organization as a trade union registered to organize poor, self-employed female workers whose livelihood is based on small businesses, whose income is earned through non-regular-salary employment, and who are without welfare benefits. Their employment is unprotected and yet constitutes 93 percent of the female workforce. Their work is a part of the informal sector, and so it is either uncounted or undercounted and is therefore invisible in census data. The fact that such women have been isolated from the general working population made it impossible for them to unionize and press for improving working conditions. However, SEWA managed to bring 315,000 self-employed women together to form a union (Chen 1983; Streenivasan 2000). SEWA has been growing and it has embarked on different campaigns, such as the campaign against police abuse of street vendors. Today, SEWA has a bank for those who do not have access to collateral and provides them with efficient savings and credit facilities, and it is designed to help the poor to remove themselves from the cycle of poverty and debt. The SEWA bank has been called "a bank of their own" and is estimated to have 40,000 members, operating similarly to a cooperative bank.[6]

The Green Belt Movement (GBM) was an initiative started by Professor Wangari Maathai (the winner of 2004 Nobel Prize) and the National Council of Kenyan Women after rural women reported that their water sources were drying up. Founded in 1977, it mobilized and facilitated the planting of 51 million trees (70 percent of which survived) by 30,000 women in an area of massive environmental degradation, soil erosion, and deforestation. Those who took part in the movement were trained in forestry and food processing. This led to further efforts to address environmental damage that have been locally led, operating on the basis of awareness. GBM has planted 51 million trees since its founding and has created seminar education initiatives designed to empower the individual on a political, economic, and environmental level.[7]

The Bangladesh Rural Advancement Committee (BRAC) was established in 1972 by Fazel Hasan Abed, a cooperative executive, and its mission was to alleviate poverty through the development of life skills and to foster community organizations and job creation through the use of local professionals. It has organized self-help programs based on local capacity around improvement of health and education through mobilization of people's resources. It is estimated to have financed 7 million microfinance group members and thousands of informal schools and health volunteers. BRAC is believed to be one of the largest NGOs in the world, employing thousands in many countries of Asia and Africa. BRAC, like other cases discussed here, has branched in other activities, such as improving the lives of landless peasants and empowering them economically (Abed and Chowdhury 1997; Lovell 1992).[8]

Se Servir de la Saison Sèche en Savane et au Sahel (Six S), was an initiative started by Bernard Lédéa Ouédraogo from Burkina Faso and Bernard Lecomte from France with a mission to provide "flexible funding." Such funding was to be approved and managed by local elders' regional networks and aimed to channel funds into income-generating activities that were self-sustaining (Lecomte 1986; Uemura 2000). Six S is also dedicated to peasant mobilization through the removal of barriers to self-sufficiency, such as the lack of technical know-how to address devastating issues such as drought and desertification, the lack of liaison with individuals who are supposed to be in dialogue with government and aid officials with regard to local issues, and the lack of funds to develop small community-oriented projects.[9]

In the conclusion we will come back to the notion of social economy/the third sector, as the informal economy, poverty, gender, and microenterprise all come together in the concept of social entrepreneurship.

Chapter 2

Gender, Micro-Entrepreneurship, and the Informal Economy

It is worth emphasizing that the reasons for waiting until the second chapter to tackle the key concepts of the book are twofold. On the one hand, the key concepts needed contextualization within development literature, to which yet another set of theories about social capital/network, social economy, and microfinance had to be introduced. The latter tends to sit on the margins of development research and literature, as we already have discussed. The two main topics of this book, microenterprise/micro-entrepreneurship and the informal sector in the context of developing countries, are closely tied and cannot be separated easily. The issue naturally becomes more complicated when it is related to countries in the Middle East and North Africa (MENA) region, where the concept of gender and the informal sector, as well as micro-entrepreneurship, remains a severely underresearched area (in contrast with areas such South Asia and Latin America). To bring such a rich literature—which tends to focus on countries and regions other than MENA—to Iran has required significant background work to make sure that readers unfamiliar with the literature arrive at the entry point from which the research for this book departed. If the transition is smooth and insightful, then the effort has been successful.

Definitions

The word *entrepreneur* refers to a person who "owns, launches, manages, and assumes the risks of an economic venture" (Greve and Salaff 2003). In recent years, as the percentage of women in the paid-employment sector has increased, many women have entered the economy as entrepreneurs. This has been documented by various organizations such as the Global Entrepreneurship Monitor (GEM) project, which estimates that women constitute close to 30 percent of total entrepreneurs. Interestingly, on a general global level, women are entering the economy as entrepreneurs a rate twice as fast as that of men (Reynolds, Bygrave, and Autio 2004). The recent Organisation for Economic Co-operation and Development (OECD) report confirms growing female entrepreneurship and emphasizes the important role entrepreneurship has for development (OECD 2012). This includes mainly large as well as small and medium enterprises (SMEs) and is more typical of rich countries (Arenius, Langowitz, and Minniti 2005).

While the issue of SMEs has attracted a great deal of attention recently, microenterprises have been research subjects within the gender and development literature in the context of the informal sector for some time. To understand the issue of microenterprises, especially in development and among those from low-income households, it will be helpful to understand the informal sector, because this sector tends to be where microenterprises are based. The *Handbook of Economic Sociology* uses Edgar Feige's definition of the informal economy: "Those actions of economic agents that fail to adhere to the established institutional rules or are denied their protection" (Smelser and Swedberg 2005, p. 12; and Feige 1990, p. 990). Alejandro Portes and William Haller define the informal economy as including "all income-earning activities that are not regulated by the state in social environments where similar activities are regulated" (2005, p. 404). A 2004 Swedish International Development Agency (SIDA) report further defines the informal economy as the "unregulated non-formal portion of the market economy that produces goods and services for sale or other forms of remuneration" (Becker 2004). The sector should include "gainful economic activity" and be considered "socially desirable" (Sethuraman 1981, p. 11) in that it aids both the workers and, in the vast majority of cases, the urban poor more generally. The term *informal economy* (or *informal market* or *sector*) refers to workers or employers that engage in informal work arrangements because either party deems formal work arrangements to be lacking or too difficult to mediate in some regard. The informal market is characterized as such because enterprises rarely comply with the legal standards and regulations that apply to their trade. It should be noted that many countries, in particular with regard to census data, consider enterprises that employ fewer than 10 to 15 employees as part of the informal sector.

Such is the case with Iran, where companies that have less than 15 employees are defined as part of the informal sector.

In 1993 the International Conference of Labor Statisticians adopted an international statistical definition of the informal sector to refer to employment and production that takes place in small and/or unregistered enterprises. In this framework, informal employment is a large and heterogeneous category, which has been divided into subcategories. First, there are types of informal self-employment that includes employers in informal enterprises, own-account workers in informal enterprises, and unpaid family workers. Second, informal wageworkers include employees of informal enterprises, casual or day laborers, temporary or part-time workers, paid domestic workers, unregistered or undeclared workers, industrial outworkers, and homeworkers. As mentioned before, all these categories are included in this research, even though some would be paid workers who are not necessarily micro-entrepreneurs. This inclusion facilitates the analysis of the data drawn from the literature on gender and informal economy.

Laborers in the informal market can be self-employed micro-entrepreneurs or work for others, the latter more commonly referred to as wageworkers. Any worker, employee, or individual working outside of formalized work or employment arrangements falls into the category of informal worker. Laborers can also cross boundaries between the formal economy and informal economy regularly; often workers use the informal economy to supplement formal work arrangements. Most scholars comment that the informal economy is highly heterogeneous by design, and consequently it defies a clear and straightforward definition, so general characteristics are often used to stand in place of a definition.

In this book, the fieldwork includes both micro-entrepreneurs as well as wageworkers at the low end of the informal sector in order to obtain a clear picture of the nature of micro-entrepreneurship and gender in the informal sector. Moreover, it should be made clear that in this book the focus is the legal informal sector, because as SIDA points out, even though the black economy is part of the informal economy, the two should be treated differently (Becker 2004). Criminal markets should not be conflated with the informal economy, as the earmarks of both are quite different, even though the informal economy's noncompliance with regulations leads to illegal activity or a legal gray zone (Timberg 1995, p. 9). For example, the nonregistration of a business might imply any of the following: nonpayment of taxes, operating a business without a license, and/or irregular working hours. The informal economy typically does not include unpaid homework, particularly by women, even though it ought to be included. Also, casual agricultural laborers are often excluded to the disadvantage of female laborers as well. Following S. V. Suthuraman, this book also excludes activities such as begging, prostitution, and trafficking. These are important topics in themselves and require separate examination. As we shall see in Chapters 4 and 5, which deal with the fieldwork findings, in the case of men, selling satellite dishes is an illegal activity, and the city of Tehran has forbidden such vending on the Metro (public transit), yet sellers are known and operate fairly publically (especially female venders).

This book's emphasis is on indicators such as the types and characteristics of informal work: temporary, unregulated, small scale, and home based, with no insurance or employment benefits. Importantly, it should be mentioned that official data do not always capture these activities. This book is focused on low-income households because the informal economy is often a vital lifeline for low-income families to survive. There is a major increase in the informal sector among the poor throughout the developing world, and millions of women are engaged in this sector of the economy—some as laborers, others as micro-entrepreneurs. The book began by looking at women, because a highly sexually segregated labor market exists, but as the fieldwork evolved, the necessity to examine males in the sector became an important part of the research as well. In the chapters to come, men also are included in the fieldwork to shed light on the nature of female work and how it differs from that of men involved in this sector.

How the Informal Economy Was "Discovered"

Keith Hart first discussed the informal economy in an African context. In the late 1960s and early 1970s, Hart, an anthropologist studying urban labor markets, "discovered" a type of economic activity that was very different from what ordinarily is thought of as economic activity. The International Labour Organization (ILO) adapted Hart's 1971 book and his work the informal sector. The work later became a widely read study of Kenya. Initial ILO reports suggested that the informal economy would be absorbed by the formal economy as countries developed their economies, and this idea is still represented in one particular school of thought. However, many studies indicate that the informal economy has expanded to the point at which the sector seems entirely fixed in some countries (Becker 2004). Since Hart's work on Ghana and Kenya, studies on the informal economy worldwide have expanded. The informal market is particularly important in Latin American countries such as Bolivia and Ecuador, as well as South and Southeast Asian countries, particularly India, Cambodia, and Vietnam, as well as in the Middle East, including Turkey and Egypt. There are different approaches to the informal economy, and what follows describes the main schools of thought.

The Modernization School. Those in favor of modernization theory hold that with development of the economy, traditional forms of work and production methods transform into modern and formal work arrangements. The informal sector is viewed as part of the economy and is considered to be traditional. However, with economic development, the informal economy is expected to disappear. Yet, as we have learned, the informal economy is far from disappearing. The informal economy in fact has grown, and not just in developing countries but also in economically advanced countries. In the context of the post-Fordist[1] era, there has been an increase in the informal sector, because many workers find it difficult to obtain work in the formal sector. According to the 2004 SIDA report, however, most modern governments still adopt this school of thought, and it informs their dealings (or lack thereof) with the informal economy (Becker 2004).

The Legalist School. Hernando De Soto's *The Other Path*, published in the 1980s, adopts and elaborates on a different approach that came to be known as the legalist school. De Soto and other Peruvian authors argue that because of excessive regulations enacted by the Peruvian government and those of the other Latin American countries, a large part of the economy has been forced into informality. This school of thought argues that unreasonable regulations were due to the mercantilism of the twentieth-century elite and were designed to create an "unfriendly" economic atmosphere for those with less means to mediate it (Sethuraman 1981). De Soto celebrates the informal economy because of its entrepreneurial spirit, though his critics see his enthusiasm for the informal economy as romanticism and emphasize the sector's social costs instead of benefits (Timberg 1995, p. 9). Others, who support free-market policies, praise his work.

In his work, De Soto documents difficulties of trying to register a small garment factory in Lima and argues that these difficulties are a major barrier to development. An economist with a background in business, De Soto became interested in the grey market during the 1980s after watching pan handlers sift for gold in the Huaypetue region of Peru. In an effort to understand how the market works, De Soto (1989) attempted to set up an informal garment factory and discovered a thick government bureaucracy, taking five full-time students 289 days to obtain an operating license that cost 31 times the average minimum wage. De Soto embarked on a three-year study of the Peruvian market, which indicated that a majority of Peru's economy was functioning on an informal level, upwards of 90 percent in the case of small industrial enterprises (Clift 2003, p. 4). Based on his experience and findings, De Soto developed a financial scheme in which the informal economy could operate by recognizing and placing value on the property of poor entrepreneurs so that they could access capital through financial institutions (Becker 2004, p. 25). De Soto's scheme reexamines and theoretically unlocks the assets in what is known as dead capital (Clift 2003, p. 3). Some proponents of micro-entrepreneurship for women draw from De Soto's work, and this has inspired policy recommendations by international organizations as a way of bringing about economic empowerment for women. However, as we shall see, the issue of microenterprise and gender is nuanced and far from simple, and there are doubts about the celebration of it as the magic bullet for poverty alleviation and/or gender economic empowerment.

The Structuralist School. This approach positions the informal economy as subordinate to the formal economy. The formal economy reduces production by decreasing labor costs and thereby increases profit margins for the capitalist entrepreneur. There is a structural relationship between the formal and the informal sector whereby the formal economy uses the informal sector for reduced labor costs in order to increase the formal sector's competitiveness and productivity. This approach to understanding the informal market was put forward by scholars such Caroline Moser and Alexandra Portes in the late 1970s and the early 1980s. They argue that the informal sector is part of the development process of a capitalist economy (Becker 2004, p. 12).

The Dualist School. There is yet another approach, dominated by the ILO, which began to be formulated in the 1970s. Dualists argue that the informal sector is made up of marginal activities and provides a safety net for the poor because it creates employment. This is particularly important and relevant in times of high unemployment and economic crisis. The literature on women in the informal economy converges with microenterprises in this school, and research on the topic has been enriched by organizations such as Women in the Informal Economy: Globalizing and Organizing (WIEGO).

Generally, many scholars view the informal economy as a sector that leaves workers in a precarious and vulnerable position. As far as the International Labor Organization is concerned, the informal economy is equated with poverty. In the literature on the informal economy, the focus is on the type of activity more common among those who live in poverty in urban areas (Sethuraman 1981; Klein and Tokman 1988). WIEGO literature notes that current scholarship advocates an integrated approach that utilizes elements of all schools of thought where appropriate to reveal the complex reasons wherein individuals turn to the informal sector and the dynamic reasons that the sector exists (Chen, Hussmanns, and Vanek 2012).

The Informal Sector on the Rise

As mentioned before, mainstream economic thought used to be that the informal sector would disappear with the expansion of the new industrial economy. However, the reality is that the informal sector has expanded and is a major provider of employment for those from low-income households, and it has contributed to a sizable share of gross domestic product (GDP). Moreover, the informal sector has become an extension of the formal sector, as it produces goods and services that are necessary to the formal sector for distribution and trade. The informal economy can be seen as trading with, distributing for, and providing services to the formal economy. In Turkey, for example, Shemsa Ozar (a prominent feminist economist) mentioned in an interview (in Istanbul, 2011) that when she was tracking down textile production for the world market in Istanbul, she found that at the low end of the production chain were women who worked at home as homeworkers. Additionally, in the face of the recent global economic meltdown, the informal sector has remained a source of employment for the growing poor, and the recent rise in informal employment is due to the decline in formal employment or to the informalization of previously formal employment relationships.

The sector has expanded beyond its more traditional vending and small-scale business into casual and part-time labor or home-based labor (referred to as homeworking) and highly technical occupations (these not necessarily low paid). More typically the sector is concentrated in nonstandard wage work as well as entrepreneurship and self-employment, which produces goods and services through irregular or unregulated means. Most entrepreneurs and self-employed are inclined to welcome reduced barriers to registration and wish to benefit from regulation, and there is reluctance to take up nonstandard wage work as they instead favor stable jobs and with workers' rights. In many parts of the world, work in the informal economy is made up mostly of activities that are vital to economic survival and tend to fall outside of economic policies (Chen, Vanek, and Carr 2004).

Table 2.1 presents the latest data on the percentage of employment in the informal sector next to those living below the poverty line. As the ILO has documented, the sector provides high employment, and in countries such as Egypt, Bolivia, and Colombia, half of the total employment is in this sector of the economy. Zambia with its high poverty rate is one of those that has more employment in the informal sector than in the formal sector.

The ILO confirms that the informal sector is expanding. Although there is no reliable data on the exact contour of the sector, the ILO has provided estimates of this sector that indicate informal employment makes up 48 percent of nonagricultural employment in North Africa, 51 percent in Latin America, 65 percent in Asia, and 72 percent in sub-Saharan Africa. If agricultural employment is added, the percentages become much larger in countries such as India and many sub-Saharan African states, where the estimate goes beyond 90 percent. Many academics from MENA (especially many Iranian academics in Iran) push for unpaid family labor to be counted as work to give a truer representation of marginalized peoples, such as women, who work in the informal economy (Povey 2005; Moghadam 2009, p. 4). Here it should be noted that in many cases, such as Egypt for instance, the ILO focuses on a small sample and extrapolates its findings. This explains why in some cases the ILO estimates are greater in the informal economy than what has been captured by country census data.

The informal sector is becoming extremely important due to structural changes in the labor market since the 1970s with the expansion of free-market policies. With the popularity of neoliberal economic policies, the role of the state in economics has been curtailed throughout the world. Deregulation of labor associated with a shrinking state role has led to the informalization of previously formal working arrangements. The informal sector has expanded more in the Southern Hemisphere than has been the case in the northern. In addition, the high fertility rate in the hemispherical south and the 1980s baby boom led to an increase in demand for work among the young, mainly urban, population. The high fertility rate in the case of Iran (as well as many other countries) has been reduced since the early 1990s, but the large number of births during the 1980s lead to a young population and mass demand for jobs, making unemployment a major problem. Also, since the 1980s, there has been an increase in urbanization in the Global South, and this is also the case in Iran. The rate of urbanization has created problems for employment in the formal sector, where job availability does not meet the demand.

Table 2.1 Participation in informal economy statistics by country

Country	Percent of persons employed in informal sector	Percent of those living below poverty line
Argentina	32.1	n.a.
Armenia	10.2	26.5
Azerbaijan	26.5*	15.8
Bolivia	52.1	60.1
Brazil	24.3	21.4
Colombia	52.2	45.5
Costa Rica	37	21.7
Ecuador	37.3	36
Egypt	51.2*	22
El Salvador	53.4	37.8
Honduras	58.3	60
Ethiopia	41.1	38.9
India	68.8	27.5
Kyrgyzstan	59.2	43.1
Madagascar	51.8	68.7
Mali	71.4	47.4
Mexico	34.1	47.4
Nicaragua	54.4	46.2
Pakistan	70	22.3
Peru	50.2	34.8
South Africa	17.8	23
Sri Lanka	50.5	15.2
Thailand	42.3*	8.1
Turkey	30.6*	18.1
Uganda	59.2	24.5
Uruguay	33.9	20.5
Viet Nam	43.5	14.5
West Bank and Gaza	23.2	21.9
Zambia	64.6	59.3
Zimbabwe	39.6	72

*These data represent the total percent of persons in the informal sector where data about persons employed in the informal sector are available.

Source: ILO 2011.

Due to a global shift toward large-scale production for the world market, labor-intensive industries have declined. Small-scale production and small enterprises, which are the motor of job creation, are being marginalized and increasingly replaced by large-scale production enterprises. In the case of Iran, although production for the world market is minimal outside of the oil sector, there has been a tendency for industrial production to become capital intensive rather than labor intensive, and unemployment remains a problem (automobile production is an example, and Iran is not exceptional, as many oil-producing MENA countries tend to focus on capital-intensive industries). Concurrent with the move toward globalization of the economy and large-scale production, cost-cutting strategies have led to an increase in subcontracting and homework, which in many cases are filled by low-paid female workers (Chen, Vanek, and Heintz 2006, p. 2133; Sethuraman 1995). These shifts have been the result of neoliberal economic policies geared to maximize profit, as we already have seen in Turkey, but the practice is very common globally. Many large factories cut back on their production costs by shifting the workplace from the factory to the living room of poor households where homework production takes place (mainly by women). Moreover, homeworking allows producers to exercise flexible labor arrangements in order further to reduce their cost (Sethuraman 1981, p. 16). Yet homework is another way of putting many workers in a vulnerable position, as they are unable to defend their rights (as we shall see later is the case with Turkey). This is just one example of how the informal sector (homework) becomes a necessary neoliberal extension of global, large-scale, formal economic expansion.

In addition, throughout the world, many firms engage in tax evasion, and this leads to hiding their real profit; using subcontract homework is an effective way of concealing their increased profit margin. Large-scale manufacturing production for the world market thrives on cost-cutting measures. The issue is interesting because, on the one hand, this expansion has increased the manufacturing enterprise market and has brought production and labor opportunities to Third World countries. On the other hand, constant competition for profit has turned wages for workers in the Global South into a race to the bottom. In many cases, manufacturing has replaced full-time employment with part-time and seasonal work. Although Iran produces only a few manufactured goods such as steel and refrigerators in addition to carpets for the world market, lowering wages in one market affects employment throughout the world nonetheless, by forcing global wages down, which, in turn, hurts those from low-income backgrounds in particular. Employees are at the mercy of their employers, who tend to create jobs that are part-time in order to avoid government regulations. This is a source of precarious labor arrangements that leave workers unprotected, an element of the informalization of work. As we shall see later, although Iran has been deglobalized due to sanctions, the informal sector has expanded partly due to rising prices at the global level and partly (and more recently) due to the impact of crippling sanctions, which take their toll on the poor.

The Positive and Negative Nuances of Gender, Micro-Entrepreneurship, and the Informal Sector

Although so far we have been dwelling on the negative side, there are two differing views about the increase of women's participation in the informal economy and as micro-entrepreneurs (the latter, of course, suggests women may have greater choice and enjoy certain economic benefits). On the positive side, the issue of choice has been emphasized as well as the fact that having some work is better than no work at all. For example, during my field research one informant indicated that her home-based salon let her take care of chores and errands during the day while managing her own time with a salon business. She also felt that she has better relationships with her clients and made more money because she did not have to pay for rental of a chair in a salon. The same informant also felt that she gained power at home by working from home, because, when she was busy, she would ask her husband to take on some household chores and errands. Meanwhile, working at home allowed her to keep an eye on household expenditures.

Successful entrepreneurship in the informal sector can lead to the creation of SMEs, and in some cases it indeed has. This became evident during my fieldwork for a World Bank–funded project on female entrepreneurs in Iran (Bahramitash, Salehi-Esfahani, and Olmsted forthcoming). Some argue that in situations where women are tied to their reproductive work and in the absence of formal employment opportunities, the informal sector, especially home-based work, provides flexibility and compatibility for women. The choice to work at home often is made for the flexibility of work hours and working arrangements as well as its proximity allowing women to combine paid work, domestic chores, and care work. For example, Julia H. Gallaway and Alexandra Bernasek (2002) found that women with infant children are less likely to take on work in the formal sector, and women with toddlers were more likely to take on work in the informal sector (Losby et al. 2002, p. 16). Other studies have shown that many women work as daily caregivers or in other similar low-paid jobs, all of which have flexible hours but are not necessarily inside the home, nor can they be viewed as typical of microenterprise activities. As we shall see in our findings, women who work in the informal sector or as micro-entrepreneurs outside of their home and their immediate network can be vulnerable in other ways.

Louise Dignard and José Havet in particular present a positive view of micro-entrepreneurship in the informal sector and women's rising economic participation. They argue that the combination of household work and paid employment for the many women who do home-based work helps them (1995). Proponents of a positive view argue that labor policy and legislation should support women who are in this sector, as the reality is that their numbers are on the rise, and instead of fighting it, one should focus on legalization, regulation, and protection of these workers (Losby et al. 2002). Naturally, in the case of micro-entrepreneurs, providing access to credit and other supportive measures by the state would be ideal. Graham Tipple also notes that for many families experiencing difficult financial times due to joblessness in the formal market, they may have no choice but to enter into this sector (2005, p. 8).

Zoë Horn discusses the feminization of the labor force in the last two decades as being directly related to women's participation in homework (Horn 2010). She notes that most often women's only access to personal income is through home-based work, and even though global statistics are sketchy, the female homework labor force makes up 50–75 percent of the total labor force where statistics are available. Increasing support for women who do home-based work would also go a long way in helping labor organizations understand the needs of women in the informal economy as well as giving a truer picture of how many work in the informal sector but are "hidden" because of gender norms.

A second school criticizes the positive view of the informal economy by arguing that women are conditioned by prevailing gender norms to assume this triple workload—that is, paid work, domestic work, and caregiving work—and add that gender norms restrict women's mobility and most women therefore do not prefer but rather are forced to work from their homes. It is not really a choice but an imposition dictated by powerful existing patriarchal norms. Critics of the positive side of the informal sector and women's initiatives as micro-entrepreneurs contend that work opportunities are gendered. These "feminine" forms of work are limiting in that they are undervalued and pay considerably less than male-oriented work. This, in fact, may be true, as we see in our discussion of the fieldwork for this book. The findings of Marilyn Carr, Martha Chen, and Joanne Vanek suggest that all these factors contribute to the concentration of women in home-based activities and to gender segmentation in both the formal and informal economies (Chen, Vanek, and Heintz 2006, p. 2136; Chen, Vanek, and Carr 2004, p. 5).

In all countries where data are available, informal traders, mainly street vendors, constitute a significant share of total employment in the informal sector. Women account for between 50 and 90 percent of informal employment in trade, except in those countries where social norms restrict women's mobility outside the home, such as Tunisia and India (Chen 2001, p. 76). Where women's movement outside the home is not restricted, such as in some parts of Southeast Asia, or where it is common for women to be street vendors, they can comprise as much as 97 percent (Cambodia) of the total street-vendor population. In countries such as Bangladesh where women are not a significant part of the visible street-vendor culture, women are still participants, often producing food in the home for men to take to market (Bhowmik 2005).

Additionally, Martha Chen finds a significant relationship between being a woman, working in the informal sector, and high rates of poverty (Chen 2001). According to Chen, gender-based differences in employment status within the informal sector have negative ramifications for relative earnings and corresponding poverty levels. Most important, there are significant gaps between men and women with regard to wages and earnings within the informal economy (this was found to be true in our fieldwork, although due to the randomness of the sample, it has not been overemphasized).

Within the literature about gender and the informal economy, it has been argued that the earnings hierarchy is such that employers have the highest earnings, homeworkers the lowest earnings, and own-account workers and wage workers earn somewhere in between, depending on the economic sector and country. Among micro-entrepreneurs, this may or may not be the case, since many microenterprises bring down their costs by operating from home. Generally, however, the net result of the impact of the labor market is a significant gender gap in earnings within the informal economy, with women earning less on average than men, especially since women are mostly homeworkers (Chen, Vanek, and Carr 2004). Richard King and Caroline

Sweetman in their 2010 Oxfam report note that home-based workers have seen a decline in available work in recent years (p. 10). Note, however, that the authors here are discussing homeworkers, not micro-entrepreneurs.

Horn argues that women already occupy the most vulnerable positions in the global workforce, but this becomes particularly pronounced during times of economic crisis. What perhaps is alarming, as Horn finds, is that 40 percent of women who responded to her survey, conducted in various regions all over the Global South, identified themselves as the primary breadwinners. The majority of the remaining respondents indicated that their income was crucial to their families' survival (2010, p. 10). The burden of financial responsibility and family duties create a great deal of stress for women, and many in Horn's survey report feeling depressed or exhausted.

To end this section, although more has been written and discussed about the negative aspects of the informal economy, the picture is far from clear. Even in the case of street vendors, who as we argued have some of the worst conditions, Bhowmik's study of them shows that women reported feelings of independence and a good self-image because they were able to provide for their families (2005, p. 55). Nevertheless, other authors report that women who work in the informal economy will sacrifice their own needs before that of their children and sometimes even their husbands. Women will forego prescribed medication, doctor's visits, or even basic nutrition so that their children can attend school (Horn 2010, p. 12; King and Sweetman 2010, p. 10). Women in King and Sweetman's 2010 Oxfam study noted that because men's jobs are more important, they deserve to eat more than women, even when the women themselves were pregnant. At the same time, a woman's income (even if it is minimal) can increase her bargaining power in the household (Braunstein 2002; Sen 1990; Roldan 1988; and Joekes 1987). It is important to examine how and to what extent, if indeed at all, access to either formal or informal employment or working as micro-entrepreneur may increase women's power over economic resource allocation and decision-making processes inside the household.

This somewhat contradictory and mixed picture calls for more in-depth research and case-by-case studies. There are clearly many different factors at work, and one of them is the type of work in which women are engaged. Generally, one can assume that when women in the informal sector engage in entrepreneurial/microenterprise activities (even in low-income households, which are the focus of this book), this means they have some kind of ownership over the means of their production, and they tend to be working under better economic conditions compared with those who are wage workers. The nuances are important, however, and it is crucial that research on the topic moves away from generalizations and aims for case-by-case documentation. Here we now turn to the MENA region and start the discussion with the case of Iran.

Where Does MENA Fit in the Complicated Picture?

According to WIEGO's analysis of the 2002 ILO report, "Women and Men in the Informal Economy," 47 percent of the working population in MENA has employment in the nonagricultural informal market. A majority—63 percent—are self-employed, and 42 percent of the self-employed in the informal sector are female (Beall 2007, p. 11). A challenge for analyzing data for MENA countries is that gender analysis is relatively new or, in some contexts, completely overlooked all together. A real problem is lack of documentation on working women. To illustrate, a United Nations Development Fund for Women (UNIFEM) report notes problems even within its own office in Lebanon—in this case, because gendered analysis was a new concept for development workers, and to make matters even more difficult, the word *gender* does not have an Arabic equivalent. In the same UNIFEM article, complications in gathering gendered business-loan information were reported because bank data were not separated by gender in an attempt by the bank to be impartial in its business dealings (Husseini 1997, p. 50).

Insight from Turkey

Of all MENA countries, Turkey is probably one of the best-documented countries in the region with regard to the role of women in the informal sector. However, the research on that topic has its own limitations, and the entire issue of work in the informal sector is a major problem when it comes to documentation. As Nurhan Davutyan notes, there are major dilemmas with regard to what small companies view as high taxation, which then translates into employers not reporting their employees, meaning that no compensation exists for their workers if they lose their employment. In order to avoid income taxes, some employees and employers collude to report only the minimum wage and pay the difference in cash and never report this payment. Due to high taxes, employees and employers often choose to work outside the formal economy (Davutyan 2008, p. 2). In the case of women, however, Belkis Kümbetoğlu et al. report that many women beg their employers to register them so that they can get social security. Many are promised registration after three months, but this never happens. Part of what may be contributing to the transient nature of the informal market is related to the inability to get social security. Women in the report by Kümbetoğlu et al. describe how they constantly are searching for new jobs that might offer them security (Kümbetoğlu, User, and Akpınar 2010). The consequence of high taxes in Turkey has translated into many workers being without social security, health benefits, legal support, and environmental regulations. Davutyan's 2008 article suggests that the World Bank's 2006 report indicates that 53 percent of Turkish workers are outside the social security system, as opposed to the 46 percent found by Kümbetoğlu et al. (2010, p. 10). Interestingly, the informal economy also includes 2.2 million male and female retirees—those who are required officially and legally to retire at rather young ages (39 for women) but continue to work informally so that they can continue to collect social security and earn supplemental wages through informal work (Davutyan 2008, p. 2).

Sibel Kalaycıoğlu's analysis shows that informal workers are at the highest risk for poverty. Those in the informal economy at the greatest risk, again, are unpaid family workers, seasonal or daily wage workers, and self-employed workers. The poverty rate for the daily wage or seasonal workers group was 45 percent. Kalaycıoğlu paints an image of the poorest families, among whom most family members are unemployed or underemployed in casual or seasonal labor, or which are female headed because an adult male is either absent or disabled. Generally these families are from rural origins but now live in the city without assets such as land or livestock. Girls' education often is sacrificed when income does not allow for tuition or school fees. No financial strategy or governmental safety net exists, as those who are employed are unregistered workers. If a family member is employed in the informal sector, they have no access to health care or infrastructural facilities. Migrant families are socially excluded and do not have access to basic information on hygiene, health, political involvement, empowerment, or government assistance.

Kalaycıoğlu also notes the importance of building family or kin safety nets, which does not solve poverty problems but at least may reduce the risk of absolute poverty. This feeds into the women's social network issue, which was discussed earlier and to which we will keep returning. Women are major contributors to the family pool of assets through their informal homework, even though wages are very low and unpredictable. The family or kin pool includes not just money but also child care, domestic work, and elderly care. This is seen as unpaid family labor, but it helps in building the familial safety net. Women are also at the center of creating opportunities to ease poverty burdens. The issue of social networks and safety nets keep resurfacing throughout this work, and in the context of Iran, they will be elaborated on in depth.

Normative views on male pride keep men from seeking government assistance, so women often are sent to social-service providers or to neighbors to ask for food or money. The family network also creates a wider social network, and women are often the messengers with regard to finding cheap food and products, employment opportunities, or government services. Kalaycıoğlu describes this structure in order to outline coping strategies, not to claim that the family structure can deal with poverty. The safety net may provide some insurance, but it also means that women are not entitled to keep their earnings or spend them as they see fit but instead are obliged through family pressure to give it over (Kalaycıoğlu 2006). These factors put women at the greatest risk for poverty.

Picking up on the familial-safety-net model that Kalaycıoğlu outlines, Simel Esim has undertaken to study how women in Turkey have begun to organize microfinance enterprises. Esim studied informal, mainly nonfinancial organizations that offer support to other informal groups (Kalaycıoğlu 2006), a subject to which we shall return later in the case of Iran and Egypt. Esim argues that support from the women's network came in the form of cooperation instead of competition in an effort to raise women's entrepreneurial profile in the buying market and their bargaining power with authorities (Esim 2000, p. 145). Women in these organizations face the same issues: juggling child care with work demands as well as discrimination in the market. Esim found that the female microenterprise operators who took part in her study were more likely to sell goods and products to other women entrepreneurs and were also more likely to hire other women compared with male entrepreneurs. Esim notes that men traditionally founded and ran most formal trade and craft organizations. Women have found that their voices are stronger together as an informal group rather than in formal male-oriented trade and crafts groups where women have limited access (Esim 2000, p. 148). This issue falls within the discussion of gender segregation, with more in-depth analysis and documentation in my fieldwork for Iran.

Esim shows that, when compared to men, women entrepreneurs were less likely to have accessed bank loans or have savings and checking accounts with financial institutions (only one-third of women had accounts, compared to one-half of the men). Also, only 9 percent of female micro-entrepreneurs and 2 percent of small entrepreneurs obtained bank loans, while most invested their own savings, others borrowed from friends and family, a small amount used retirement savings, and 9 percent started with zero capital (Esim 2000, p. 146). Esim looks at two groups: first, 3B, a marketing cooperative in which women support one another in coming up with design ideas for craft, clothing, and food products and that also provides members with a stall one day per week at the local market (2000, p. 146). 3B also provides contacts for members to attend trade shows. Esim found that cooperation among 3B members to be quite healthy, with communication flowing horizontally instead of vertically. The second group is Corum Women's Cooperative, which provides stall space at markets as well (Esim 2000, p. 148). However, Esim found this group to more hierarchical. According to Esim, these organizations are born out of the lack of resources in formal channels for marketing, legal advice, and government support, with NGOs proving to be unreliable sources for support as well (2000, p. 149).

Similarly in other informal economies worldwide, women often do temporary, sporadic, home-based, and seasonal or piecework jobs. Compounding this issue, however, is an assumption that men are the breadwinners, and if women work at all, it is before they are married. Kümbetoğlu et al. notes a predominant stereotype that Turkish women see marriage as the means to making a living. This stereotype has been used as a means to justify the bias against hiring women in the formal economy and their mistreatment in the informal economy, especially when it comes to registering employees for social insurance. As of 2005, women made up only 24 percent of the formal economy but made up 75 percent of the informal economy (Kümbetoğlu, User, and Akpınar 2010). Another issue that arises for women in the Turkish economy is that women largely are concentrated in agriculture and unpaid work, both of which further obscure them from economic recognition (Spidla 2012, p. 3). Though Vladimir Spidla notes that Turkey has made advances in gender-equality legislation, Aysit Tansel (2000) points out that women's wages are still generally below men's in both the formal and the informal economy, but to the greatest degree in the informal market.

Tansel suggests that these findings indicate systematic discrimination against women in the Turkish employment economy, both informal and formal.[2] Spidla also finds that women in Turkey do not have equal access to education, and illiteracy is prevalent among them

(Tansel 2000, p. 2). In fact, Kalaycıoğlu puts the total illiteracy rate for women at 11.4 percent (Spidla 2012, p. 4). These are factors that may push women toward the informal economy. Kümbetoğlu et al. reports that industries that operate informally in Turkey are notoriously difficult and dangerous places to work. Work conditions often are cramped, dark, loud, and toxic. Female workers, who very commonly work in textiles, a gendered occupation, toil long hours, sometimes through the night. One informant reported going to work on a Thursday and not leaving until Saturday (Kalaycıoğlu 2006). Another informant, who worked in a mushroom-growing enterprise, reported many incidents of rheumatoid arthritis from working in cramped, humid conditions, because employers did not install appropriate ventilation systems for fear of being caught by authorities (Kümbetoğlu, User, and Akpınar 2010). Tansel notes that the fine for having an unregistered worker is 360 US dollars, twice the rate of the legal minimum wage at the time the research was carried out. Yet, whatever extreme steps employers take to conceal their employees (i.e., not installing proper ventilation), Tansel also notes a very low probability that employers will be caught, and if they are caught, they likely will not comply with paying the fine.

In fairly sharp contrast to Spidla's 75 percent female participation in the informal economy, Bulutay and Tasti place women's involvement at only 11 percent, based on census data gathered in 1999. One might question their work, because it relies entirely on national census data, which may not capture the whole picture. The authors attribute this low involvement with the informal economy not to low education rates (they note that women in urban areas without high school education is only at 9.9 percent), or solely to Islamic views on women, but more to the idea that it is not usual for women to take on work for a secondary income (Bulutay and Tasti 2004). It is noted that this burden generally falls on young male members of the family when more income is needed. The focus of these findings does draw attention to the value that unpaid labor adds to the economy, but it doesn't seem to fit with prevailing thought on women's involvement in the economy.

Insight from Egypt

Many authors note that a major barrier to women's success in the formal sector is the breadwinner model: Men are the breadwinners in families, and women's main responsibility is to stay home and raise children. This ideology stems from, in some cases, the Islamic worldview, and in Egypt (Elgeziri 2010) and Iran (Povey 2005) it is propped up by state law. Women are allowed to work to varying degrees, and freedom to choose to work also varies. We will return to the topic of the male-breadwinner model and the patriarchal bargain.

In the case of Egypt, the Egyptian Labor Bureau gives a similar picture of women in the informal market. In 2002 the ILO reported that informally self-employed Egyptian women were 67 percent of total women wage workers. Moushira Elgeziri's 2010 study looks at the experiences of a number of women with technical degrees but who either are unable or choose not to utilize their degrees. The article, "Wading through the Treacle: Female Commercial School Graduates (CSGs) in Egypt's Informal Economy," follows the experiences of sixty women working in the informal sector after graduating from commercial schools. Elgeziri cites a 2006 Egyptian Labor Market Panel Survey indicating that unemployment rates had declined compared with 1998 data, yet women's unemployment remained quite high. This is similar to Iran, where since 2000 there has been a high unemployment rate for women despite increasing employment opportunities. Elgeziri notes that the Egyptian government's hiring was at 30 percent of the total labor force in 1988, lowering to 23 percent in 1998, and further decreasing to 15 percent in 2006. She argues that women prefer to be hired by the government because of work stability, benefits, and social security. Women did not seek jobs in other formal sectors, such as industrial work, because the hours and working conditions were not tolerable for long periods of time. It is unclear, based on the two articles cited here, why women's wages in the informal market also decreased rapidly between 1988 and 1998, but Women in Informal Employment Globalizing and Organizing (WIEGO) confirms that women's wages were significantly lower than men's in 1998 regardless of education levels (Chen, Vanek, and Carr 2004, p. 51).[3]

The informal market in Egypt is estimated to make up 55 percent of the total workforce; this includes not only microenterprises but also workers who are registered but are not supported or recognized by the government and therefore have no social protection. Most of these workers are technical school graduates who take work in order to survive because of work shortages in their field (Elgeziri 2010, p. 7). Female employment in the informal economy is not always about survival, however. Many women from affluent families say that they take employment to alleviate boredom when living at home (2010, p. 13). Elgeziri notes that the pressure to marry is not as great as it was ten years ago, and so recent grads may live at home for longer.

Even women from less affluent families will often also say that their informal work is "passing time" so as to distance themselves from appearing financially needy, or if they fail to find jobs, they are able to "save face" (p. 13). We shall return to this issue later when we discuss the topic of class in Iran, and in many ways Iran shares some of the findings general to the issue of women's work in the informal sector in Turkey and Egypt.

Iran: Documentation and Information

An overview of the informal sector by the 2003 United Nations Country Assessment for Iran places the country's informal sector at 65 percent of the gross national product (GNP; UN 2003, p. 40). This is similar to other southern hemispherical numbers: informal employment makes up 48 percent of nonagricultural employment in North Africa, 51 percent in Latin America, 65 percent in Asia, and 72 percent in sub-Saharan Africa. Iran, however, has the largest informal economy in the region. Iran's government, like many others, tolerates and in some cases encourages the informal sector in an effort to alleviate poverty and diversify the economy away from mainly oil revenues. The effort to diversify came after the Iran-Iraq war, which had a devastating effect on Iran's unemployment rate.

Mohsen Ranani argues that there has been significant growth in Iran's informal sector in the ten years following the revolution and during the Iran-Iraq war. Before the revolution, the informal sector could be placed at 21 percent of all employment. Directly following the revolution, the sector rose from 21 percent to 29 percent, and it rose another 29 percent following the war (Ranani 2001a). The Ministry of Labor puts the overall informal sector at a full 30 percent, meaning that 7.5 million laborers out of 25 million work in the informal sector.[4] Again, Iran is not unusual in this regard when it comes to the ever-expanding informal labor sector worldwide.

While there is little information on the informal sector in Iran, there is even less written about women in the informal sector. Where there is literature on the topic, the focus is on the rural informal sector.[5] For example, Khojasteh Arefnia (1993), Jaleh Shaditalab (2005), and Mohsen Ranani (2001a, 2001b) focus on rural informal economies rather than urban ones. Others have emphasized women's unpaid work at home as part of the informal sector and its contribution to surplus value (Lehsayi-Zadeh and Omidi 2001). They assert that women's reproductive labor is an important part of the economy, yet there is no recognition of its value as part of the national economy.

All these aspects of women's role in the informal sector are important, but increasingly with urbanization, the rise of mega cities, and rural-to-urban migration, urban informal economies are becoming more and more salient. Yet, the topic remains underresearched, in spite of some work by academics such as Firozeh Jamal, Mirsatar Saddr Mosavi, and Parvin Dokht Libarjani (2009), and there is a dearth of literature on the urban informal sector in general and the position of women in particular.

Some of this is due to sexual segregation and the fact that what many women do takes place at home and can easily be overlooked. On the whole it seems that research and literature on the topic is quite general and has not been able to document women's important roles in the informal sector. What little research does exist on the informal sector in Iran often focuses on men, and women's role continues to be left out. In two major works on the informal sector, by Mahmood Jomehpoor and Said Nayeb, the focus of the first one was men only, and in the second, no gender desegregated analysis was done (Nayeb 2001; Jomehpoor 2001).[6] There is research that examines gender and the informal sector, but it is limited. The existing focus on the informal economy that excludes urban women has left a gap in the research on the informal economy in Iran in general. There is a need for data on women's employment, especially as micro-entrepreneurs in the growing urban economy.

One of the façades of employment in the informal sector is undercounting and underreporting, as we already have seen in the case of Turkey, where private enterprises did not report workers to evade taxes. This is true of many developing countries and also of Iran. It is especially applicable for upper-income women who work as micro-entrepreneurs. For example, Fatemeh Moghadam (2011) gathered data on women's microenterprises in higher-income areas of Tehran by distributing anonymous surveys through a network of friends and acquaintances to locales and offices that had a high number of female clients, customers, and volunteers and also recruiting a number of women volunteers to fill out the surveys. Locations were chosen based on the likelihood that working-age women with a variety of educational backgrounds would visit, such as travel agencies, dress makers, private language classes, a cancer-related charity, an engineering consulting firm, newspaper/magazine offices, and photography studios.

GENDER SEGREGATION MATTERS

Gender segregation is another factor in the low documentation of female employment. Because women often carry out their work in the private domain, it easily is overlooked. Moreover, in the case of home-based businesses, and especially if a woman is not a wage earner, she may tend not to think of her work as work. This was found among low-income women who did food processing, for example. When such work is viewed as being extremely close to their reproductive roles, it tends to be unreported, and this is a problem that has been mentioned about data gathering on female employment.

Iran has one of the most gender-segregated labor markets in the world. I have discussed in my earlier work that generally, worldwide, documenting women's work is a challenge. Moreover, gender continues to be at a disparity in matters of skilled labor, employment opportunities, benefits, and stability (Bahramitash 2005). Men are overrepresented in high-paid, skilled labor, whereas women are overrepresented in low-paid, temporary jobs that offer no benefits (Joekes 1987; Anker 2001; and Loutfi 2001). Despite these "facts," in Iran the issue is more complicated than it is globally, and one cannot automatically assume that just because gender segregation is more prevalent, it is necessarily and categorically worse for women. In the case of Iran, it is worth mentioning that, similar to many other countries in the region, a double segregation (in public life as well the labor market) has provided a more complex economic and social environment. Sexual segregation can hinder women's access to well-paid, formal employment, although the issue is related to women's class position. In the case of Iran (and also in Turkey and Egypt, as well as in much of the MENA region), while sexual segregation may have closed some employment doors, ironically—and especially in the case of the self-employed and micro-entrepreneurs—it has opened others. This is because women entrepreneurs in a highly segregated society tend to focus on all-female-clientele-based businesses, and this can provide some freedom from male competition, increase their access to the market, and at the same time reduce cases of sexual harassment. Furthermore, in Iran, rotating credit and saving associations (ROCSAs) are common among women. These credit associations in some cases solve the problem of lack of female access to credit, especially for those who do not possess collateral, and they are a potential venue for women's entrepreneurial needs. We shall return to this later in this book with documented cases.

There is also greater diversity of activities among this group of women, who work with other women and make a decent income without working outside the home. For some own-account workers, working from the home also makes greater economic sense, contrary to what some argue about the global picture. Women micro-entrepreneurs who are from middle-income households save on overhead costs, like rent or utilities. Women's entry into micro-entrepreneurial activities started in Iran after the 1979 revolution; among middle-class women who were forced or compelled to leave their jobs, the choice to work as micro-entrepreneurs became an alternative option. Women's activities are extremely varied, from providing rentals for wedding celebrations, to interior design, women-only art exhibitions (particularly among the high-income households), dressmaking, home day care, and tutoring, among middle-income households. Among the low-income households we find women working in sales in particular (Bahramitash and Kazemipour 2011, p. 231). By showing the range of activities in the informal sector, one can get a sense of the delicate line between working in the informal sector and micro-entrepreneurship.

CLASS MATTERS

With regard to urban women, Fatemeh Moghadam's "Women, Gender and Informal Sector: Iran" (from *Encyclopedia of Women and Islamic Cultures*, 2007) suggests there is a large informal labor sector in Iran, and it is made up of women who do not fit the profile of informal laborers as being poor, uneducated, and therefore unable to find formal employment. In my 2011 research with Shahla Kazmeipour, we documented how women from different class backgrounds are engaged in the informal sector, some as micro-entrepreneurs. In our survey based on cluster sampling, using a map of Tehran to pick a representative sample, we discovered that women from the high and very high-income brackets made up 11.7 percent and 9.5 percent, respectively, in the informally employed and micro-entrepreneurs categories. This finding contrasts somewhat with much of the literature on gender and the informal sector, which focuses largely on uneducated women who work in the informal market.

Women's participation in the formal labor force in MENA countries is low when compared to participation rates elsewhere in the world. Moghadam suggests that there is "a sizeable unmeasured and hidden informal female economy that is inclusive of not only poor and unskilled female workers but also middle- and upper-class educated and skilled women" (2011). In my previous work on the informal sector (Bahramitash and Kazemipour 2011), my survey of more than four hundred women in the city of Tehran showed that 68.9 percent were working in the formal and informal sectors, and the rest were homemakers. The results indicated that women preferred to work in the formal sector, and if they entered the informal sector, they did so as micro-entrepreneurs.

This survey was followed by another research project in Tehran and Mashhad, where several unstructured, open-ended interviews and focus groups were organized. All in all, the research project included interviews with sixty female low-income workers, half of which were street vendors, and the other half being home-based workers. The research also included women from both medium- and low-income households. The aim was to examine the impact of class in preference for formal versus informal work, and the results showed that women enter the informal sector in many cases because of their lack of access to formal work. Yet, when their activities were in the domain of micro-entrepreneurship, they preferred the informal sector. Moreover, some reported that microenterprise, when home based, has several advantages. Working in the informal sector and/or as micro-entrepreneurs can provide many women with feelings of satisfaction, but this feeling was more common among women in the high- to very-high-income category. In general, the survey revealed that those women who were very successful, high-income micro-entrepreneurs had a good sense of work satisfaction and also preferred working in the informal sector. Close to 80 percent of female micro-entrepreneurs from the middle- and high-income brackets reported being either highly or fairly satisfied with their enterprises. Some of them preferred self-employment because of the freedom it provided from male harassment and the ability to stay at home rather than travelling to work, which gave them the liberty of not observing imposed public dress code (there is a tendency among middle- and upper-class urban women not to observe Islamic *hejab* when in homes). Additional reasons for working as micro-entrepreneurs, such as general independence and personal interest, ranked high among this group. These reasons could be attributed to the fact that many upper- and middle-class women have the luxury of choosing the type of economic activity in which to become involved, and they can afford to hire women from low-income households to take care of their domestic chores.

There is an interesting contrast with what we shall see among low-income women, who reported mixed feelings, some not liking their work at all, others liking it, and some liking the extra income because of the negotiating leverage it gave them but not the nature of their work. The survey showed that low-income households were unsatisfied in their employment at a rate of 31.6 percent, and many of them were in business due to the lack of other options. Obviously, they did not have the advantage of having paid daily care, because this is costly and is the privilege of the middle- and upper-class women, but they drew on their social network and extended family to provide them with assistance with their household chores. My earlier survey and the research for this book found similar results.

Many of our interviewees from both the middle- and high-income brackets said they had not provided information about their employment to officers who were collecting data for the national census because they wished to keep the government from interfering with their financial affairs. This was why in this book I have tried to include household data as well. For the low-income women, the reasons for not reporting their financial income was in part because they did not see themselves as really "working" due to the temporary nature of many of their jobs, or they viewed much of their work as part of their roles as homemakers and thus downplayed it. This has been a challenge, and, as discussed before, it is not just a problem for Iran but rampant throughout the developing world.

Generally and due to low pay, the informal economy is overcrowded by those from low-income households. This is why the survey focused on those from low-income groups. The sample in this book is comprised of 30.7 percent and 27.7 percent respectively from low- and very-low-income women. Ironically, however, many described themselves as primarily housewives (33 percent), and this is related to the types of production they are involved in, which is very close to their role as homemakers. What is intriguing is the class difference between high- and middle-income women and low-income women: Low-income women can facilitate the work of middle-class and upper-class women. This means that women from low-income households subsidize the reproductive work of high- and middle-income women by working for them as maids and/or nannies. Low-income women must rely on family and friend networks or their older children for the care of younger ones when they are working out of the home. All the same, among our sample the low-income women had to work harder to make up for the double workday, since in a busy city like Tehran the extended family network is not as strong.

SOCIAL NETWORK MATTERS

In Chapter 1 we had some discussion about the importance of social networks. We saw how they can work for as well as against women by reinforcing inequalities (especially emphasized in the work of

Bourdieu). In Egypt, for example, it has been argued that a major problem that women face in finding formal-sector jobs is the lack of influential connections in the social network, or *wasta* (in Persian, *vaseteh*). Women in Elgeziri's work reported losing opportunities for stable employment because their families are not well connected in the formal sector.[7] One informant tried to find a *wasta* and instead found herself to be more of an escort to the man with whom she was trying to make connections. The informal economy is also somewhat dangerous for women, as one woman reported showing up for an interview despite warnings from neighbors about the address for which she was looking. Finally arriving at the address, she found an upturned office and a half-dressed man there to greet her (Elgeziri 2010, p. 14).

However, in my research the issue has been viewed from a different angle. As discussed in Chapter 1, there exists the shadow/Other market, which mixes and overlaps with the informal market and, in some cases, is in the third sector. This theme will be elaborated in the conclusion after the fieldwork has been discussed in full. The shadow/Other market also feeds well into the sexually segregated labor market, because women who work informally in the service and production industry have created separate and parallel markets that have come to be dominated by women. In fieldwork conducted in Tehran, I found women-run support networks, which functioned based on contacts with extended family and neighborhood networks. In just one hairdressing salon I found a number of economic activities being conducted, including a women's underwear sale, fortune telling, advertising for dressmakers, buying and selling of real estate, and referrals for rental opportunities and day-care and domestic-care providers. In later research, I found that many women come together through their religious activities in the form of *sofrehs* (a religious meeting group in homes), for instance. The *sofreh* is a major networking event, and in some cases I have observed women finding clientele for their goods and services.

In my earlier survey (2007), many women reported that they received business through word of mouth. Since the informal economy's nature is to be somewhat underground, yet accessible to potential clients and customers, word of mouth is the most important form of marketing for women in the sector, close to 70 percent of them indicated that word-of-mouth marketing was their primary method, while the rest cited it as the secondary method. Some women also relied on promotion in private gatherings, as well as advertising in residential buildings, art galleries, and showrooms. In the case of low-income and religious women, religious gatherings fulfilled the same function. These methods were largely noted as secondary, with 37.1 percent of women noting private promotion and 20 percent noting advertisements as their secondary methods. Further, in more recent research (2012), I have found that the social network, especially among low-income religious women, is an important part of the social safety net. With regard to women's work both as employees and as micro-entrepreneurs, the network is highly critical in providing access to mainly female-dominated markets. The social network also has an important function with regard to access to credit through rotating credit and saving associations (see Chapter 1 for a detailed discussion of ROCSAs).

Education, Age, and Marital-Status Matters

One of the factors that seemed to affect women's presence in the informal sector and as micro-entrepreneurs was their level of education, an issue also linked to their class. Higher education among the sample brought more access to formal employment. The findings were generally in line with other literature on women in the informal economy, as it is thought that women with low levels of education are able to find employment in the informal sector when they are shut out of formal employment. Levels of education for women in Iran have increased, and these numbers may change with an increase in overall education levels (Bahramitash 2007). Similar results were found in the research for this book, as we shall see later.

Moreover, in all research groups, across classes, and for women of all walks of life, gaining economic decision-making power in the family was an important factor. During the course of research on this topic, I found that many women, especially older women working in the informal sector and micro-entrepreneurs, secured powerful places for themselves within the social network; working informally helped them maintain contacts within extended families and social networks. For this reason, Chapter 3 will present information on the issue of social capital and social networks.

To end this chapter with an interesting concept while we are on the topic of education, age, and marital status, it is important to discuss an insight concerning the patriarchal bargain. Throughout this chapter, I have mentioned the breadwinner model. The term refers to how mainstream literature views men as the breadwinner and women as homemakers. The issue in the context of the Middle East was first articulated in the work of Deniz Kandiyoti in her 1988 article "Bargaining with Patriarchy." Kandiyoti articulated the idea in terms of how women negotiate their position not just domestically but also socially. The topic has been used in many writings on women in the Muslim world and articulated in other academic research. Here the focus will be on employment and how women negotiate their reproductive and productive work. When fieldwork is analyzed in this book, we will come back to this issue, since many women are ambivalent about the fact that, despite bringing an income, they continue to be responsible for domestic and reproductive work. This is even more pertinent to women who are married. Some interviews showed that not all women wanted to enter paid employment out of choice; for some it was an economic survival strategy. In the case of widowed and single mothers, however, the fact that the mainstream stereotypes women's work as primarily that of a homemaker is obviously a major hindrance to their economic status as independent workers, since their income is assumed to be supplementary. Increasingly women are divorcing their husbands, and in some cases men either are absent or are a drain on family income because of drug addiction. This issue poses a major challenge to women who are the main breadwinners (Bahramitash and Olmsted 2012a, b).

Chapter 3

Women's Employment in Iran

Entering the Formal Sector

Until the mid-twentieth century, the urban economy was limited in scope, and much of Iran's economy was concentrated in agricultural production. As a result, where the issue of women in the informal economy is concerned, much of the focus was on the rural economy. In Iran, much like the rest of the world, women have been, and continue to be, part of the agricultural and pastoral economy as well as its cottage industry. With respect to rural production, as Lois Beck and Nikki R. Keddi documented, women long have been involved in the production of the famous Persian carpets (1978, p. 358), and Fred Halliday demonstrated that women were responsible for 70 percent of cloth weaving (1979, p. 191). What is important to remember here is that, in preindustrial Iran, as was typically the case elsewhere, there was little or no separation between the workplace and the home, and since there was not much of a formal economy, there was no real formal employment either.

In my previous work I have argued that the process of modernization/industrialization undermined women's economic status in the early stages of development, as women lost access to means of home-based economic production (Bahramitash and Salehi-Esfahani 2011). Many academics have argued that the transition to modernization is coupled with a redefinition of male and female work and their responsibilities in and outside home, at least initially, which led to loss of status and access to economic resources for women. This can be seen not just in the Third World but also in the First World (Benería and Sen 1981; Hall 1996). Judith Tucker documented that the economic history of Egypt indicated controls on which women had access to means of production as well as the sale of goods produced (especially in the Nile Delta). Her research showed that women's roles were undermined by colonization. Furthermore, records about women in the late nineteenth century show that women were engaged in a variety of occupations, such as midwives, servants, pastry cooks, cotton workers, singers, and dancers (1985, 1976, 1993).

There is evidence to show that industrialization under Muhammad Ali (r. 1805–48) led to the taking over of entire workers' guilds that had provided workers with raw materials, compensated them, and taken control of the sales of their finished products (Keddie 2007). The process of colonization and industrialization in Egypt marginalized women from the textile industry in favor of British goods and the production of raw material, which replaced the textile industry. Singerman also points to women's involvement in trade (Hoodfar and Singerman 1996). The colonization of Egypt crippled the cottage industries—women's guilds in particular, which were never able to regain their economic significance (Hoodfar 1997). One could argue that in the case of Iran, similar to other urban economies of the region during the nineteenth and early twentieth centuries, women were able to participate in the gender-segregated, petty professions of the informal urban economy. In Iran, one found women participating in the informal sale of goods and products made in the home, working in public baths, hairdressing, and dress making.

Until World War I, Iran was primarily an agrarian society. However, the change and transition from an agricultural to an industrial market began after the 1921 coup d'état that led to the rise of Reza Shah Pahlavi (r. 1925–41). He embarked on a rapid modernization program, including building public infrastructure such as schools and hospitals, which opened new types of occupations for women. Reza Shah, a military man, much like Ataturk of Turkey, became a major force in bringing women into the formal labor force. Secular education became an important venue for incorporating women into the public sphere and the creation of a new professional class. Most of the changes applied to those belonging to the urban middle class, and for the most part the rural and pastoral society remained on the periphery. After the outbreak of the World War II in 1939, Reza Shah did not join the allies and instead declared Iran a neutral country. After Germany invaded the Soviet Union in 1941, thus making the latter an ally of Great Britain, a joint Anglo-Russian army invaded Iran to seize control of the railroad Reza Shah had constructed, quickly defeated the Iranian army, sent Reza Shah into "exile" (house arrest) in British South Africa, but allowed his son, Mohammad Reza

Shah, to reign, even as Iran remained under allied occupation until March 1946. After the war and a decade of political turmoil caused by Iran's efforts to nationalize its oil industry—which British Petroleum claimed to own—Mohammed Reza Shah continued with the modernization agenda, initiating during the early 1960s a "White Revolution" that focused on industrial development and land reform. However, the White Revolution's modernization plans for agriculture led to a decline in employment in the rural areas (Hooglund 1982). Modernization continued after the overthrow of the monarchy in 1979 and its replacement with an Islamic Republic, and it still remains official policy, even though its focus now is on urban areas, because the population in rural Iran has declined from 75 percent in 1950 to 30 percent in 2006.

Between 1920 and 1960 Iran's population doubled to 23 million, and by 1979 the equivalent to the entire population of the country in 1920 had been added. Most of the population migrated to urban centers and found jobs in industry and services. In 1960, about one-third of the population lived in towns, but by 1979 nearly half the population was urban. Tehran became the center of government, higher education, and industry; in 1976, it contained two-thirds of all university students and nearly one-third of high school students, and about half of all factories were in or around Tehran. After the revolution of 1979, this trend continued, although at a slower pace, as industrialization spread out to other urban centers, such as Esfahan, Mashhad, Shiraz, and Tabriz, as well as to smaller cities. Currently, more than 65 percent of the Iranian population lives in towns. Tehran remains the principal political, economic, and industrial center, with a population of 7 million, according to the 2006 census, and at least 5 million more in the suburban communities to the east, west, and south of the capital.[1]

The Shah's Era (1941–79)

The shah's era was marked by rapid industrialization through several programs packaged as the White Revolution, which partially was an effort to avoid a peasant uprising and the spread of socialist ideas. A massive land redistribution program was carried out in order to create the preconditions for capitalist agriculture and to encourage "surplus" landless peasants to migrate to cities to become workers for accelerated industrialization (Hooglund 1982). As part of the White Revolution many educated young men and women were sent to rural areas to bring formal education and basic health-care services; this was part and parcel of women's entry into the formal economy. However, the White Revolution had an impact on these young women, who did not wear *hejab* and primarily belonged to the middle class. Partially the White Revolution was an attempt to modernize not just women's economic way of life but also their ideas about what it meant to be working women in the new industrialized Iran. While land redistribution generally can be an important step toward income redistribution, as far as the position of women and their access to economic resources are concerned, there were several dilemmas. The program distributed land to men as heads of households, thereby reinforcing male control over land and property and diminishing the concept of community ownership, where women tend to exercise more power over economic resources. Moreover, by overlooking landless peasants—who made up half of the rural population, it overlooked women as simple wage workers, and they became invisible workers. In addition, it fell short of assistance to 75 percent of peasants obtaining land, because the plots they received were too small to provide adequate livelihoods for a family, thus impoverishing many women who no longer had any role in the production and sale of harvested crops. Thus, similarly to many parts of world, the effectively capitalist commercialization of agriculture undermined women's control over economic resources, forced them into marginal production processes, and reduced their economic role.

This process not only marginalized women; it also informalized their work, since women became unpaid family workers, and the state recognized men alone as heads of households. The heads of the households then received all assistance, and their role in the economy and their access to economic resources were enhanced. Additionally, commercialization of agriculture led to pulverization of landless and small landowning peasants, many of whom left for the cities, often with their wives and children, and settled in shanty towns around Tehran, Karaj, and other cities (Hooglund 1982). From the early 1960s until the mid-1970s, the agricultural sector continued to decline, and as thousands of women migrated to the cities, their share of urban employment in the formal sector increased consistently, but this does not include their undocumented informal employment, which also experienced a huge increase.

Part of the invisibility of the rise of women's role in the informal sector was due to the fact that often what they produced was consumed within Iran's economy; this incidentally is not a uniquely Iranian experience, as it is a fairly common experience of the Third World. As discussed in my previous work, sometimes what women produce does not enter into the market, and since it remains outside the market, it is not regarded as having value and thus falls into the invisible, informal economy (Bahramitash 2007).

The White Revolution also affected the pastoral portion of the rural economy, as many livestock-raising tribes were forced to settle because their seasonal migrations did not accord with the urban political elite's vision of nation building. As sociologist Mostafa Azkia has noted in the case of various Fars tribes, forced settlement had disturbing effects on women's political and economic well-being (Azkia 2002). He points out that, as families were settled on former pasture lands that were not suitable for cultivated agriculture, men migrated to the cities to find work in the formal or informal urban economy, leaving behind women to care for homes and children while they waited for remittances from their husbands or other males but no longer had their once-important productive roles in the processing of animal products. This new modern economy coupled with the gendered ideology of the White Revolution had the effect of economically marginalizing all rural women. This policy no doubt reinforced the vision of the male as breadwinner, but it had the effect of isolating women from their extended family support system just as they were losing their access to the means of production and being forced to work as wage or seasonal workers. At the same time, the low wages that the men earned meant that they really could not be model breadwinners. We will come back to the breadwinner/homemaker model in later chapters of this book.

On the positive side, the expanding manufacturing economy opened up some employment opportunities in the formal sector for women, with the major exception of the Persian carpet industry, which had already existed before the 1960s (many girls in the 10-to-15 age group were in this industry). Formal employment expansion took place mainly in textiles, food processing, chemicals and steel production, and consumer durable goods.

While rural and tribal women's employment suffered and their role in the informal economy declined, their role in the urban formal economy grew. The many village women who migrated with their men to the cities constituted the bulk of low-paid formal and informal female labor in the economy by the mid-1970s. They were mostly unskilled and low-ranking workers, and if they were lucky enough to find a job, it would be in textile factories or domestic work. In many cases, women were forced to find employment, because wages for men were not sufficient for the costs of urban living.

The process of industrialization and urbanization brought benefits mainly to middle- and upper-middle-class women, who received formal educations not just at the primary level but also at the secondary and tertiary levels. In contrast, women who had migrated from rural areas had a tendency to become marginalized, not just economically but also culturally, and in the absence of their extended family networks, they also became isolated. Moreover, they tended to respect religious norms, and unlike their middle- and upper-middle-class counterparts, who generally were deveiled, rural migrant women wore the *chador* [veil] in public, a further barrier to their entry into education and well-paid jobs (the introduction of imposed veiling associated with the Iranian Revolution is discussed later). Generally speaking, women's representation in professional jobs remained low, even though many women entered into the public sector as teachers and nurses. Iran's Women's Organization data illustrated that professional women had little presence in the high-ranking professional job market.

THE IRANIAN REVOLUTION (1978–79)

Generally, the shah's era brought some degree of modernization as measured by an increase in urbanization and a transition from an agricultural and rural economy to a semi-industrial economy; one result was that many women entered the formal economy. Yet the ideology of the state was based on modernization, as discussed in Chapter 1, with all the problems associated with a Western-imitated modernization agenda. As was the case with other countries of the Southern Hemisphere, which had been either colonized or semicolonized, the path to economic development prescribed by the West was based on the way the West had been transformed into an industrial society. Similar to the early days of modernization in the West, poverty and income disparity increased during the transition, and, as we have explained, these contradictions were brought to newly urbanized and industrialized countries. Iran itself was plagued by the fact that the trickle-down effect was limited, and the revenue generated by the export of oil was largely concentrated among the top 1 percent of the population.

However, it was not just economic transformation that created a rupture in society but also the Westernization and cultural transformation imposed on the urban and rural poor, which gave rise to discontent. The imposition of this model was facilitated by the nature of the government, for the shah became increasingly authoritarian after the 1953 coup against the popular prime minister Mohammad Mosadeq. The latter had risen to political prominence in the late 1940s by leading the campaign to nationalize the oil industry. Proshah officers in the army overthrew Mosadeq in accordance with a coup plan designed and supported by the US Central Intelligence Agency (CIA), approved by the shah, and subsequently utilized for similar coups against nationalist governments in Latin America, Africa, and South Asia (Hooglund 1989). The subsequent close strategic relationship between the shah and the United States enabled the former to establish a secret police force, SAVAK, which during the 1960s and 1970s clamped down on all political organizations suspected of threatening "national security"—that is, opposing the rule of the shah. Ironically, opposition efforts largely came from the middle-class student population, which, despite their prosperity under the shah, opposed his autocratic rule. Many women of all classes, again rather ironically, participated in opposition movements, even though the shah had given women the right to vote in 1963.

At the same time, many people were experiencing disenchantment with Western-style development because of its failures in many parts of the world—namely, Africa, Latin America, and the Middle East, where dictatorial rule backed by the United States and its allies not only had failed to deliver economic prosperity for all but also had deprived people of the ability to choose their own leaders. A clear example was Chile and the assassination of Salvador Allende in 1973. Western models of both the American style of leadership and that of the Soviet Union were increasingly becoming unpopular among people in many parts of the world. In the absence of political alternatives, a more indigenously inspired political ideology was awoken instead. As in the case of Latin America where liberation theology became popular, in the Middle East in general, and in Iran in particular, a quest for a new ideology was started.

The writings of the sociologist Ali Shariati, inspired by the French Caribbean postcolonial writer Franz Fanon, became popular, especially among the young. Shariati presented a new interpretation of Islam that emphasized its role as a religion of social justice (Rahnema 1996; Gamari-Tabrizi 2009). Shariati believed that it was only possible to create a successful revolutionary movement by using the religious vocabulary that resonated with the average Iranian and by comparing current instances of political corruption and oppression with that of hated rulers who centuries ago had persecuted the revered Twelve Imams of Shi'a Islam, the religion of 90 percent of Iranians. His public lectures in the early 1970s attracted large audiences, especially among middle-class youth, including many young women, and his implicit critiques led to his arrest and imprisonment by SAVAK. Shariati did not limit his criticisms to unjust political rulers but also condemned the clergy who supported them. In this way, one can compare him with the Catholic liberation theologists who argued that Catholicism must oppose injustice and criticized those priests, bishops, and cardinals whom they saw as supporting unjust political systems in Latin America.

Although Shariati's ideas had widespread popular appeal, they were controversial among the clergy. However, Iran's most respected cleric, Ayatollah Ruhollah Khomeini, who had been sent into exile in 1964 for criticizing the shah's policies, declined to criticize Shariati's views, even though some of his followers entreated him to do so. Shariati himself was freed from prison and allowed to go to London for medical treatment, but he died there in 1977, several months before the start of mass demonstrations against the shah's regime. Clerical organizers, whatever their views about Shariati's religious interpretations, understood the value of his slogans as important mobilizing tools. In fact, the Islamic language of the demonstrations legitimized the participation of women, especially lower-class women, and facilitated the nationwide strikes in all sectors of the economy after September 1978. By the end of the year, even secular groups, including feminists, leftists, and nationalists, accepted overall coordination of the opposition by religious organizations.

Continued demonstrations and clashes between the army and people continued until the shah agreed to leave Iran for medical treatment in January 1979, leaving behind a weak caretaker government. Two weeks later, Ayatollah Khomeini arrived back in Iran, after more than 13 years in exile. He refused to recognize the shah's government, appointing instead a provisional government; Mehdi Bazargan, a longtime antishah activist and a founder of the progressive Islamist National Freedom Movement, was the prime minister. This government came to power on February 1979, after the top military officers ordered all troops to return to the barracks and remain politically neutral. In a referendum one month later, an overwhelming majority of people voted to replace the monarchy with an Islamic republic.

Soon after the revolution, *hejab*, or proper covering for women in public, became a major issue. The standard covering in the 1970s was the all-enveloping *chador*, which religious women and all urban lower-class women wore when in public. A 1936 law had banned women from wearing it, although that law was not enforced after 1941, except for women in the families of government officials. Nonreligious women of the middle and upper classes in Tehran did not wear the *chador*, and this practice was followed in several other large cities. Many such women regarded it as old-fashioned, a symbol of backwardness or even repression of women and their rights to equality. However, the majority of Iranian women did wear the *chador*, which became one of the visible symbols of the revolutionary demonstrations and marches during the long months of the revolution. Indeed, the *chador*, because it exemplified their piety, actually legitimized their presence in the revolution, and many of these women were determined to continue their activism after the revolution. This attitude put pressure on the minority of women who did not wear the *chador*, especially middle- and upper-class women in Tehran who worked in various government offices. Should women working in the formal and even informal sector be encouraged or even required to observe proper *hejab*, and if so, what constituted proper *hejab*? The debate over *hejab* during the spring and summer of 1979 was conducted in the press, and women were on both sides of the issue. Eventually, a law was enacted requiring women to observe *hejab* in public, with proper *hejab* being defined as a covering for head hair and clothing that did not reveal the feminine shape of a woman's body. In practice, for women opposed to wearing a *chador*, this meant wearing a headscarf and a *manteaux*: a very loose, ankle-length, trench-coat-like outer garment over one's clothes.

Some of the legal reforms that had helped women, particularly the 1967 Family Protection Act, were reversed. This led to major opposition against religion, particularly among those middle-class women who believed religion ought to be a private matter and/or were very casual in their own observance of religious rituals. However, low-income and working-class women, as well as those in the religious middle class, continued to find Khomeini's ideas appealing. Many responded to his call for women to participate in the building of an Islamic society, and they worked as volunteers for various state-sponsored programs, such as the nationwide literacy campaign, the Jihad Against Illiteracy.

The Khomeini-approved provisional government seemed unable to control extremist revolutionaries in the months following the revolution and finally resigned in November 1979, after only nine months in office. There followed two years of political instability, which ended in the fall of 1981 when the Majlis (Iranian parliament) approved a government headed by Mir-Hosein Musavi. Its agenda over the next eight years was to bring social justice in the form of economic redistribution and economic nationalism. Unlike the shah's era, the postrevolutionary government emphasized rural development and agricultural production, the latter policy having the aim to increase self-sufficiency in food crops. Import substitution was pursued, but due to 1980 Iraqi invasion of Iran and the subsequent eight-year war, as well as US sanctions against Iran, international trade was severely restricted, and this had negative effects on employment for men as well as women.

However, the Islamic Republic's new social policies, especially comprehensive health and educational programs, as well as food and shelter subsides, helped to mitigate the economic problems related to the war and international politics. Nevertheless, because many economic and management experts left the country in 1979–81, implementation of these programs was difficult. Khomeini called on his followers, many of them low-income and religious women, to subsidize the state welfare program, and these women worked as volunteers (Povey 2001). These programs effectively relied on social capital, but at a national level they were effective. By 2010, three decades since the revolution, we have witnessed a major improvement in educational attainment, with the greatest increase among young women (Salehi-Isfahani 2005, UN 2003).

In September 1980, Iraq leader Saddam Hussein, with tacit US support, invaded Iran, and the war, which lasted for eight years, changed postrevolutionary Iran. Politically, it mobilized a part of the opposition to support the government against a foreign aggressor. On the level of economic performance, the government relied more on people's assistance for its social programs. For example, many women, in rural areas and small cities in particular, provided volunteer support for the war effort by preparing food and clothing and donating money. Moreover, for the first time the informal sector in urban areas started to expand rapidly, because while food and other subsidies for essential goods were being distributed equally throughout the nation, some people preferred to pay others to stand in queues or to buy their coupons for essential goods on the black market. Some industries had closed down or were running at lower efficiency, so unemployment was high, and many men and some women found employment by selling their coupons as *vultures*, or they would spend time in queues for scarce goods.

Ten years after the revolution, the war with Iraq ended and the charismatic but elderly Khomeini died—two developments that initiated a new chapter in the history of the Islamic Republic. Ali Akbar Hashemi-Rafsanjani was elected president on a campaign platform that focused on reconstruction and rebuilding the economy. The programs of his government created employment opportunities and encouraged women to enter the labor market not as volunteers but for pay. Universities were expanded to meet the growing demand for postsecondary education, and there were major annual increases in the number of women enrolled in colleges.

In some ways, Iran's postrevolutionary governments can be compared to the European Christian Democratic parties that favor income redistribution. Iran's governments were not run by one authoritarian ruler (although Ayatollah Khomeini certainly was an authoritative figure), as the mainstream Western media has suggested. Rather, from the very outset there was an intense competition among different factions at the top of the political elite, although the clerical class remained at the top of the power pyramid as manifested in the office of *velayat-e faqih*. Although sometimes the religious leader (*faqih*) can be viewed as the ultimate authority because he has the power to overrule the Majlis and the president, in practice he rarely used this power. According to Mehdi Moslem, Iranian politics is dominated by factional politics; he uses "left" or "radical" for lack of better words (2002, p. 5). President Rafsanjani championed business interests after coming to power. He supported the transition to neoliberal economic policies, including industrialization programs that generated employment in both the formal and informal sectors.

Here it can be noted that the probusiness faction among Iran's political elite is (and historically has been) strong due to its support from the Bazaar, which had provided Ayatollah Khomeini with monetary and political support while he was in exile and during the revolution. Yet the most conservative faction of the elite old merchant class felt its interests were being threatened by the policies of the Rafsanjani government. After the death of Ayatollah Khomeini, his successor Ali Khamenehi, seemed more in favor of the merchant class than Rafsanjani. However, political tensions between Rafsanjani and Khamenehi were muted during 1989–97. Instead, tension grew between Rafsanjani and Ayatollah Mesbah-Yazdi, as it was the latter cleric who actively represented the interests of the old merchant class.

Rafsanjani was an astute politician who proved capable of navigating the different political factions. Importantly, it was his policies that paved the way for the reformist movement, which relied on the dynamic jurisprudence (*fegh-e-poya*) of progressive clerics for its rise to power. The reformists, whose moderate vision of Islam favored a moving away from strict adherence to religious interpretations and practices, advocated for the rule of law, and beginning in 1992 they slowly emerged as a new elite faction. During the 1997 presidential election campaign, Mohammad Khatami, a good speaker and open-minded cleric, won a landslide victory. In his campaign, Khatami successfully appealed to women and young people and promised reform, and thus women became a major force in shaping Iran's policies during the eight years that Khatami was president.

Nonetheless, conservative clerics in the judiciary and the Council of Guardians opposed many of the reformist policies and used their authority to interpret laws in ways that effectively cancelled much reformist legislation. After reformist candidates won a majority of seats in the 2000 Majlis elections, the Council of Guardians, an appointive legislative body that can veto legislation that it deems to contradict Islam and that also vets all candidates for Majlis elections, disqualified the majority of reformist deputies from running for reelection in 2004. The inability of Khatami or the reformist politicians to counter the conservatives was one of the factors that ultimately led to the public's disappointment with the reformists and the defeat of the reformist presidential candidate in 2005, when Mahmud Ahmadinejad was elected.

During the reform period of constant struggle between elected members of the executive and legislative branches on the one hand and members of the judiciary branch on the other hand, issues related to women were among the foremost contentious ones. A great deal of gender-rights advocacy was promoted by those who had joined the reformist government, as well as those who were outside of it and working independently. The two groups came together as a united front on issues such as women's constitutional right to be presidential candidates. Even Islamist women, such as the daughter of Ayatollah Taleghani, Azam Taleghani, and Rafat Bayat (Bayat was a member of parliament during the 2000–2004 session), in protest against women's lack of constitutional rights, campaigned for the presidency in 2005. On June 12, 2005, just before Iran's presidential election, approximately two thousand women from different political factions organized a demonstration and signed a petition for their constitutional right to run for president. Their activism during the early 2000s demonstrated that women have become a major political force in postrevolutionary Iran (Kian 1995; Poya 1999; Povey 2001; Halper 2005; Tohidi 2007).

Another aspect of Khatami's presidency was the financial assistance his government provided for the formation of civil society activities, also known as nongovernmental organizations (NGOs). These NGOs experienced a major setback once his term of office ended and especially with the beginning of Ahmadinejad's term. During Ahmadinejad's first term, from 2005 to 2013, many NGOs were dismantled due to lack of funding or were uprooted by the imprisonment of their leading figures.

Despite these negative political tendencies, it is also true that during both the Rafsanjani and Khatami presidencies, which spanned a continuous 16-year period, the economy experienced some degree of recovery from the war, which translated into improvements in some of the basic economic indicators and lead to a balanced budget. This happened despite the 1994–95 drop in world oil prices. However, by the late 1990s and into the early 2000s, the economy improved due to rising oil prices. Generally, during the two decades after the revolution, oil prices were low and the country suffered some economic setbacks due to US sanctions. These sanctions increased during Ahmadinejad's presidency because of his political posturing against the United States and his emphasis on developing Iran's nuclear program. As a result, Iran's economy slowed down considerably after 2005.

It should be noted that despite a great deal of dissatisfaction with the overall economic performance of postrevolutionary Iran, there have been major improvements in some of the basic indicators. For instance, despite sanctions and the eight years of war, a United Nations report in 2003 indicated that "Iran's 65 million inhabitants enjoy an average quality of life, which when quantified by the Human Development Index (HDI), is near the top of the middle-level human development category. With a value of around 0.72 in 2002, Iran appears to be within reach of the level of medium human development index (starting at 1)" (UN 2003, p. 14). If we take into account that Iran has absorbed the world largest refugee population from Afghanistan, this becomes a more significant achievement and indicates the extent of the informal sector, since the majority of Afghan workers work informally.

As far as a general postrevolutionary picture of female employment is concerned, some academics have argued that the decline of female employment after the revolution was due to Islamization processes (Moghadam 1988, 1995; Moghadam 2004; Afshar 1996; Alizadeh and Harper 2003; and Nomani and Behdad 2006). Others have challenged this idea by stating that Islamization in fact may have facilitated education, mobilization, and participation in public life for women who came from low-income families or religious backgrounds (Paidar 1995; Kian 1995; Poya 1999; Mehran 2003; and Bahramitash 2007). However, as we shall see in this chapter, several factors have contributed to the transformation of the labor market for women in the decades following the revolution.

One of the important factors affecting the female labor market is population. Iran's ten-and-older female labor force has grown more than sixfold, from 0.57 million to 3.62 million according to the

2006 census (Bahramitash and Salehi-Esfahani 2011, p. 124). This growth was much greater than that of male workforce, which saw a 3.6-fold increase. Between the mid-1960s and mid-1990s, the Labor Force Participation (LFP) rate declined steadily from 9.9 percent to 8.1 percent in the urban female labor market. In rural areas, the LFP rate continued to rise in the 1960s and most of the 1970s, reaching 16.7 percent in 1976. After the revolution it then dropped sharply, falling to 7.9 percent in 1986, before it started to rise again, albeit at a slower pace during the past two decades (Bahramitash and Salehi-Esfahani 2011, p. 126). Compared to some countries where the rate of female labor is at 60 percent, Iran is low, being at 33 percent. However, the female LFP rate is above average for MENA countries, which in 2004 was placed at 27 percent by the World Bank Group (2007; and Haghighat-Sordellini 2011).

One may attribute this generally low LFP rate partly to undercounting, which is something Marilyn Waring (1990, 1999) documented well in the gender and development literature. But in the case of Iran, undercounting has an added dimension; Valentine Moghadam (1988) and Jennifer Olmsted (2011) both argue that during the time of the shah, there was an incentive to have better documentation of women's work as proof of the shah's success in modernization. After the revolution, however, this is not the case, as many women work as volunteers, which by definition is not captured in statistical data.

Yet it should be noted that barriers to female employment outside the home due to gender segregation are key to understanding the issues (Kian 2002; and Khosrokhavar 2011). Gender and development literature has documented that the impact of development has had adverse effects, and Iran has been no exception. For example, between the 1960s and 1990s, women were excluded from the development process (as mentioned earlier in this chapter). Some of the overall female LFP decline in Iran may well be related to the decline of the urban women's LFP rate between the 1960s and the 1970s, perhaps due to an increase in educational opportunities for women. However, it seems that the rise of the male breadwinner and female homemaker model proves to be more relevant, particularly when seen in correlation with the rise of urbanization. While male employment continually increased, female employment declined as modernization intensified in the 1970s. This is despite the fact that the economy was booming and there was a significant shortage of labor. However, after the revolution, the reason for decline in women's LFP within the urban middle and upper classes was that women were either banned from or encouraged to leave jobs.

The ups and downs of official labor force participation data of women is a fairly complex business. There are many interesting factors at work, such as the rise of women's volunteer work as a result of free public education and Khomeini's proclamation of a literacy Jihad (which meant that it became a religious duty to be literate), which sent many girls and young women to be educated and away from the employment sector. There were some additional factors, such as allowances for households, which were given to the heads of the household, and as Fatemeh Moghadam notes, some working women in rural areas stopped working, at least officially, in order to be eligible for *tarheh rajai*, or pension after the age of 65.

Ironically, postrevolutionary Iran has a female labor force that is more educated than in previous eras. The new generation of women entering the urban job market was and is far more educated than those retiring, since nationwide campaigns to increase educational attainment levels for women have been successful. Moreover, as is the case with many wars, particularly the two world wars, the Iran-Iraq war led to an increase in female labor participation in the two decades following the war.

In my previous work on census data, the results showed a steady growth in the female labor force, particularly in the urban setting from 1956 to 2006, notwithstanding a slight drop in 1986 during the Iran-Iraq war. After the war, however, the greatest growth in female labor force participation was at a rate of 4.4 percent and 5.8 percent in 1996 and 2006, respectively. For women in the rural setting, employment has been somewhat less steady, and rural women saw a greater decrease in their employment during the Iran-Iraq war when the LFP rate dropped from 16.6 percent in 1976 to 7.9 percent in 1986. Rural LFP rates have not recovered to the same rates that were seen prior to the 1986 figure, but, as we will see, there are many possible reasons for this (Bahramitash and Salehi-Esfahani 2011).

The role of Islamization in the decline of the female LFP rate is unlikely to have been significant. This is because much of the decline in employment in the two decades following the revolution occurred in rural areas where people had never been secularized under the shah and had remained religious. Postrevolutionary Iran did experience a decline for some women, mainly among those who belonged to the middle and upper class, but jobs opened for other women, particularly due to a gender segregation policy. What did affect the decline in rural female employment has been the decline in the carpet-weaving industry due to the international embargo (Karimi 2011), as well as an increase in educational opportunities (Paguntalan 2002; Pearson 1997; and Elson and Çağatay 2000).

To repeat an earlier point, some academics argued that the shah was politically motivated to create a rise in employment for women to illustrate that industrialization and Westernization had been successful and that women's access to employment was due to cultural and economic changes. However, given the revolution's anti-Westernization ethos, there was no such incentive to conflate female employment with Westernization, and thus a decline in female labor followed. Nevertheless, in 1956 the female labor force in urban areas was 0.19 million, and in 2006 it had grown to 2.5 million, a significant 13.5-fold increase, compared to the 7.9-fold increase for men. This resulted in an increase in women's share of the urban labor force from about 10 percent in 1956 to almost 16 percent in 2006 (Bahramitash and Salehi-Esfahani 2011, p. 125). Since then, there has been another census that has gathered data based on different definitions of employment and unemployment, making it difficult to make comparisons with previous decades.

Overall, women's role in the Iranian economy illustrates an initial decline in the 1980s, but from then on, there is an upward trend in the rate of women's involvement in the labor force. In my book on female employment, the following results were drawn. First, the decline in the 1980s and in postrevolutionary Iran is a rural phenomenon, and we already discussed some possible explanations for it. Second, female employment in the urban economy has continued to grow, particularly during the 1990s, and this growth has further accelerated into the 2000s (2006 national census, Bahramitash and Salehi-Esfahani 2011). This has been coupled with rising urbanization. Currently almost 70 percent of women live in urban areas, and many of those who find employment find it in the service sector. This is important when we come to review the fieldwork findings, and it is not surprising to see that many in our sample work in the service sector.

In the three decades following the revolution, universal education and health care in general, as well as other services, provided opportunities for a female labor force unique to other non-Muslim countries. During the time of the shah many religious families refused to send their daughters to schools and universities, but with Islamization and sexual segregation, this barrier was taken away. For example, more girls were sent to school because many male teachers in girl's schools from during the shah's era were replaced with female ones, since primary and secondary schools became female-only places. Initially, a shortage of math and physics teachers for secondary school was seen, which forced young girls to wait to take these subjects in their secondary and tertiary education. Today the number of female engineers is very impressive, and many young women enter traditionally "male" subjects such as physics and math. Moreover, currently women constitute more than half of the employees in education, health care, and social services (Bahramitash and Salehi-Esfahani 2011, p. 136). We will return to the theme of gender segregation in the informal sector later in this book, as the informal sector is much more gender segregated than the formal sector, and there is a tendency to underrecord women's labor participation, particularly in the service sector.

Since the mid-1980s, the data show that the percentage of women as employers, executives, and managers in the private sector has increased. Though the overall increase is small, the trend shows an upward slope. There are currently two female business associations, an indication of a coming of age of women's interests in entrepreneurial activities. The increase in the country's female executives is partly due to women's rising educational levels (Moghadam 2004) and partly because of women's own drive to achieve economic success, as demonstrated by active women's business networks.

While women's educational attainment has increased and their presence in highly skilled labor is on the rise, the number of those who are unemployed is also high, at 1.8 million according to the 2006 census; this is a 5.8 percent increase since 1986 (Bahramitash and Salehi-Esfahani 2011, p. 128). This is an important point to remember, as unemployment is one of the main factors driving women to the informal sector. It is particularly significant to bear in mind that for those who come from low-income households, the type of jobs available/created in this sector of the economy are their lifelines, whether they are married, the heads of households, or single.

A Contemporary Picture

A picture of contemporary Iranian women shows that in the past few decades women have taken large strides toward gaining education, and they constitute close to 60 percent of university students. In 2012, 3.340 million women, compared to 1.708 million men, finished university. Women not only enter university programs more frequently than do men, but they more often complete their education, and all in all, women's education rates are close to three times higher than that of men.[2] Many educated women are unable to find jobs matching their education, and this creates disappointment and frustration. Moreover, women find it difficult to find men of the same educational level, and this could explain why the rate of single women and divorce is high. As we shall see in our sample, women have higher education levels, even in the low-income, informal-sector bracket, than is the case for men. Moreover, the article continues, women who continue their education postpone their marriage, and this results in a tendency for women to remain single. This is rational, since spending several years in higher education gives women a sense of independence and autonomy that could be lost if they get married to men of a lesser educational background.

As we will see in later chapters, attitudes among low-income men toward their wives' work are very negative. However, men are not against a university education, and as stated in at least one interview, the husband was even providing economic means for his wife to attend university, but he was against her working outside the home. Many young men leave university because highly paying jobs are not related to high education. Not only do men have to sacrifice many years at schools with high tuition fees in the case of private universities, but they also end up falling behind in the business world, where it is possible to make money in occupations such as real estate or trade.

A recent debate over types of education open to women at tertiary levels engaged several members of parliament as well as other policy makers who argued that the discrepancies between job availability and women's rate of education need to be addressed, as it is posing a threat to the institution of the family. Similar issues may be at stake in Western countries, as the percentage of women in higher education is rising more rapidly than it is for men (Hakim 2003). From primary up to tertiary, girls tend to have a much higher performance than in the past, and, as a result, attitudes toward love and courting need to adapt to the changing role of women in society (Beck and Nashat 2004).

Policy makers' concerns over the issue of inadequate opportunities corresponding to the type of university training women receive include such fields as engineering and agricultural sciences and industries, where there are few job opportunities for employment in general. This has alarmed authorities to the extent that there are discussions about gender-justice programs that would make it more difficult for women to enter university. As a result, there are debates over issues such as setting quotas for women in certain courses. Clearly, however, the issue at hand is a lack of employment opportunities more generally, which is a critical challenge in many parts of MENA, especially where oil tends to dominate the economy. It should be mentioned that some kinds of restriction already have been imposed, such as those the Ministry of Science and Technology imposed in 2007 in an attempt to curb the rise in female medical students. The rising number of female doctors was such that soon far more women would be receiving medical training than men, thereby posing a challenge to gender segregation, as men would be forced to be treated by female physicians.

The role of the Open University (a private university) in providing educational opportunities for women has been immense. The Open University has opened branches throughout the country, transforming the face of many small cities, as young women from metropolitan areas come to study as single female students and, by doing so, challenge the traditional values of female home confinement.

A rising number of educated women, some of whom may have lived away from home during their university education, have had a major impact on the family. To give an example, young women who live away from home tend to challenge family authority. In fact, an attitude survey illustrated that there has been a decline in male authority over the course of five years. The data compared prevailing attitudes toward male authority in 1995 with those in the year 2000 and concluded that there has been a decline in the perception of the father as the primary authority figure (Mohseni 2000).

Factors Contributing to the Increase in the Female Labor-Force Participation Rate

One of the significant factors increasing the female labor-force participation rate is the age of the female population. Iran has experienced two population booms: one after World War II (similar to many parts of the world), the other beginning a few years before and continuing for a decade after the revolution, partly due to the postrevolutionary government's population-growth program. This policy was reversed after 1987, leading to a drop in the fertility rate. The second population boom led to rising labor-force participation in the late 1990s. In the case of teenagers, the number of young women in the labor market increased between 1950 and 1970, and again during the mid-1990s. The increase in the labor-force participation rate in rural areas was less than it was in the 1960s and 1970s due to the fact that education, particularly at the secondary level, became more available for rural women. However, as mentioned before, Iran experienced a massive population increase as the result of postrevolutionary/war circumstances and state policy, and this has translated into a high number of young females joining the labor force.

Moreover, there has been a recent tendency for women to marry later. The number of single women in the labor market among our sample gives a glimpse of what might be a national trend (as we will see with our findings later). On average, women in 2006 married at least four years older than they did in 1966. It is interesting to note that this is contrary to the commonly held assumption about the impact of the revolution and the Islamization process, but the census data clearly illustrate this trend (Bahramitash and Salehi-Esfahani 2011, p. 104). For example, in 1966 for women in urban areas, the average age of marriage was 19, whereas in 2006 it had risen to 23.2 years. In rural areas the corresponding figures are 17.9 years for 1966 and 23.4 years for 2006, which shows a greater change in rural areas. This affects the labor market situation, because some of those rural-raised, young unmarried women may remain unmarried and migrate to cities. During my fieldwork, I met young women who had left their rural areas to live with relatives in cities to search for better marriage prospects and also for better work opportunities.

In my previous book on employment, the 2006 census showed that there has been an increase in the percentage of women aged 15–19 who are single, rising from 65.7 percent to 85 percent between 1976 and 2006. For women in the 20–24 year age bracket, the increase was from 21.4 percent to 53.6 percent during the same period. These young women increase labor-force participation and thereby increase unemployment rates because the market cannot support them, and thus their desire to enter the informal sector also rises.

Some women are single due to divorce, and the rate of divorce has increased to a 2006 level of 11.5 percent (Bahramitash and Salehi-Esfahani 2011, p. 105) from 9.1 percent in 2001 (Kazemipour Sabet 2007). Due to unfavorable marriage laws, the likelihood of women having to rely on their own resources for survival has increased in places like Tehran and its suburbs, which have a population of 14 million. The divorce rate in the urban areas more generally is 21.4 percent. Among our sample during fieldwork, I came across women who were divorced, but there were also some who were abandoned by their husbands or had husbands who were drug addicts or in jail.

In fact, the issue of single-headed households has gathered a great deal of attention. The percentage of female-headed households has increased, according to a 2005 United Nations Development Programme report. Even in developed countries, female-headed households (FHH) fare far worse than single-income, male-headed households; for example, in the Netherlands, women head 62 percent of poor households. The global disparity of wages between men and women (with women making slightly more than 50 percent of what men make) compounds the issue of single-income households where women alone are responsible for the home.[3]

The Statistical Center of Iran defines a FHH as one where women are responsible for securing and managing a household's means of subsistence. Such a home may include an adult male who due to disability is unable to contribute financially; unfortunately for disabled men and their families, a social stigma attaches to disability, and this leads government assistance programs to regard disabled men in the same way as men who have abandoned their families, are imprisoned, or are drug addicted. Men who are unable to provide for their families face the same level of poverty and powerlessness as do female-headed households. FHHs in Iran also include a number of refugee women from Afghanistan, and fieldwork conducted in 2004–8 confirmed that Afghan women prefer to stay home. Also, many female-headed households are headed by widows who are aged 65 and older (Sekhavati 2004). According to the 2006 census data, the current rate of FHHs is 9.6 percent, and in 1996 it was estimated that there were about 100,060 FHHs in Iran, although this is probably an underestimate (Bahramitash 2011, p. 196). Between 1996 and 2006, there was a notable increase in FHHs, from 8.4 percent to 9.6 percent, and overall there has been a steady increase in the rate of FHHs beginning in 1966, when the rate was at 6.4 percent. Male-headed households show a corresponding decline from 93.6 to 90.5 percent over the last four decades. By far, women who describe themselves as homemakers make up the largest percentage of women who head households. The most recent census showed that only 14.7 percent of women who are the sole breadwinners for their families are employed. For those who are employed, their work tends to be consistent with the type of work among women in the very-low-income category—that is, seasonal, temporary or piecework and domestic care work for other families—and they have low education rates. This seems counterintuitive to what might be expected of women who are the sole breadwinners to provide comfortably for their families, yet they are no more employed than women who do have male breadwinners. This indicates a problem not only for FHH breadwinners but also for women in the Iranian labor market overall. To end this discussion, one needs to bear in mind that although FHHs may be at a disadvantage, at the same time one cannot assume that those households with a male breadwinner provide more access to economic resources for women.

The economic vulnerability of women who head households was raised directly after the revolution and during the war with Iraq. Both the revolution and the Iran-Iraq war resulted in causalities (significantly more so in the case of the war), and many injured men came to depend on their wives or mothers because they could not contribute to the family's resources. Iran's constitution does deal with the precariousness of FHHs by providing special insurance for female-headed households, widows, and elderly women, but the state's ability to deliver and manage these programs has not been effective. As a result, women may also have access to microcredit programs, NGOs that support women who head households, and other various charitable and religious programs (Bahramitash 2011). These programs, while of benefit to women of FHHs, also distract from a greater problem within the Iranian labor market. As noted before, a spectrum of women are un(der)employed or exploited in their work, and programs that exist to help women whatever their marital status are lacking. Criticisms of state programs and NGOs have ranged from lack of resources to effectively help those in need, to a too-dense bureaucracy, as well as to a overemphasis on charity without facilitating an environment of self-sufficiency. A focus on women who are heads of households is an oversimplification of poverty issues not just in Iran but also throughout the MENA region.

Moreover, women's life expectancy has increased, especially in urban areas. According to the 2006 census, women's life expectancy is 72.8 years, whereas men's life expectancy is 69.6 years (Bahramitash and Salehi-Esfahani 2011, p. 107). This increases the likelihood of widowed women and the likelihood that some of these women have to rely on their own income. Additionally, the fertility rate has dropped significantly, from 7.0 (births per woman) in 1960 to 2.1 in 2005 (ibid, p. 108, table 7), which translates into less child care and more free time to work for pay, which pushes the unemployment rate higher.

Women as Self-Employed/ Micro-Entrepreneurs

As far as statistics are concerned, microenterprise is not always registered, for reasons previously discussed. In the case of low-income women, fieldwork suggests that many women tend to underreport their work. Throughout fieldwork, I came across many women who said something along the line that they did something (processed food, knitted, or worked as handy women) but that it was not work.

This is not unique to Iran; throughout the developing work in particular, undercounting women's work by women themselves is a data-gathering problem (Waring 1999).

The 2006 Iranian national census results show that the share of female private-sector employment in the category of urban self-employment as an employer has increased from 0.8 percent in the 1950s to 4.61 percent (Table 3.1). The most significant increase occurred in the past decade. This was somewhat reflected in another survey conducted on gender and entrepreneurship in Iran (Bahrami-tash, Salehi-Esfahani, and Olmsted forthcoming), which showed that many educated women of middle- and upper-middle-class background have been venturing into the world of entrepreneurship in the past decade.

Table 3.1 Distribution of female employment across private-sector positions (percentage of total female employment in each area)

Census year	1956	1966	1976	1986	1996	2006
PRIVATE SECTOR—URBAN AREAS	86.3	78.9	50.0	20.4	31.2	48.8
As employers	0.8	1.01	0.59	1.04	0.92	4.61
As self-employed	10.9	12.8	8.7	9.2	12.7	16.6
As private employees	72.5	59.5	29.8	7.8	13.1	25.3
As unpaid family workers	2.1	5.6	11.0	2.4	4.4	2.3
PRIVATE SECTOR—RURAL AREAS	98.5	98.6	96.2	87.1	86.5	85.2
As employers	0.5	0.44	0.35	1.79	0.92	2.82
As self-employed	28.5	26.5	12.1	28.8	28.6	34.6
As private employees	44.1	41.3	24.6	12.8	15.6	15.9
As unpaid family workers	25.4	30.3	59.2	43.8	41.5	31.9

Source: Statistical Center of Iran, various years.

Table 3.2 Distribution of individuals 16 and older by job types and gender in 1986 (by percentage)

	Men			Women			Total		
	Urban	*Rural*	*All*	*Urban*	*Rural*	*All*	*Urban*	*Rural*	*All*
Job									
16+ Self-employed (principal)	13.6	3.1	6.4	2.3	0.2	0.5	12.4	2.3	5.1
16+ Self-employed (independent worker)	65.0	66.9	66.3	53.5	19.4	24.0	63.7	53.9	56.6
16+ Self-employed (family worker)	0.0	0.0	0.0	0.0	0.0	0.0	0.0	0.0	0.0
16+ First wage and salary	100	100	100	100	100	100	100	100	100
16+ Wage and salary (public sector)	53.5	24.5	32.1	75.5	15.5	57.2	56.3	23.9	41.8
16+ Wage and salary (private sector)	45.0	74.1	46.8	21.9	79.3	39.4	42.1	74.5	56.5

Note: "First wage and salary" implies the first job reported by the individual being a wage and salary job.

Source: 1986 Household Income and Expenditure Survey (HIES), Statistical Center of Iran.

Table 3.3 Distribution of individuals 16 and older by job types and gender in 1997 (by percentage)

	Men			Women			Total		
	Urban	*Rural*	*All*	*Urban*	*Rural*	*All*	*Urban*	*Rural*	*All*
Job									
16+ First self-employed	100	100	100	100	100	100	100	100	100
16+ Self-employed (principal)	16.7	13.4	14.5	2.6	2.1	2.2	15.1	10.2	11.7
16+ Self-employed (independent worker)	76.0	68.7	71.2	53.7	22.7	27.2	73.5	55.6	61.0
16+ Self-employed (family worker)	7.3	17.9	14.3	43.7	75.2	70.7	11.4	34.2	27.4
16+ First wage and salary	100	100	100	100	100	100	100	100	100
16+ Wage and salary (public sector)	46.6	26.3	35.6	73.1	21.5	51.8	50.2	25.7	38.9
16+ Wage and salary (private sector)	53.4	73.7	60.4	26.9	78.5	48.2	49.8	74.3	61.1

Note: "First self-employed" implies the first job reported by the individual being a self-employed job. Similarly, "first wage and salary" implies the first job reported by the individual being a wage and salary job.

Source: 1997 Household Income and Expenditure Survey (HIES), Statistical Center of Iran.

Table 3.4 Distribution of individuals 16 and older by job types and gender in 2009 (by percentage)

	Men	Women	Total						
	Urban	*Rural*	*All*	*Urban*	*Rural*	*All*	*Urban*	*Rural*	*All*
16+ First self-employed	100	100	100	100	100	100	100	100	100
16+ Self-employed (principal)	15.1	11.8	13.0	4.9	1.5	2.1	13.8	9.0	10.7
16+ Self-employed (independent worker)	76.9	71.0	73.3	50.2	19.8	25.5	73.7	57.1	62.8
16+ Self-employed (family worker)	8.0	17.3	13.7	44.9	78.7	72.4	12.4	34.0	26.6
16+ First wage and salary	100	100	100	100	100	100	100	100	100
16+ Wage and salary (public sector)	28.3	10.7	24.0	57.0	17.7	42.6	32.1	11.3	22.3
16+ Wage and salary (private sector)	0.4	0.5	0.5	0.3	0.4	0.3	0.4	0.5	0.4

Note: "First self-employed" implies the first job reported by the individual being a self-employed job. Similarly, "first wage and salary" implies the first job reported by the individual being a wage and salary job.

Source: 2009 Household Income and Expenditure Survey (HIES), Statistical Center of Iran.

According to the census's Household Data, the share of self-employed among employed women has increased from 10.9 percent in the 1950s to 16.6 percent. The sharpest increase has been in the last decade, from its lowest rate in the mid-1980s at 8.7 percent, to 12.7 percent in the 1990s, and then ten years later to 16.6 percent. This documents some of the figures on women as micro-entrepreneurs. There has also been an increase in women as employers, which has reached 4.9 percent (see Table 3.1). These are women who own small businesses, such as shops in urban areas (see tables in the Appendix). These owners are the focus of Chapter 4, where I review a survey conducted about women and microenterprises in the informal sector.

Moreover, the tables in the Appendix show that most of the employment for women (especially since women in Iran do not work as construction workers) is in the service sector. The result confirms fieldwork findings, where those interviewed, although randomly selected, tend to be by and large in the service sector, in areas such as sales. It should be added that the rising share of female employment as micro-entrepreneurs and in the service sector is to some extent one of the facades of the unemployment problem. Although the female employment and labor-force participation rate has increased, women's unemployment has also increased in the last decade, particularly among those in urban areas. Indeed, unemployment is a major issue in Iran, and some of it is due to the fact that the economy is oil based and capital intensive. For example, Iran has invested heavily in the automobile industry, which tends to employ men and generally is capital intensive rather than labor intensive.

After the revolution, female unemployment spiked in urban areas, and the ratio of female to male unemployment rates showed the difference between women and men in this respect. In 1986, this ratio was 2.1, which means that at the time the probability that a female participating in the labor force remained unemployed was 2.1 times the probability for a male participant in the labor force. This ratio decreased in the 1990s with the economic recovery of the postwar reconstruction plan, but in the last decade the female unemployment rate and its ratio to the male unemployment rate rose again. In 2006, unemployment for women in urban areas was 2.3 times more than that of men (Bahramitash and Salehi-Esfahani 2011, p. 126).

During the last three decades, the unemployment rate has been high, although lower among those with tertiary education. However, the unemployment rate for those with high school degrees tends to be higher than for those with lower levels of education. This has also been reflected in fieldwork, where a high percentage of those with secondary education work in low-paid informal jobs; this is true for both men and women, although it is more common for women to be overqualified than is the case for men.

Veiled Employment (2011, p. 161) demonstrates unemployment rates for women in 1976 through 2006 across age groups. Unemployment in general is the problem, and this no doubt affects those from low-income households more. Unemployment among women aged 35 and over is higher than that of younger women. Ironically, however, in one of the focus groups an interviewee complained that young women do not have to work because they are supported by their families, so they work to purchase consumer goods while "we [married women over 30] work to feed our family." It seems that the new cohort of women who arrived in the urban labor market in the 2000s, as illustrated in chapter 4 of *Veiled Employment*, faced a much higher risk of unemployment and were at a greater disadvantage compared with men. Older women already have some kind of employment, but for those who are entering the labor force, it is a challenge to find jobs.

Chapter 4

Low-Income Female Workers, Micro-Entrepreneurs, and the Informal Sector

Sorayya Nouri, a delightful 35-year-old woman who works as a domestic helper, was born in Tabriz and is married to a young man from Tehran. The combination of the global economic crisis and national sanctions led to her husband's bankruptcy after he had taken out a loan to open a mobile phone store. His shop was vandalized during antigovernment protests in the aftermath of the 2009 presidential election. The windows were broken and the phones damaged, leaving her husband with considerable debt. Lacking insurance, Sorayya's husband was unable to recoup his losses. The family was left in a desperate economic situation and Sorayya decided to start working: from dress making to food processing and becoming a domestic helper. The neighborhood, fully aware of the family's economic situation, came to aid her by providing her with odd jobs—keeping their business within their neighborhood.

She lives in Naziabad, an old working-class neighborhood in the south of Tehran. Her social network brings her odd jobs, and she accepts them all while wearing a smile, pleased to find some extra income. Indeed, throughout the interview a pleasant smile remained on Sorayya's face, except when she told me about her son being unable to attend Olympiad, a national academic competition whose winner is invited to the world finals. Her son had won the math competition, but the family could not finance his international trip.

I asked why she was not able to apply for a loan. The answer was obvious: with what collateral? In the absence of collateral, the bank will grant you a loan if you have a guarantor. The guarantor must be a public employee in case there is a default in repayment. The public employee must prove that he or she is able to make the payments in case of default, and as a result every public employee can vouch for only one borrower at a time, unless his or her income is exceptionally high. I asked why no one would become her guarantor, and the response was that most people she knew had already become the guarantor of someone else. I asked about her family in Tabriz; she was reluctant to ask her own family, because she did not want them to know that she was in financial difficulty.

This chapter is based on fieldwork conducted in Tehran and reports the findings of ninety interviews carried out through standardized and open-ended questions. The fieldwork was focused in southern Tehran, where those from the lowest-income stratum reside, except in the case of street vendors, whose work takes them throughout the city.

The research started in 2009 with focus groups, the results for which are included at the end of the chapter. The initial questionnaire was pretested during the winter of 2010, in the aftermath of the June 2009 election crisis. This was problematic since the authorities were sensitive about social research; long interviews were carried out under extremely difficult circumstances. The nature of the topic required confidence building, and for this reason snowball sampling was used, as personal contacts were essential. Fortunately, low-income neighborhoods are often closely knit, so one interview usually leads to another. The questionnaire was finalized in 2011, and the research took place that spring.

The research relied on the interviewees' willingness to participate. In my previous fieldwork, I found that women from low-income households are more comfortable in sharing information than women from middle- and upper-middle-income brackets, particularly when the topic is the source of income. Nonetheless, it had to be made clear that (1) the research was unable to provide monetary compensation for the time of the interviewee (since the research had no funding) and (2) the interview would not lead to improved working conditions or pay. Those who agreed were most generous with their time and patiently responded to a long questionnaire, while at times volunteering extra information as part of the open-ended questionnaire.

This book has been the result of several previous research projects on female employment in Southeast Asia and the Middle East, including very recent work on gender and entrepreneurship (focusing on women owners of large businesses as well as small and medium enterprises), and therefore some assumptions were made: (1) women enter into this sector of the economy because they lack access to the formal sector; (2) employment in the informal sector is an indispensable part of their social safety net; (3) employment in the informal sector is supported by the family and kin network, which provides employment opportunities as well as access to markets; (4) sexual segregation has closed some economic opportunities while it has created others in all-female spaces; (5) working conditions in the informal sector are characterized by long hours, low pay, and a lack of unemployment insurance or other labor benefits; (6) women whose work space is close to their home enjoy more support from their social network than those who live far away from their place of work; (7) the informal sector includes the exchange of goods and services that do not enter into the cash economy (this will not be measured, however, only observed); (8) street vendors are the least protected, particularly when they are working in areas outside their neighborhood; (9) because of their reproductive and domestic roles, some women prefer the informal sector, as it allows more flexible hours and working arrangements, in some cases allowing one to work from home (this is more true of home-based enterprises); (10) some women use rotating credit and saving associations as interest-free credit that acts as part of their social safety net; and (11) work in the informal sector can provide access to community leadership and increase women's social roles within their community.

The sample was selected through personal contacts that linked the research to those living in low-income neighborhoods such as Naziabad, Khaiabad, Javadieh, Islam-shahr, and Sultanabad. Each of these neighborhoods varies slightly in its degree of poverty, from low-income households to those living in shantytowns. In order to have access to the sample, I hired research assistants who were sociology graduate students, were familiar with working in the field, and had personal contacts in low-income neighborhoods. They were trained to gather information, and I was usually present during the process. Generally, however, I tried to avoid conducting interviews myself, because my demeanor as a hyphenated Iranian, who had lived most of her life outside of Iran, had the potential to be off-putting; during the interviews, I remained quiet and wore clothes similar to what the interviewees would wear and that therefore would not separate me from women of low-income homes. We briefly explained the purpose of the interviews to the interviewees, but since snowballing was used to select interviewees, most were already familiar with the interviewer. After explaining the aim of the research, we obtained their agreement before conducting the interview.

FINDINGS

As to be expected, many did not own their own homes and lived in substandard housing. Most were tenants unless their dwellings were provided by various government-run programs and foundations, owned by family members who did not collect rent, or they lived in various forms of charitable housing. The sample interviewees were workers in diverse low-income occupations. The majority of interviewees were hairdressers and saleswomen; other common low-paying occupations included home caregivers, food processers, cleaning ladies, Metro vendors, massage therapists, assistants (usually to home-based productions), arts and crafts producers, and short-term contract employees of offices or sport centers still within the low-income category.

Occupation

The sample was made up of women from all stages of life: 4.4 percent were below the age of 20; 26.6 percent were between the ages of 21 and 30; the largest number—38.8 percent of the sample—were between the ages of 31 and 40; 26.4 percent were between 41 and 50 years of age; 9.9 percent were 51 to 60; and 2.2 percent were older than 60 years. In terms of their education, they mostly had secondary education (close to half of the sample; 49.5 percent) and those with

Table 4.1 Line of activity

Line of activity	Frequency	Percentage
Sewing	12	13.2
Metro vendor	10	11.0
Hairdresser	14	15.4
Employee	11	12.1
Home caregiver	2	2.2
Arts and crafts	4	4.4
Saleswoman	14	15.4
Food processer	8	8.8
Massage therapist	5	5.5
Cleaning lady	11	12.1
Total	91	100.0

middle school [*raynamai*] were 18.7 percent. Women who had tertiary education made up 12.1 percent of the sample. However, 12.1 percent of the sample had only primary education, and 7.7 percent were illiterate (see Table 4.2).

These figures correspond to the general findings on education and unemployment documented in my previous book, *Veiled Employment* (2011), which discussed high unemployment among educated women. They also relate to Chapter 3 of this book, which describes the informal sector as being where those who are unemployed find the most likelihood of having access to employment. Furthermore, a cross-tabulation between education and occupation showed the following results: 57.1 percent of those with middle school diplomas worked as hairdressers; and 42.9 percent of high school graduates worked as saleswomen.

Table 4.2 Education and reasons for work

	Education level					
Reasons for work	*Illiterate*	*Primary*	*Middle school*	*Secondary*	*Tertiary*	*Total*
Economic necessity	7	8	15	33	6	69
	10.1	*11.6*	*21.7*	*47.8*	*8.7*	*100.0*
Personal interest	0		1	3	0	6
	0.0	*33.3*	*16.7*	*50.0*	*0.0*	*100.0*
Economic independence	0	0	0	3	3	6
	0.0	*0.0*	*0.0*	*50.0*	*50.0*	*100.0*
Female-headed household	0	1	1	6	2	10
	0.0	*10.0*	*10.0*	*60.0*	*20.0*	*100.0*
Total	7	11	17	45	11	91
	7.7	*12.1*	*18.7*	*49.5*	*12.1*	*100.0*

Note: The numbers in italics are percentages of row totals for each row group.

Age and Line of Activity

The mean age of women in the sample was 38, and 47 percent were 31–45; 29 percent were 16–30, and 24 percent were 46–60. It is noteworthy to mention that 3 percent of our sample was below 18 years of age. The sample was primarily young and middle age (probably representative of the working population, at least in Tehran). However, one point of concern is that social programs for the young and the elderly are inefficient. We shall return to this theme later in the chapter when we examine why women enter into this sector of the economy.

With regard to our sample's marital status, the majority were married (52.7 percent); this is, as we shall see, significant, as it partly challenges assumptions about women being dependent on a male breadwinner. Single women made up 19.8 percent of our sample, and the percentages of those who were widowed, divorced, or abandoned by their husbands were 11 percent, 9.9 percent, and 6.6 percent, respectively. Age of marriage and marital status were cross-tabulated, and the results are shown in Table 4.3.

Those women between the ages of 21 and 30 who never had married had the highest percentage of work—54.2 percent—among all those who never married. There are currently a high percentage of young educated women in search of employment, and since formal venues are more limited than the informal ones, this explains their significant percentage. In the next age categories, 31–45 and 46–60, married women were the most likely to be in the informal sector: 60.7 percent and 70.8 percent, respectively. Among those 51–60 and over 60, the percentage was high as well: 66.7 percent and 50 percent, respectively. This is an interesting finding because it contradicts the assumption that women with breadwinner spouses are less likely to enter the labor market (at least the informal sector). We will examine later the issue of female-headed households, as the combined percentage of those widowed, divorced, or abandoned by their husbands was significant.

ECONOMIC NECESSITY AND THE MALE-BREADWINNER MODEL

With regard to the question of why our interviewees have chosen the informal sector, many women responded that they would have preferred working in the formal sector because of the security and protection it affords, even though it might well be low-level office

Table 4.3 Age and marital status of the survey sample

	Marital status						
Age group (years)	*Never married*	*Married*	*Divorced*	*Abandoned*	*Widowed*	*Total*	*Share of age group in total sample (percentage)*
11–20	4	0	0	0	0	4	4.4
	100.0	*0.0*	*0.0*	*0.0*	*0.0*	*100.0*	
21–30	13	7	1	2	1	24	26.4
	54.2	*29.2*	*4.2*	*8.3*	*4.2*	*100.0*	
31–40	1	17	4	2	4	28	30.8
	3.6	*60.7*	*14.3*	*7.1*	*14.3*	*100.0*	
41–50	0	17	2	2	3	24	26.4
	0.0	*70.8*	*8.3*	*8.3*	*12.5*	*100.0*	
51–60	0	6	2	0	1	9	9.9
	0.0	*66.7*	*22.2*	*0.0*	*11.1*	*100.0*	
60+	0	1	0	0	1	2	2.2
	0.0	*50.0*	*0.0*	*0.0*	*50.0*	*100.0*	
Total	18	48	9	6	10	91	100.0
	19.8	*52.8*	*9.9*	*6.6*	*11.0*	*100.0*	

Note: The numbers in italics are percentages of row totals for each row group.

and clerical work. Among the sample, those who worked for economic independence made up 50 percent of never-married women; 33.3 percent worked because of their personal interest, while only 10 percent worked because they were heads of households. Ironically, a relatively low 17.4 percent of the never-married worked because of economic necessity (see Table 4.4). Among those who were married, however, 58 percent responded that they worked because of economic necessity, and 20 percent of married women stated that they worked because they were heads of households, which overlapped with those who stated they worked because of necessity. Sometimes women who have a breadwinner in the family work because their husband's income is insufficient; sometimes it is due to lack of a breadwinner. Interestingly, 66.7 percent of all interviewed women reported that they worked out of personal interest, and 33.3 percent worked to gain economic independence.

When the interviewers asked women the open-ended question, "Why do you work?" they received a variety of responses, a few examples of which are presented as follows:

- Masumeh said, "My husband had a financed car with which he worked as a driver, and then he had an accident. We were left with huge expenses, paying our rent, etc. I had no skills, but I tried to find a job and couldn't. I ended up selling kitchen cloth in the Metro."
- Marjan said, "My husband is a drug addict, and what he makes goes for his drugs. I have to pay for everything my children need. My parents can't help me and I am left by myself."
- Somayeh said, "My husband and children were against me working, because being a vendor is a source of shame. But what my husband earned could not put food on the table. I told them, 'If you don't like my work, you bring money!'"
- Zahra said, "I was separated from my husband and needed money. Although from the start I always worked, my husband was always suspicious and paranoid, and he beat me up from time to time. I don't like divorce, but I had to get a divorce because of all the beating. I am happy now sewing for a charity foundation."
- Roya, an unmarried young woman who sells perfume in the Metro, said, "I needed money and had too much work at home. My brothers were bullying me and I had no freedom. I couldn't even use the phone or listen to music. Now that I work I have more freedom. When I was at home my brothers would get on my nerves and we had fights. Now I am happy working."

Table 4.4 Marital status and reasons for work

	Marital status					
Reasons for work	*Never married*	*Married*	*Divorced*	*Abandoned*	*Widowed*	*Total*
Economic necessity	12	40	6	4	7	69
	17.4	*58.0*	*8.7*	*5.8*	*10.1*	*100.0*
Personal interest	2	4	0	0	0	6
	33.3	*66.7*	*0.0*	*0.0*	*0.0*	*100.0*
Economic independence	3	2	0	1	0	6
	50.0	*33.3*	*0.0*	*16.7*	*0.0*	*100.0*
Female-headed household	1	2	3	1	3	10
	10.0	*20.0*	*30.0*	*10.0*	*30.0*	*100.0*
Total	18	48	9	6	10	91
	19.8	*52.8*	*9.9*	*6.6*	*11.0*	*100.0*

Note: The numbers in italics are percentages of row totals for each row group.

One significant factor of women's work in this sector of course is their earnings. For this reason a cross-tabulation between income and line of activity was done. The findings showed that those who had the lowest income earned an equivalent at the time of the interviews of 50,000 rials per day. In 2010, approximately 10,000 rials were equivalent to 1 US dollar. After the imposition of EU sanctions in 2012, however, the rial lost its value almost daily, finally stabilizing at around 40,000 to 1 USD by early 2013. The depreciation of the rial and the resultant inflation of prices for imported goods effectively lowered the value of earnings, especially for low-income wage earners. Thus earnings of 50,000 rials per day were equivalent to $5 in 2010 but worth less than $1.50 in 2013. This is relevant because earnings of 50,000 rials per day are typical for such low-income work as sewing, which is the occupation of 33.3 percent of the sample. Other low-income occupations included working as a helper for other people (performing odd jobs) at 12.1 percent of the sample; arts and crafts producers, 4.4 percent; and food processors, 8.8 percent.

In terms of their earnings, most women earned $11–$15 per day in 2010. Among them, many were caregivers and hairdressers, as well as those who produced arts and crafts, and some women worked as massage therapists. Interestingly, women who earned more than $15 a day primarily worked in arts and crafts (which shows the widest range of income); 10 percent were vendors; 7.1 percent were in sales; and 9.1 percent were cleaning ladies. As we see in Table 4.5, among our sample most women earned between $5 and $10 a day. This, as we shall see in Chapter 5, is lower at least by $5 compared to their male counterparts.

Table 4.5 Income and line of activity

	Income range in US dollars per day				
Line of activity	*$0–$5*	*$6–$10*	*$11–$15*	*$16–$20*	*Total*
Sewing	4	5	3	0	12
	33.3	*41.7*	*25.0*	*0.0*	*100.0*
Metro vendor	1	6	2	1	10
	10.0	*60.0*	*20.0*	*10.0*	*100.0*

	Income range in US dollars per day				
Line of activity	*$0–$5*	*$6–$10*	*$11–$15*	*$16–$20*	*Total*
Hairdresser	3	8	3	0	14
	21.4	*57.1*	*21.4*	*0.0*	*100.0*
Employee	4	7	0	0	11
	36.4	*63.6*	*0.0*	*0.0*	*100.0*
Home caregiver	0	1	1	0	2
	0.0	*50.0*	*50.0*	*0.0*	*100.0*
Arts and crafts	2	0	1	1	4
	50.0	*0.0*	*25.0*	*25.0*	*100.0*
Saleswoman	4	8	1	1	14
	28.6	*57.1*	*7.1*	*7.1*	*100.0*
Food processer	4	4	0	0	8
	50.0	*50.0*	*0.0*	*0.0*	*100.0*
Massage therapist	1	3	1	0	5
	20.0	*60.0*	*20.0*	*0.0*	*100.0*
Cleaning lady	4	4	2	1	11
	36.4	*36.4*	*18.2*	*9.1*	*100.0*
Total	27	46	14	4	91
	29.7	*50.6*	*15.4*	*4.4*	*100.0*

Note: The numbers in italics are percentages of row totals for each row group.

These figures are in stark contrast to a law passed in 2010 that sets the minimum daily pay at 100,000 rials ($10 USD) and the minimum monthly income at 3,966,000 rials (close to $400 USD), as a base wage to be complemented with benefits. Here we should mention that the law regarding employment of workers, inspired by the Islamic Republic's Constitution, stipulates that every worker will receive 20,000 rials per day ($2 USD) in addition to the base salary, as well as monthly child benefits for the first two children in the sum of 404,000 rials ($40 USD) and shelter allowance equivalent to 100,000 ($10 USD) per month. This makes the base monthly salary of a worker between $396 and $600 USD.

The contrast between what the minimum wage law mandates and the reality of low-income life is highlighted further in the following extracts from the interviews:

- Fereshteh, a street vendor, said, "I only sell as much as I need for daily food, rice, or something for that day, because I don't want my husband to get used to the idea of me being responsible for housekeeping money. It is his responsibility to provide, and I only make 50,000 rials. As soon as that is done I pack and leave."
- Soghra, an immigrant from a small town from Azerbaijan province who works as a street vendor, saved most of her earnings for her daughter: "I don't give a penny of what I earn to my husband. My husband is responsible for housekeeping money. I save what I earn and it all will go to my daughter. He does not ask how much I earn and I don't bother to tell him."
- Mahtab, a vendor, had started working because of her husband's disability: "We were rich and had a house in an uptown neighborhood, but my husband had a car accident, and he has been handicapped ever since. I have to pay for everything, including his medication. And my son is into drugs, so he not only does not bring an income, but I have to pay for his addiction, too."

Earlier in this chapter we saw that the majority of women who are in the informal sector are married women. Therefore it is worth emphasizing that what seems to be a commonly held assumption about the traditional family model of the male breadwinner, at least in low-income Tehran, is more of a myth than a reality. To develop a deeper understanding, husbands' occupations were reviewed: 49.9 percent of the men to whom the women in our sample were married were employed, which means half (50.1 percent) of these men were not income earners. Of those employed, 60.4 percent worked in the informal sector, while only 19.8 percent worked in the formal sector. When husbands are employed, it tends to be in the informal sector, which puts the entire family in an economically precarious situation, and this could explain why married women have to work—common characteristics of incomes in the informal sector are irregular, low-paying wages and workers lacking protection such as unemployment benefits. Of our sample's husbands, 9.9 percent were declared by their wives to be unemployed (I use the word *declared* because we never interviewed the husbands, just the wives), 6 percent were retired (presumably without a pension or on a low pension), 1.1 percent were handicapped, and unfortunately 13.2 were reported to be drug addicts.

In terms of the types of jobs men held, many were part of the service sector of the informal economy. The result of the initial pretest in 2009 showed that they worked primarily as street vendors, janitors, repair and handymen, or delivery men. A minority of them worked in low-level office or clerical jobs, or worked in various health clubs, as either cleaners or training assistants. Only a few were in the formal sector, albeit in low-paying jobs such as cafeteria workers. We will return to this with more detail in Chapter 5.

INFORMAL WORK: CHOICE VERSUS SKILL AND EDUCATION, EXPERIENCE VERSUS PERSONAL INTEREST

A cross-tabulation between education and line of activity showed that those who were illiterate were engaged in sewing, vending, food processing, or working as cleaning ladies. Most respondents had middle school [*rahnamai*] and secondary school educations. Among those with secondary school diplomas, 80 percent were vendors and massage therapists; all home caregivers had secondary degrees, as did 75 percent of those who produced arts and crafts. Ironically, there were some low-income women with college education, and 10 percent of them worked as vendors in the Metro (which tends to be a part-time job for some university students); half of them worked as employees, and among massage therapists, 20 percent of them had college degrees.

With regard to personal choice and line of activity, only 21.4 percent of those who were working as hairdressers declared that they worked because of personal interest. The 27 percent who worked odd jobs also stated that they worked for personal interest, while the corresponding statistic among saleswomen was 7.1 percent. Those who

Table 4.6 Line of activity and reasons for occupational choice

	Reasons for occupational choice							
Line of activity	*Personal interest*	*Work experience*	*Good skill match*	*Easy access*	*Through metro*	*Lack of choice*	*Social network*	*Total*
Sewing	1	2	4	1	0	0	4	12
	8.3	*16.7*	*33.3*	*8.3*	*0.0*	*0.0*	*33.3*	*100.0*
Metro vendor	0	1	0	2	5	0	2	10
	0.0	*10.0*	*0.0*	*20.0*	*50.0*	*0.0*	*20.0*	*100.0*
Hairdresser	3	1	7	0	0	1	2	14
	21.4	*7.1*	*50.0*	*0.0*	*0.0*	*7.1*	*14.3*	*100.0*
Employee	3	2	2	0	0	0	4	11
	27.3	*18.2*	*18.2*	*0.0*	*0.0*	*0.0*	*36.4*	*100.0*
Home caregiver	0	0	0	0	0	0	2	2
	0.0	*0.0*	*0.0*	*0.0*	*0.0*	*0.0*	*100.0*	*100.0*

Arts and crafts	0	2	1	0	0	0	1	4
	0.0	*50.0*	*25.0*	*0.0*	*0.0*	*0.0*	*25.0*	*100.0*
Saleswoman	1	4	0	4	1	0	4	14
	7.1	*28.6*	*0.0*	*28.6*	*7.1*	*0.0*	*28.6*	*100.0*
Food processer	0	2	1	3	0	2	0	8
	0.0	*25.0*	*12.5*	*37.5*	*0.0*	*25.0*	*0.0*	*100.0*
Massage therapist	0	1	0	1	0	1	2	5
	0.0	*20.0*	*0.0*	*20.0*	*0.0*	*20.0*	*40.0*	*100.0*
Cleaning lady	0	2	0	2	0	0	7	11
	0.0	*18.2*	*0.0*	*18.2*	*0.0*	*0.0*	*63.6*	*100.0*
Total	8	17	15	13	6	4	28	91
	8.8	*18.7*	*16.5*	*14.3*	*6.6*	*4.4*	*30.8*	*100.0*

Note: The numbers in italics are percentages of row totals for each group.

stated that they work in their occupation due to lack of choice had the highest percentage: 25 percent of food processers, 20 percent of massage therapists, and 7.1 percent of hairdressers.

Among the sample, it seems that skills, easy access, and experience were much more important factors. Among hairdressers, skill plays an important role in the choice of occupation (50 percent). Of those who worked in sewing, 50 percent had chosen it because of their skills; the corresponding figure among those who worked in arts and crafts was 25 percent, and it was 12.5 percent for food processers (37.5 percent of food processors also stated that the reason was easy access). Food processers are among the lowest-paid workers, and they also declared that a lack of choice brought them to this work. Among those in sales, 20 percent of Metro vendors and 28.6 percent of saleswomen entered the jobs because of easy access.

A cross-tabulation between work experience and line of activity illustrates a rather alarming picture: most of these workers have been in their businesses for only one to five years. However, on the bright side—and from my personal field observation—many women have come into the labor market in the last five years, which may explain why the majority of our sample tends to fall in that category. Within other services, with 57.6 percent of workers in the one- to five-year category, most are in traditionally "female jobs" such as cleaning and home caregiving. Tradition likewise applies to the category of sewing and knitting, which is the sector with the most experience (28 percent).

FORMAL VERSUS INFORMAL AND GENDER SEGREGATION

Gender segregation, as discussed earlier, is an impediment to women's access to employment. Although gender segregation closes certain jobs to women, however, it also opens other work opportunities. This is certainly true of home-based business activities. For a closer examination, our research looked into the nature of women's work. It was found that a quarter of our sample worked from home (25.5 percent), while the rest worked outside of their homes (74.5 percent).

As mentioned, even when women work outside of their homes, their work tends to be clustered around goods and services whose clientele are exclusively female. In the aftermath of the revolution, and with progressive gender segregation in areas such as education, the formal sector created opportunities for female teachers at the primary and secondary level. The experience gained in the informal sector is similar to that of the formal. A gradual move toward the expansion of all-female spaces has taken place, including an all-female restaurant (currently there is only one in Tehran) or women-only concerts. All-female spaces have become places of work—for instance, the mosque and other religious gatherings were traditionally not spaces where sales would take place, but this has changed.

Moreover, all-female spaces have become platforms for multiple sources of goods and services. Health clubs, for example, used to be places for women's sports only, but now they sell sports clothes as well. I have witnessed these gradual changes for the past five years; today in many women's sports clubs, a wide range of goods such as underwear, makeup, and even health food and other items are being sold. According to interviews, all-female spaces are among the most lucrative sources of income.

In Tehran's sexually segregated Metro, female vendors are tacitly permitted by the city. The authorities adopt a much softer attitude toward female Metro vendors by the very fact that women vendors in the Metro are tolerated while male vendors are not, and crackdowns are far less frequent than is the case for street vendors. This has been attributed to lobbying by the mayor's wife, who campaigns against female poverty.

Our sample Metro vendors stated that their incomes were sufficient to meet their families' basic needs. Nonetheless, one of the major hazards of Metro vending is that the authorities can confiscate their inventories at any time. However, nearly all those interviewees whose inventory had been confiscated by the authorities stated that their goods were later returned. There are no regulations and no official policy to protect these workers, and the lobby efforts by the mayor's wife have remained at the level of the city's discourse: legally, Metro vendors are similar to all vendors and remain without any labor protection. One could argue that these all-female spaces have provided a venue for women who cannot enter formal employment to gain access to unskilled jobs. In this sense, these all-female spaces effectively turned gender segregation on its head, and women are using it to their own advantage.

Most of our respondents entered the job market as low or unskilled laborers to deal with the rising cost of living, and they tended to work wherever they could. In the case of Metro vendors, when asked what they considered to be their best skills, they responded that it was their qualities as saleswomen. When asked what was essential to their success, they indicated that it was social skills and persuasive advertising of their goods and services. Some stated that such qualities are not a given but are acquired, and that without them one cannot operate in this sector of the economy. We will return to Metro vendors in a separate section.

PROBLEMS WITH WORK

As discussed in earlier chapters, informal employment can be among the most precarious. In this research, many respondents complained about long hours. This is to be expected, since, as noted, many work below minimum wage and so need to work longer hours to make up for their low base pay. Worse, long hours often coincide with unfavorable conditions, such as standing on one's feet for the entirety of the day. The main sources of dissatisfaction were a lack of protection regarding their employment and the low social status inherent in their occupation.

According to Law 51 concerning working hours, it is stipulated that working hours must not exceed 8 hours per day. In addendum number 1, employers are permitted to extend the hours of work in any given day providing they reduce the same number of hours from another day of the week, and the total number of hours worked per week must not exceed 44. Yet, according to Table 4.7, many women work between 7 and 9 hours daily, and in some professions more than 10 hours. A cross-tabulation between line of activity and hours of work showed that 60 percent of massage therapists, 100 percent of home caregivers, and 50 percent of food processers worked more than 10 hours a day, as did 66.7 percent of those in sewing and knitting, 20 percent of vendors, 57 percent of hairdressers, 54 percent of handy women, 50 percent of those who worked in arts and crafts, 57.1 percent of saleswomen, and 63.6 percent of cleaning ladies.

- Mino worked in a house as a seamstress: "I have to work many hours. I don't have time for other things that I have to get done. It's very boring and it really puts a lot of pressure on my nerves. Some of my customers are demanding and never happy. And some don't pay me for a long time."

Table 4.7 Hours of work and line of activity

	Hours of work				
Line of activity	*1–3*	*4–6*	*7–9*	*10+*	*Total*
Sewing	0	3	8	1	12
	0.0	*25.0*	*66.7*	*8.3*	*100.0*
Metro vendor	0	2	2	6	10

	Hours of work				
Line of activity	*1–3*	*4–6*	*7–9*	*10+*	*Total*
	0.0	*20.0*	*20.0*	*60.0*	*100.0*
Hairdresser	1	5	8	0	14
	7.1	*35.7*	*57.1*	*0.0*	*100.0*
Employee	0	4	6	1	11
	0.0	*36.4*	*54.6*	*9.1*	*100.0*
Home caregiver	0	0	0	2	2
	0.0	*0.0*	*0.0*	*100.0*	*100.0*
Arts and crafts	0	1	2	1	4
	0.0	*25.0*	*50.0*	*25.0*	*100.0*
Saleswoman	0	2	8	4	14
	0.0	*14.3*	*57.1*	*28.6*	*100.0*
Food processer	0	3	1	4	8
	0.0	*37.5*	*12.5*	*50.0*	*100.0*
Massage therapist	0	2	0	3	5
	0.0	*40.0*	*0.0*	*60.0*	*100.0*
Cleaning lady	1	1	7	2	11
	9.1	*9.1*	*63.6*	*18.2*	*100.0*
Total	2	23	42	24	91
	2.2	*25.3*	*46.2*	*26.4*	*100.0*

Note: The numbers in italics are percentages of row totals for each row group.

Table 4.8 Insurance type and line of activity

	Insurance type					
Line of activity	*No insurance*	*Compulsory insurance*	*Optional/ voluntary*	*Spouse's coverage*	*Parents' insurance*	*Total*
Sewing	7	0	2	3	0	12
	58.3	*0.0*	*16.7*	*25.0*	*0.0*	*100.0*
Metro vendor	8	2	0	0	0	10
	80.0	*20.0*	*0.0*	*0.0*	*0.0*	*100.0*
Hairdresser	5	1	1	7	0	14
	35.7	*7.1*	*7.1*	*50.0*	*0.0*	*100.0*
Employee	6	2	1	0	2	11
	54.6	*18.2*	*9.1*	*0.0*	*18.2*	*100.0*
Home caregiver	1	1	0	0	0	2
	50.0	*50.0*	*0.0*	*0.0*	*0.0*	*100.0*
Arts and crafts	2	0	1	1	0	4
	50.0	*0.0*	*25.0*	*25.0*	*0.0*	*100.0*
Saleswoman	8	1	0	3	2	14
	57.1	*7.1*	*0.0*	*21.4*	*14.3*	*100.0*
Food processer	3	0	3	1	1	8
	37.5	*0.0*	*37.5*	*12.5*	*12.5*	*100.0*
Massage therapist	3	0	0	1	1	5
	60.0	*0.0*	*0.0*	*20.0*	*20.0*	*100.0*
Cleaning lady	6	1	1	3	0	11
	54.6	*9.1*	*9.1*	*27.3*	*0.0*	*100.0*

	Insurance type					
Line of activity	*No insurance*	*Compulsory insurance*	*Optional/ voluntary*	*Spouse's coverage*	*Parents' insurance*	*Total*
Total	49	8	9	19	6	91
	53.9	*8.8*	*9.9*	*20.9*	*6.6*	*100.0*

Note: The numbers in italics are percentages of row totals for each row group.

- Mahin, a masseuse, said, "I spend many hours travelling back and forth, and massage is hard work. I have to stand many hours and give massages. I travel a long way but sometimes I don't have a client. There's no fixed salary, I get paid if there's work, and if there isn't then I've got nothing coming in."
- Parivash, a sales woman, said, "I'm always standing all day and my employer is a man. He's always in the shop and I don't feel comfortable with him around. We don't have a toilet here, and I try as much as possible not to drink so that I won't have to use the toilet."
- Azam, a janitor in a female health club in a wealthy area of Tehran, said, "Sometimes people are very snobbish, they treat me like I'm their servant, and they make feel bad about myself and my job."
- Fatmeh, knitting from home, said, "When I'm knitting and I have a problem, I go to see friends or attend a religious function. As soon as they start to ask about my problem, my friends know I'm working. I'm ashamed of having to work and to earn so little. They start to feel sorry for me and I feel bad."

Cross-tabulation between problems with work and line of activity shows that it is hairdressers who complain the most about their terms of employment (76.9 percent). This could be due to an oversupply of hairdressers. In a field trip to Sultanabad, a shantytown on the outskirts of Islamabad (itself a shantytown until a decade ago), there were at least three hairdressing salons within two blocks. Following hairdressers are those in the Other Services category, especially cleaning ladies and home caregivers, who complain about being at the mercy of their employers' needs (63.6 percent). In contrast, those in the high-end kind of Other Services had far fewer difficulties (6.1 percent). Complaints about a lack of unemployment protection was consistent across all lines of activities, from around one-fifth to one-quarter, which is unsurprising given that informal work is typically without unemployment protection. As for low social status, 12 percent of those in Other Services complained, some of whom were Metro vendors, which we will discuss in the next section.

Add to this lack of insurance. Among respondents, 53 percent had no insurance at all, while 20.9 percent had insurance through their husbands, 8.8 percent had compulsory insurance, 6.6 percent had insurance because of their fathers, and only 9.9 had insurance they paid for (Iran allows people to purchase their insurance at a subsidized rate). These figures indicate how the government fails to provide the sector with insurance.

- Fereshteh suffered from a skin condition related to sun exposure working outside as a vendor: "Some people say standing under the sun, I might get skin cancer."

Table 4.9 Problems with work and line of activity

	Which of the following are problems with your work?					
Line of activity	*Low income*	*Unfavorable working conditions*	*Not having enough time for other work*	*Being caught by officials*	*Physical and emotional fatigue*	*Total*
Sewing	5	5	1	0	0	12
	41.7	*41.7*	*8.3*	*0.0*	*0.0*	*100.0*
Metro vendor	1	8	1	4	0	10
	10.0	*80.0*	*10.0*	*40.0*	*0.0*	*100.0*
Hairdresser	7	7	2	0	2	14
	50.0	*50.0*	*14.3*	*0.0*	*14.3*	*100.0*
Employee	5	7	1	0	0	11
	45.5	*63.6*	*9.1*	*0.0*	*0.0*	*100.0*
Home caregiver	2	0	1	0	0	2

Which of the following are problems with your work?						
Line of activity	*Low income*	*Unfavorable working conditions*	*Not having enough time for other work*	*Being caught by officials*	*Physical and emotional fatigue*	*Total*
	100.0	*0.0*	*50.0*	*0.0*	*0.0*	*100.0*
Arts and crafts	1	2	0	0	0	4
	25.0	*50.0*	*0.0*	*0.0*	*0.0*	*100.0*
Saleswoman	4	9	0	1	0	14
	28.6	*64.3*	*0.0*	*7.1*	*0.0*	*100.0*
Food processer	4	3	1	0	0	8
	50.0	*37.5*	*12.5*	*0.0*	*0.0*	*100.0*
Massage therapist	3	4	0	0	1	5
	60.0	*80.0*	*0.0*	*0.0*	*20.0*	*100.0*
Cleaning lady	4	8	0	0	0	11
	36.4	*72.7*	*0.0*	*0.0*	*0.0*	*100.0*
Total	36	53	7	5	3	91
	39.6	*58.2*	*7.7*	*5.5*	*3.3*	*100.0*

Note: The numbers in italics are percentages of those in each line of activity who respond affirmatively to column questions.

- Soghra, a vendor, said, "City officials are for sure a problem, but they do not bother me because I am old woman. When they come to confiscate other people's goods, they leave me behind and don't bother me."
- Akram, a homeworker, said, "I do piece work for my husband and he does not pay me."

- Shokat, who sold flowers with her daughter, complained about city officials but also male passersby: "When they are too stubborn and don't leave us alone I tell them, 'Look my husband is at the corner in his car. If you continue, you will get a good beating. Are you ready?' Then they disappear."
- Davari, a Metro vendor, complained that sometimes people take her goods and walk away without paying, and because her work is illegal, she cannot complain. On one occasion she was robbed while busy selling.

As a researcher I have travelled by Metro and have noticed that vendors give their items to their customers so the latter have a closer look. It is a difficult task to keep track of which customer has what item, while vendors also are advertising, selling, and making sure they are not in the way of other people. It is fairly easy during busy times for customers to walk away with their goods because of the high traffic and short distance between stops. The fact that a vendor often has at least three customers looking at her merchandize at the same time makes it hard to watch carefully.

Street Vendors

Our research shows that even in jobs such as street vending, which is the least protected environment, women can create protection through a network of those who work alongside them. To some extent this depends on being able to establish a face-to-face relationship and being in a stable situation. Some vendors are part-time workers; some work only during particular times, such as just before the New Year, and tend to be alienated from the rest of the vendor community. The research found that those who had been in this profession for a long time could establish better relations with other vendors and build solidarity.

During open-ended interviews, some women believed that solidarity and support was important in difficult situations. Masumeh, for example, said, "Some of the other single-headed households understand each other. They support each other because they know that the husband has either left or is a drug addict and they have to provide for their children, and this brings them together." While she was speaking she pointed out other women; one of them was divorced from a drug-addict husband and was selling flowers, and she had two children. She said that the two of them started working around the same time. They exchanged their goods, and when they had time they talked about their common problems.

Fieldwork in the Metro showed that the vendors know each other well and, at times, even give each other small gifts for their children. When business is slow they sit by each other's side providing support and discussing family matters. They try not to compete for sales, as one vendor works at a time in the Metro and taking turns is respected. One starts to advertise one's own goods only when another has finished, asking permission from the other to start advertising.

Most vendors complained about city officials, but there were cases in which the vendor was known and respected by the people, and the street corner had turned into a familiar place with a network of support from the shopkeepers and city officials.

- Zahra, an elderly vendor who worked opposite of Tehran University, reported that her old age draws students to help her: "My books are second hand and are given to me by bookstores nearby, and I know sometime students buy from me just because they want to be kind and helpful." She sat outside a shop, and if she had to step out or stop work, the bookstore sales person would look after her merchandise. "Sometimes other bookstore people give me tea and feed me, they are really kind to me."
- Davari was not as bitter as some of the other vendors about city officials: "They have to do their job, but they know we need the money. You can see some of them are kind and don't want to do this, but they have to, and whenever they can, they let us off."
- Razieh said, "When one of us is in trouble and doesn't have money, we help her and give her things to sell and she can pay us back. We understand each other and help out when we can. Sometimes even the police feel sorry for us and leave us alone. They know we have to do this and we are poor."

Working in the Metro is very different from working in the street, and it has created its own neighborhood and social network. In a study of street vendors that focused on vendors who constituted female-headed households, similar findings are reported. One respondent stated that when she was working in a company and the owner found out she was a single woman, he asked her to leave, and she was forced to become a Metro vendor. In other cases, women reported feeling comfortable being in an all-female space and free from male harassment; they enjoyed the support of some of the women who buy from them in solidarity with their situation (Nahavandi and Ajavarlo 2009).

The Informal Sector, Social Networks, and the Safety Net

Jaleh, a massage therapist from Khaniabad (a low-income neighborhood), is a single mother of two children. She lives in her father's house, pays no rent, and started working as a masseuse before enrolling in courses with various alternative health-care providers and becoming a massage therapist. With her deceased husband's pension and her participation in credit clubs, she was able to save money. Now that her eldest son is able to contribute to the household, she is only giving massages to select customers. In her tightly knit community, many neighbors were fellow-migrants from Tabriz and lived in solidarity with one another. She told me about how she took care of her cousin Solmaz.

Jaleh had mobilized her friends and family members to give financial assistance to her cousin, whose husband, Hussein, was a drug addict. Hussein had gone through several rehabilitation programs but was unable to leave his addiction. He had sold everything he could to finance his addiction, but with the help of the local realtor, who was a distant relation to Jaleh's family, Solmaz's house was put under her name in order to prevent Hussein from being able to sell it.

Nonetheless, Solmaz had to rely on the assistance she received from her family network for her daily survival. At the time of the interview, Jaleh, together with her sister-in-law, had gathered close to $2,000 USD for the marriage of Solmaz's daughter. Although this financial assistance is critical to her cousin's life, Jaleh said, "My cousin is not happy and feels that she is the recipient of charity from the family." I asked Jaleh to take me to see her, and she accepted, provided there would be no mention of why I was there. Jaleh told Solmaz that I was an academic interested in the role of women in the informal sector and that I wanted to visit some sights in Sultanabad. Solmaz spoke Persian with a heavy accent, and at times we spoke in Azeri. She was very generous and served us tea. Her house consisted of two rooms and an indoor toilet. One of her rooms was full of *Jahizieh* (household goods bought by the bride's family) for Solmaz's daughter. From bedroom furniture to a fridge and stove, the entire room was filled with enough goods to furnish a small apartment and give the young couple an easy start in their new life. The young bride was happy and showed me a picture of her future husband. When I asked her if she loved him, she became bashful and laughed.[1]

As discussed previously, social networks are important to the informal sector. In our findings, 79 percent of respondents found their jobs through their network of extended family and neighborhood friends. Social networks not only help women find jobs but also help them find clientele. Our research found that many respondents developed their clienteles through relatives, friends, and neighbors, and advertised for their goods and services through their networks. The network was important for exchange and bartering, and it gave subsidized goods and services as well as provided credit. Among our respondents, 25.3 percent received loans from their relatives and 5.5 percent from their friends. Only 7.7 percent reported getting loans from charity, while 4 percent had access to bank loans. However, *Garzol Hassaneh*, or rotating credit and saving associations (ROCSAs), provided 7.7 percent of the respondents with access to credit; needless to mention, membership in these clubs depends on one's social network. On the down side of the social network, whereas 9.9 percent thought their work brought status to them, the vast majority of our respondents—90.1 percent—reported being ashamed of their jobs.

In Table 4.6 we cross-tabulated line of activity and social network when reasons for occupational choice was discussed. The result showed that 33 percent of those in sewing and knitting chose this job because of/through their social network. Among Metro vendors, 20 percent used their social network (this includes getting credit from wholesalers to advance them inventories for sale). Among hairdressers, only 14 percent relied on their social network, while 36 percent of those who worked as employees found their jobs because of their social network. All home caregivers found jobs through social networks. A quarter of those who made arts and crafts received access to this job through their network. Among those working in sales, 28 percent reported that their reason to choose the occupation was because of the social network. Aside from home caregivers, the highest percentages among those whose reason to choose their occupation was their network were massage therapists at 40 percent and cleaning ladies at 63 percent. The finding among the sample confirms the literature on the importance of social networks in the informal sector.

Fereshteh, a street vendor, said, "I often get my goods [women's underwear] on credit. When I can't afford to pay for them, I get them as credit, then once I sell, I pay back, and if I don't sell, I return them." Fereshteh continued, "I can't spend too much time selling because I look after my old aunt who has lost her son in a car crash. My husband was against it, but now he knows my aunt has no other person to take care of her." In most cases, our interviewees had some kind of charity. Charity seems to be almost a part of the low-income household life. Shahrbanoo, an elderly vendor, had difficulties making ends meet; nonetheless, she collected money for the elderly and organized religious gatherings regularly and encouraged charitable donations to the poor.

One's social network and extended family sometimes can work against a woman. Soghra, for example, complained about in-laws and how they interfered with her life: "My husband thinks about his own family, and his sister always is telling him to divorce me and to sell his house. He is a little aggressive sometimes (verbally) but he is always helping with chores around the house." Another negative side of social network is shame. Fereshteh said, "My biggest problem is being seen by a family member while sitting in the street putting out my stuff. Many times when I see a familiar face, I take my stuff and hide in the close-by shopping center. This is while we are being harassed by the city officials."

In the case of homeworkers, some thought that working from their home was limiting and provided little opportunity to draw customers, although close to one-fifth (20 percent) enjoyed support from their neighborhood and thought it a very positive factor in finding work and clientele. The opposite was held to be true for vendors who worked in places outside of their homes and thought that being outside brought more clients. In the case of one saleswomen, certain places such as Berlin Street (famous for being the center of inexpensive goods such as fabrics, sewing, and knitting items) in the old downtown reported that being in such locations was very important when selling specialized women's consumer items.

Following are some of the responses from interviewees who worked outside of their homes:

- Shireen, in charge of a coffee shop in a women's health club, responded, "I like working here because I get a lot of customers from the club and it is convenient for people to drop by."
- Mahtab, a masseuse in a women's health club, responded, "I wouldn't know how to get customers if it was not because of the club."
- Shadi, a street vendor on Berlin Street, said, "I sell very well here because of the location."
- Shohreh, who sells clothes, dolls, and makeup in a mosque, said, "Since people come for prayers I get a lot of customers. It is better to sell in a mosque than at home."

And here are some of the responses from home-based workers that highlight its advantages and disadvantages:

- Zohreh, a hairdresser who worked from her house, said, "Everyone knows me here and I have a lot of customers. I have made a name here and built my customers from among the neighborhood."
- Sima, another hairdresser, said, "I prefer to work at home because of my small children. Here I can keep an eye on them and do my work. If I were working outside, I would have more customers. Being at home, some think my work is not good enough to work outside and I lose customers."
- Tahereh, who makes handkerchiefs, said, "I have made a name selling high-quality handkerchiefs, and they tell each other and come back to me for more."
- Marzieh, a dressmaker, said, "Because I am at home, I don't have too many customers, not many people get to know my work. My clients are my close relatives, friends, and neighbors."
- Haleh, a dressmaker who specializes in wedding dresses, said, "Working at home is not good for my business because I cannot allow strangers into my home. I have to know them well, and this is not good for business."
- A food processor said, "Many of my neighbors know that I prepare vegetables, and they bring their vegetables for me to clean, wash, and prepare for them."
- Fatima, a Qur'an teacher, said, "Everyone knows me well and they call me for religious ceremonies. I am called if people want to go on a pilgrimage or if there are ceremonies for mourning."

As testified by our interviewees, the results vary. Generally, women benefited from their social networks based on their neighborhood and kinship. In other cases women preferred to work in public places where it is easier to be seen and to advertise. Normally shopkeepers resent having vendors working by their shops because their price is much lower, but in the case of Fereshteh, they did not mind her and were very friendly with her. During the interview one of them dropped by to greet her and find out how she was doing. Soghrah was a vendor who had earned a certain respect and used it to help others: "Because I am old and I use the respect I have earned, I help others and sometimes go to the city to negotiate and return other person's confiscated goods." Mehnoosh, who worked at home processing food and did odd jobs, anything she could do to bring extra cash, reported that because she was barren she chose a new wife for her husband. She was happy with the arrangement and liked the second wife, who brought children, and the three lived happily. She had no problem earning money and paying for the second wife's children because the second wife was very respectful of her and took care of household chores and freed her from those duties. Mahtab, a vendor, was grateful that her street-corner vending place was a point where people knew her and respected her. She even had the nearby shop ready to help her by storing her goods (she sold scarves), saving her from having to bring them back and forth, and letting her customers know when she is away and when she will be back. And Davari, a Metro vendor, lived in a room offered by a relative for free. "I am even told that I should not do anything in return, it is something she is offering because I need a place to stay." She has a room to herself, but she tries to be away and keep herself out of the way when her relative's husband is home.

Informal Economy, Double Days, and Flexible Hours

Working a double day is a major problem for married women. Our research shows that despite the fact that generating an income is vital to the family's economic survival, their responsibilities at home as homemakers remain unchanged. They continue to cook, clean, and take care of the children. Our research shows that 52 percent of married women stated that their outside work did not reduce their responsibilities at home, and they had to work hard to meet the demands of two jobs. Close to half (48 percent) of our sample reported that they had to rely on help from other family members, often relying on their own mothers or sisters (19 percent) or their eldest children (18 percent). Only in a minority of cases (8 percent) did men help with the housework.

In our research, 38 percent of respondents preferred to work from home, and 59 percent preferred to work outside. The most important reason for wanting to work at home was being able to take care of their children and being able to combine their productive labor with their reproductive labor. Some 26 percent preferred home because it was more peaceful, while 4 percent thought home was a more protected space and felt safe and free from male harassment.

When we asked if working at home allowed them to have more control over their expenditures, 68.1 percent responded that working outside of their homes offered higher social status and gave them more opportunity to socialize, which was more important. Some preferred working outside because of higher economic opportunities and an increase in their clientele (16 percent), while others felt they had more freedom (5 percent). The latter was more applicable to those who were unmarried.

In-depth interviews showed that many of these women suffered from depression and were under a great deal of stress. This is especially true of women who were abandoned or divorced. Masumeh, a piece worker in a sewing workshop, said, "I hated to divorce. But my husband was paranoid and had obsessive thoughts about me betraying him and beat me up, so I had to get divorced. I had a son and a daughter-in-law and was ashamed of getting divorced. I insisted on not divorcing and staying together, but he would not accept that and we finally separated. I was very depressed for a long time until I came to work in this small workshop. Since I left home, I feel a lot better. My husband returned and begged me to get back with him, but I wouldn't."

Despite all the pros and cons of working in the informal sector, half of our respondents preferred not to have the obligation to work at all, the most important factor being that they wanted to spend time with their families. Here it may be important to refer to the work of Catherine Hakim, who found that some women prefer to have more time with their families than a career (in this case access to economic resources). Hakim's work is about women in the context of European countries, but it seems to apply to our sample, too (Hakim 2000, 2003, 2006).

Perhaps our results are not surprising; working in a low-paid, unprotected job with long hours can hardly be desirable when one has the extra work of being a wife and a mother. It may be fairly obvious that among single women there was a tendency to work for independence and self-interest while among married women work was considered an economic necessity. Yet this could not be generalized, and there were cases of married women wanting to work and viewing it as an important part of their economic empowerment and independence. They saw their work as a means to gain self-confidence and to increase their bargaining power within their households. We will expand on this in the next section.

Informal Work and Empowerment

Despite the fact that our research showed that women working in the informal sector faced low pay and long hours under sometimes unfavorable conditions with little or no protection, half of our respondents thought that their job was a source of empowerment in terms of self-confidence, economic decision making, and intrahousehold bargaining power. Even when the sole reason for entering into the sector was economic necessity (19 percent), there was nonetheless a sense of economic empowerment. When we combine social and economic empowerment, 53 percent of our respondents felt that their job provided at least one of the two. What's more, most women (57 percent) stated that their work brought them recognition and credibility in their immediate community.

The impact of how the immediate and extended family members viewed our respondents' work was distinct. More than half of our respondents stated that their family respected and admired their effort, and that the work gave them credibility and decision-making power within their households. Close to one-third felt that they enjoyed support from their family and friends, and almost one-quarter of respondents stated that their work has provided them with greater respect and that their opinions now are considered important, as others turn to them for advice. Zahra, for example, said, "My family is proud of me now because they know I can take care of myself." Zeynab said, "My family looks at me with more respect and thinks of me as a strong woman, someone who can organize her life." Masumeh said, "They tell me that I am a strong woman and resourceful and respect me for what I do. They tell me, 'You are a man.' I love working hard and paying for myself."

When expenditure patterns were examined, it was found that 57 percent of household items were paid for by women's income, and the corresponding figure for children's education was 54.5 percent. Women also paid for 43 percent of necessary items, such as food and family clothing, as well as installments on various loans, and 32 percent paid rent. Women could also save, and our respondents reported that they could save one-fifth of their earnings; 7 percent of their income was spent on buying gold, which is a traditional form of saving for many women of low-income backgrounds.

With regard to general decision making, one-third of our respondents stated that they are in charge of the most important economic decisions in their lives, while 24 percent said that they would consult their husbands before taking decisions. The majority of working women felt they were in charge of major decisions; just under one-quarter responded that their husband or parents were in charge. Our research shows that, generally, women have been able to increase their power in their households mainly because of their work and the income they have brought into their families. By and large there was a sense of empowerment among women, except for a minority who felt they still had little power vis-à-vis their husbands and parents.

The results of our research show that while traditional male-female roles persist, there is a major transition in process. Gender-role transformation is, to some extent, related to the changing role of women in the labor market. In terms of decision making, women made the majority of decisions with regard to the welfare of the children (62 percent), and this was coupled with some decision making about household resource allocation (43 percent). Men had more decision-making power over the purchase of items such as a family car (35 percent); the corresponding figure was one-fifth among women. Men made decisions related to expenditures for purchasing or renting a home 33 percent of the time compared with 21 percent of the time for women. This is showed a dramatic change when we asked women how decisions over housing or car purchases had been made a decade ago.

Some women voiced their sense of empowerment and solidarity. Working in the Metro is very different from working on the street, and the Metro vendors have formed a social network of their own kind—a neighborhood of a different nature.

- Golnar, who was a student, said, "I need to work to pay for my university. I wanted to pay for myself and stand on my own feet, but because of my university, I could not work full time. I took a course in artificial nails and now I work in a hair salon."
- Parivash said, "I saw how women sell in the Metro, and to pay for my university [she was attending the private Open University], I began selling makeup. Now I sell makeup and I make enough to pay for my education."
- Rafiyeh said, "Since I began to work in the Metro I have been able to keep up payments for my daughter's wedding gift."
- Tayebeh said, "I started working in the Metro because my parents would not allow me to study and live with them if I didn't pay them."

Others gave other examples of empowerment:

- Mehnoosh, who worked as food processor and had brought a second wife for her husband because she was barren, said, "My husband doesn't have much say in the way the household is run. I rule."
- Simin, a masseuse, said, "My husband wanted me to give me a massage. I resented that and thought, 'This is great after a day of work. Sir wants his massage.' So I gave him a very hard and pain-

ful massage. He said, 'God, you women, how can you pay for such a painful thing?' That was that, and he never asked for another massage again. I was free from giving him a free massage."

- Shokat, a street vendor whose husband was an informal driver (someone who does not have a taxi permit but works as a taxi driver), said, "My husband does not speak to his in-laws because they say this house is matriarchal. I rule and I make all the decisions. My husband's family does not like it and they are not welcome into my house." She and her daughter sold flowers.
- Jamileh, a cleaning lady aged 39, reported that she rules in the house. She is in charge of all the income that the household generates. "When we first married, he was in charge, but slowly I gained control. He is now forced to take a shower every morning; I've told him if he doesn't his day will be ruined and he listens. At first he would not listen, but I kept repeating, when you have a nice shower in the morning your day is fresh and everything goes well. He slowly started to realize the benefits of nice fresh shower in the morning . . . He is sometimes short tempered because of the side effects of chemical bombing [the husband fought in the Iran-Iraq war where chemical bombs were used on Iranians], but overall he is kind."

The fieldwork shed light on an important institution very common among women of low-income households: rotating credit and saving associations. There has been some discussion in the Introduction, and here we include more information about these all-female clubs.

Rotating Credit and Saving Associations (ROCSAs)

ROCSAs have become highly popular, perhaps due to difficulties related to obtaining loans from formal institutions. They seem to be vital to women and transcend different socioeconomic categories. In this section, because of easy access to middle-income households and ROCSA-head-organizer Shireen, I discuss one that is more typical of middle-income neighborhoods, but the basis of all ROCSAs are the same; the difference among them is the amount of cash that members of individual ROCSAs have invested.

Shireen, a newly widowed mother of three, kindly and generously accepted my request for an interview, and she graciously offered my research assistant and me tea. Our interference with her son's watching of his favorite program was not well received by the young boy.

She had two daughters, and after I explained my research and plan to write a book, the atmosphere changed, as my visit became more welcomed by the family, especially by the two young women. Shireen had a rotating credit club business (a ROCSA), which was a source of income, as she took a percentage of the loans as payment for her service. The loans operate by each person purchasing one or more shares at a fixed amount. For example, one of her clubs had a five-year period for a total number of sixty women, each of whom paid a monthly installment of 100,000 rials ($10 USD). This provided credit of $600 each month for one person. She had several rotating credit clubs, from 1.5 million *toman* ($1,500 USD) to $2,000, $4,000, and even up to $6,000. Every month on a certain day, sixty women come to her house for a social gathering, and a name is drawn from a box. Shireen then takes a percentage from the winner for her pay. (These figures are much higher than the average of what can be found in low-income neighborhoods, where the actual credit in ROCSAs is between $500 and $1000). When I asked Shireen whether there were any risks involved, she responded,

> This can be a risky business. Sometimes people default in their payments, some lose their husbands and cannot pay their installments, or their husband becomes unemployed, and I have to buy their share. There are also a lot of costs. I have to call them all to remind them and my phone bill is often very high. I have to make sure that the cash flow is smooth, members pay on time, and the right amount is collected. Some use bank transfers and I have to keep track. The different credit clubs meet at different times and it means that I have to have four or five social evenings and invite everybody. Now that, thank God, I have several rotating credit clubs, I am dealing with a lot of shares, and if there are defaults in one I can make it up with earnings from the other clubs.

Her apartment looked large enough to accommodate maybe twenty people, and I thought that it must be hard to have sixty members attend each draw. I posed that question to her, and she responded, "Not all members attend, but most do to make sure the process is smooth. And in some cases it is a time to socialize."

Shireen chose this job when she was living with her parents. Her mother had several rotating clubs, and she helped her to run them for many years by taking charge of the bookkeeping. Later, she started her own clubs while still living with her parents, but they were separate from her mother's clubs. Once she married, she expanded her clubs. Her husband was not always happy with her work. His main complaint was that they had no privacy—club members felt free to drop in and out, call at inappropriate times, and every month there were nights when he could not come home because of the ladies' club. Shireen's work became a point of tension. "Why can't you do something else?" her husband would ask. Her response was that the income was high and she could stay at home and take care of their family. Shireen had tried sewing and hairdressing, but being in charge of credit clubs was far more lucrative. Now that she had lost her husband, her pension and credit-club revenue would enable her to sustain her and her children's standard of living. The business had even brought enough cash for her to buy another apartment to rent out. But for Shireen, as for many other women whom I interviewed, these clubs are not just a way of raising cash but a way of being part of a self-help community. Shireen, like other women, believes that as the funds are interest free, it is religiously *halal* [permissible] and is in fact an Islamic good deed (*savab darad*) because the funds are used for helping its members to enrich their families' lives. As with similar credit clubs, Shireen said that since members of a club know one another, if someone is in trouble—if someone's husband has died or if someone has had an injury or a sickness in her family—the winner gives her turn to the member in need.

Shireen is a very efficient and resourceful woman, and since she has several clubs and is dealing with a fairly large number of people, she asks every member to give her a bond as a guarantee that they will continue their payments after they have won. Technically a bond is much more cashable than a check—it is possible to obtain a court order to cash a bond or seize the possessions of the person in debt. But Shireen said that in the twenty years she has been in business, she had never taken anyone to court. Shireen admits that she had never told her husband about defaults, because he was always nervous that someone would default and that he would have to bear the cost. When it did happen, however, she managed to carry on the payments and continue to make a profit. I asked her why she didn't take the matter to court, and she said,

> It is not fair to take people to court because they are poor and unable to pay. It isn't fair to give someone a bad name in the community. Poverty is not a sin. God is great, and if someone is in a difficult time then I am not going to take her to jail or have her assets seized. The whole idea of these clubs is to help people. I had a friend who was going through a difficult time. I asked her to start saving only $100 a month and

> encouraged her to join our club. She did and won on the first month. She then put that 100 dollars into a savings account and received $25 in interest, which she then reinvested. Gradually her husband joined in, and they took larger shares. She has managed to earn a living and has used some of the cash to continue with her education. Now she has a secondary school diploma. One of her interesting encounters was when she started to open a bank account and brought in large sums of money on a regular basis. The bank teller thought that she had joined Gold Quest [a pyramid scheme which had become popular at the time]. We all laughed!

Again, this is more typical of lower-middle-income households and not the poor. Of course, some members are against investing their money in a bank because they regard interest rates from banks as *haram* (not *halal*) and against Islam. Instead they entered into mutual-fund investments with religious and pious members of the bazaar.

Our research findings show that one-third of our respondents were part of rotating credit clubs, of which 37 percent belonged to a family-based credit club, another 37 percent belonged to a club with neighborhood friends, and the rest used mosque-based credits or funds from different foundations. These credit institutions are based on traditional models and personal trust. Some clubs operate through a rotation, and in others they hold a lottery; in emergencies, loans are provided based on a woman's need. During our interviews we found that in most cases women started these clubs as a way of dealing with the economic difficulties of their friends and family members.

In some cases, credit clubs are a way for the rich to reach out to the poor. In Muslim culture giving charity must remain anonymous to save the dignity of the recipient, and so some wealthy persons use credit clubs as a mechanism for charitable giving. During one of my observations I found a case of a woman from a high-income household who was a member of a low-income club; she indicated that her purpose there was to help the poor without taking away their dignity.

In addition to these credit associations, many of our respondents received support from their close family such as their parents (42 percent), and some received interest-free loans from charity organizations (15 percent). Receiving an interest-free loan from a charity organization, however, requires a guarantor. This often is not hard to find, and it is generally far easier than borrowing from a formal lending institution, including formal charities. Most of what is borrowed is spent on household expenses, such as a down payment for a home, or paying for unexpected costs such as weddings and bride gifts (*jahizieh*). These loans are therefore a vital resource for the poor.

Mina gave a different picture of rotating credit. While she runs a ROCSA and belonged to another association, she reported that she knew of a ROCSA that was a scam and in which all its members lost their savings. The person in charge disappeared with an amount equivalent to $80,000. She invited me to attend court to hear about another scam. She also related that, after her husband had passed away, she was very lonely and joined her local Qur'an reading group, where she met a highly charismatic female Qur'an interpreter. The female Qur'an reader and ceremony holder had just moved into their neighborhood in Javadieh, and they had quickly gathered a crowd of followers who were inspired by the reader's religious teachings and attended her sermons at different religious gatherings. She then started a credit club, and because of her popularity and community trust, was able to gather a great deal of club members. Mina continued,

> In the beginning she was full of charisma on *Ashura* [the tenth day of Muharram in the Muslim calendar and the day that commemorates the martyrdom of the Prophet's grandson, Imam Hussein]. Her preaching would melt everyone into tears and we all loved her. She was invited to every religious gathering to speak for an eager crowd. And soon enough she became rich and bought a house and a car and slowly changed into a rich woman who wore a miniskirt and makeup to dinner parties. She was a total hypocrite and she made me turn against religion. I felt I was being used. Why are miniskirts and makeup bad for me but not for her?

Mina had recently joined a Sufi group and attended regular Sufi sessions. She was in contact with a large community and was a big help in locating interviewees.[2]

Focus Group in Shahid Harandy Neighborhood (Molavi and Darvazeh Ghar)

The women in this focus group included Akram, widowed, 43 years of age; Rahimeh, married, 32 years of age; and Fatimah, unmarried, 22 years of age.

Akram's husband, who had been in the carpet business, had passed away, so now she worked in a sweatshop packaging women's underwear from 8:00 in the morning until 8:00 at night, with a one-and-a-half-hour lunch break. She earned 15,000 rials (equivalent to

$150 USD) per month. She did not own her house and had a monthly rent equivalent to $200. Her daughter helped with the packaging.

Rahimeh was married to a man two years older than her; she had two daughters and was pregnant with her third child. Her husband worked as a piece worker and earned $250 per month. They lived in Rahimeh's mother's house and had only one room with a kitchen. She was a piece worker in a sweatshop.

Fatimah had not married. She lived in her father's house with her brother and his family. Her mother did facial hair threading and her father was retired.

On the issue of breadwinner model, Akram said, "All laws are in favor of men. If I go to the court and complain about my husband not paying housekeeping money, they will not listen; as long as he pays something, anything, even $10, they will let him off. I am very much against the inheritance law. Why should a son inherit twice that of a daughter? In traditional society, the family supported women, but now that we are away from our families [she was an immigrant from Azerbaijan province], we have no support. Women have to work and stand up for themselves."

Rahimeh said, "I work because I have a contract with the bazaar. I used to be a hairdresser; I learned that from my mother because that is what she did, too. But hairdressing was not bringing enough income, so I started to learn to work with a sewing machine. Now I work from home because I borrowed a sewing machine from my employer. I spend some money on the household but keep the rest and save and sometimes spend on the children."

Rahimeh had managed to save money together with her husband to buy a house, and they were in the process of moving out of her mother's place. The house was in the name of Rahimeh, and they were paying a $150 monthly mortgage. Her mother was a source of help, and moving out meant she would have difficulty looking after her children (particularly now that she was pregnant with a new child).

I asked if she was able to get any loans. "I had no help here. There is a *garssol hassaneh* [credit club] for Khalkhal [a city in East Azerbaijan Province from where she had migrated]." However, it had not granted her any loan because she needed a guarantor. Akram said, "These credit clubs do not give a lot of money; we have our own credit club with 30 members, and if we win we get $50. It held a monthly lottery. For me it is like a kind of saving." When I asked her on what she spends her money, she responded that she uses the funds for buying new household items or paying tuition fees for one of her children, who is a university student. Rahimeh was very thankful to her credit club, because once her father had to go to an emergency hospital, and the person who had won the lottery for that month gave her turn to her. Akram added that this is not part of the deal; people do it out of their kindness and are not obliged to do so.

I asked about their relations with their husbands. Rahimeh said that in the beginning she had some problems with her husband, but now she was in charge of most decisions at home: "He first was against me working, but we had no choice. If I don't work, we cannot live. My daughters help me with the work around the house; one of them is 10 and the other is 12. My husband also helps, and, if we don't have dinner or the house is untidy, he starts cooking and cleaning. He doesn't think of working around the house as being *zan zalil* [a henpecked husband]."

Akram said, "Women pretend to be submissive, but they are really in charge most of the time. They get their way one way or the other but do it in a subtle way and let men feel they are the boss. Who cares as long as what they [the women] want to be done gets accomplished." Akram had cut ties with her in-laws completely and kept her family more or less limited to her own family. After her husband had died, she preferred to be away from them, because her brothers-in-law were young and handsome and she thought there would be gossip about her and her brothers-in-law, particularly because she was also young herself when she lost her husband. Rahimeh's husband had lived in Moghan and had little contact with his relatives.

On the question of the workplace, Rahimeh said, "I am happy working at home where I am with my family. They help me, and I don't have to go to the bazaar where there are lots of men. Men from the bazaar are very macho and think women are second-class citizens. I would not be comfortable there. Plus no one can gossip about me working with other men." Akram added that many women feel like Rahimeh. For this reason, many sweatshops rent a large apartment so that women can be together and not have to work in the bazaar. "I much rather work at home, and the employers prefer us to work at home because they save on space and other costs. They hire an Afghan to bring the work to our house and have him collect it, and they pay little to Afghans." She continued, "It really is better for me to work at home, there is no gossip, and you know I am a single woman and people love to talk, but with me working at home they can't. Sometimes relatives and friends like to gossip, and they think we are after their husbands, but we have to work, and working at home is good because then we don't have to deal with gossip."

Akram also said,

> Sometimes the pay is so low I wonder why these young women bother. Some of these young women have to wear this and that clothes and have to be fashionable, so they work just to pay for their clothes and makeup. But married women come to work because they need the money, you can see it, they just wear the same clothes and they work because they have to. But when you see a young woman wearing a pair of jeans costing $35, you know why she's there. Her father cannot buy it for her, so she comes and works to pay for her taste in fashion.

They said that the number of women working in sweatshops has increased even in the bazaar, because living costs are high. Also, a lot of men are on drugs now, and many women have to work.

I asked about their luxuries. Akram said, "I like reading, going to parks with my daughter and sister and their daughters, but I don't attend any religious gathering and dislike them because they are occasions for *khalezank basic* [women getting together to gossip about one another]. I believe in praying in my own house. Having a party in my own house, mixing and mingling [men and women], brings gossip." Rahimeh replied to Akram, "I am sorry you think that way; this is because you are widowed. I don't feel like that at all, I love mixing and mingling." Both women agreed that being single is a problem when it comes to mixing and mingling with extended family as well as people from the neighborhood.

I asked them about their jobs and their health. There were complaints about long hours of work, but they were realistic about the fact that earning an income is not easy. Akram said that she wants to make sure that her children do not feel deprived as a result of having lost their father, and she spends most of her income; her savings is only through the credit club.

When I asked for whom they had voted, Rahimeh said that she voted for Ahmadinejad because he was like Rajai, another president who was also conservative. "Iran is not Europe, Iran is an Islamic country. Have you seen the way some young men dress? They put lots of gel on their hair and make it stand up. I am ashamed to look at the vanity of some boys." When I asked her what she thinks of economic problems and inflation, she responded, "There is a lot of corruption and this is a major cause." But she added, "I am very happy with Mr. Ahmadinejad because he goes to the root of the problems. He goes to small cities and to rural areas and fights with economic corruption."

On the question of charity and social safety nets, Rahimeh said that she always keeps track of who has enough to eat and who does not. "We always help each other in the neighborhood."

Fatimah was relatively quiet, and I had to encourage her to share her experience. She lived with her father and worked as a hairdresser. She learned to be a hairdresser from her mother, and then she went to get her diploma. I asked her why she had not married, and she responded, "My family did not force me to marry, and I did not care much about being married. I am the oldest child, and now I make all the decision around the house and take care of my parents. I have helped all my brothers and sisters to get married and helped them pay their mortgages by mortgaging our own house, and I have been paying toward their homes. I am happy to look after them and make between $10 and $30 a day." She had no sign for her shop but was well known enough among her customers that she was successful.

The neighborhood where we held the focus group was an old neighborhood known for prostitution and drug abuse (*Shahid Harandy*), and I asked them about that. Fatimah said, "Yes, there are some sex workers, and we know them, but they are so kind and generous and harm no one, so we live with them, and we look at them because that is their job: I am a hairdresser and she is a sex worker. They are such kind people that we are ashamed to mention anything about their doings." Fatimah also mentioned that the drug trade is rampant and "sometimes women are involved in drug trafficking; they hide it in their bra, even in their children's clothes."

"How can religious people live with this?" I asked. Fatimah responded, "Here people don't take religion seriously, religious believers are blind to these things; they pray but don't pay attention to what really is going on." "What about the *Basijj*?"[3] I asked. "We don't have any *Basijji* here, and people have a lot of solidarity. They protect each other. If the authorities raid a house, other neighbors help to clear out drugs before the police gets here, and by the time they come there is nothing to confiscate and no one to be arrested."

Fatimah, like many other women I had interviewed, was involved in charitable activities and worked in the Kahrizak Foundation and for the elderly. She also had a credit club based in her house and was in charge of one.

Focus Group in Moradabad Neighborhood

This focus group took place in Moradabad, on the periphery of West Tehran, a new neighborhood of low-income households. The five women whose interviews will be presented were Mehry M., a 28-year-old unmarried woman; her sister Maryam, 32 and married (the two worked in packaging, daily help, and embroidery); Mehry K., 40, with two daughters and a son, working in food processing and daily help; Sarah, 36, married with two children, working as a hairdresser; and Soraya, 32, with two sons, working as cleaning lady but also preparing herbs. Mehry M. worked in a sweatshop in a packaging assembly line and also worked on embroidery (but since she had bad eyesight she had troubles and was doing less needle work). Maryam worked on embroidery for bridal dresses. Mehry M. lived with her sister Maryam and helped her.

Mehry M. and Maryam lived with their mother, who did not charge them any rent, although they in turn contributed to the expenditures of their mother (an income-pulling extended family household). They both complained about low income and long hours from 9:00 in the morning until sometimes 10:00 at night (in the case of needle work), and each received $150 USD a month. They supplemented their income with seasonal work, such as during the New Year holidays (the New Year in Iran always coincides with the spring equinox), when they also worked in food processing and cleaning herbs. Cleaning and frying herbs can bring about $8 for a ten-hour day, although the rate varied from customer to customer, since they relied on individuals who knew of their work to hire them. They complained about not having job stability, insurance, or benefits (a New Year bonus, for example, is common in Iran). They both did house chores after 8:00 at night. Maryam made sure the house was clean and dinner was ready at 9:30 when her husband came back from work. Although most of the time their mother took care of the household, recently she had become sick and the sisters had to take over, sometimes even taking care of their mother.

Soraya's income was less; she only earned about $2–$3 a day. "Some people have machines which help them clean and cut herbs fast; I don't, and I have to work hard." Her income was low because she worked as a cleaner inside the neighborhood. In a low-income neighborhood, people tend not to hire daily help. Nonetheless, she earns close to $150 a month, just enough to make ends meet. Her husband also works in the informal sector and is in the construction industry making window glass. "The work is not steady, sometimes he has jobs, sometimes he doesn't," she said.

All three women reported that they exchange services with friends and family members. Mehry K. makes dresses for a friend, and her friend prepares herbs in return. Another friend makes her doctor's appointments and pays for her glasses, not expecting to be repaid immediately, as she knows the situation of the family. Mehry K. continues to provide herbs for her and sometimes lends a hand with cleaning the house, even though her friend tells her she does not have to and it all can wait. "Once I worked very hard for her, cleaning until 10:00 at night, and her husband wanted to pay me but I refused. She was there for me when I needed the money and I worked for her when she needed help." Clearly these women did multiple types of jobs according to the demands.

Maryam, who was mostly quiet (we found out later she was suffering from diabetes and was very sick), entered into the discussion and talked about emergency loans: "I have received emergency loans for my illness. I have lost sight in one of my eyes and my kidneys work only 30 percent. I lose a lot of protein during the day and my friends always are helping me. I repay my loans but it takes a long time. I have close to $500 in debts. No one asks to be repaid, but I feel awkward about it. My mother helps out." Getting loans from banks is difficult, and one needs a guarantor who is a public servant (this is to ensure that, in the case of default, the loan can be deducted from his or her salary). She added that she lost her marriage loan (a loan given by the government) because she did not have a guarantor or collateral. She explained, "My daughter was sick and we tried very hard to get a loan, but we couldn't because my husband is self-employed. You have to know somebody who knows somebody or have someone who is rich. There is a lot of corruption in loan giving."

Mehry M., who was very concerned about her sister's health and an eye operation that she needed badly, said, "I kept going to the bank insisting, crying in the hallway, begging for a loan. Finally, one of employees came to me and gave me the address of a doctor who would give a discount to people who were low-income, and he is an excellent eye surgeon. We ended up going to see him, and he gave us a half-price deal. That is how we could afford Maryam's operation. But we still had to borrow money." I learned that a distant relative who wished that her name not be revealed had donated the money for the operation. It was part of a *nazr* [charitable gift].

Sarah spoke last (I tried to generate a discussion and speak and interfere as little as possible, and Sarah felt comfortable to talk only after she heard other peoples' stories). She was a hairdresser who worked at home; she had bought her equipment with her and her husband's own savings. Her husband worked at the *Sharvand* journal and had a steady income, but they did not own a house and had to spend a huge part of their income on rent. "We have been struggling to buy a house, had term deposit to get credit for mortgage, but it is hard and we still need a guarantor [despite the fact that *Sharvand* journal is owned by the city]. The bank wanted us to bring a guarantor and to give them an authorized check."

I asked her if she had used loans for the self-employed, since the government had a policy to give loans to the self-employed as a way to increase employment opportunities. "Even for these loans you need to know people of influence. Also I had to have a diploma from a certified hairdresser, lots of bureaucracy. It isn't worth it, and I didn't bother."

She then continued complaining about rental laws and why it was important for them to own their house: "We have rented a small apartment, but every year they can ask us to leave or raise the rent. For the past few years, we have had to rent a new place every one or two years because the landlord wanted to raise the rent and we could not afford it. It is impossible to be a tenant. Mortgage rates and loans are high, as high as 15 to 20 percent, and still, if you do not have a guarantor, you will not get it." The women reported that landlords write one-year contracts to be free to increase the rent, or if they are in conflict with the tenants, they can force them to leave. "Every move costs at least $200, and the real estate agents charge," Mehry M. said. Sarah replied to Maryam, "I left my previous house because the landlord was rude and I could not stand him. I have lost a son and have no patience with aggressive people."

The subject could have continued for longer, but I interrupted and asked them if bringing home an income gave them power in their households.

- Sarah said, "My husband does not do housework, and I work outside and inside. Mind you, he comes home very late and works until late at night."
- Mehry K. said, "Sometimes my husband gives me no housekeeping money, and then I am grateful that I have an income and don't have to rely on him. He says he has made no money. I do all the housework except when we have guests, as in front of guests he does a lot of housework and everyone thinks I am lazy and idle. He likes it if people think he is *zan zalil* [a man who is humiliated and ruled by his wife, and has no authority or will to stand up for himself]; they think I rule the house."
- Soraya said her husband helps especially when there is too much work. People say he is *zan zalil*, too: "But I wish he would appreci-

ate all the work I do. I dream that one day he would come home and say, 'you worked so hard.' He always is telling others how hard I work, and sometimes he is close to having tears in his eyes, but he never says anything to me. I don't understand my husband: How can he be so thankful about my work when I am not around to hear, and I have to hear it from other people. It is so much easier if he could say it to me."

- Mehry K. said that her husband went bankrupt, and she had helped him to rebuild his assets. She also received an inheritance from her relative in Ghazvin, from which she had managed to buy half a property, which she then put under her daughter's name. "I don't want my daughter to go through what I did, this half property is my daughter's. And you wouldn't believe what my in-laws said! They said, 'You [the husband] have become the wife and she is the husband and head of the household. You are gonna need permission from your wife now, she rules. You don't have a house, and your wife gave half a property to her daughter, what is this blab blab blab? But I do what I want with my money."
- Maryam said, "My mother-in-law says I am more competent than my husband. She said because you are competent you rule the house. She means, 'It is always your word and you take the final decision.' I must agree with her. We have been living here for six years. Ask people around if they know Mr.———. Will they say anything? But ask around if they know Mrs.———, and they will say, 'Yes, we know her.' He does a lot of housework; he even washes my clothes."
- Soraya added to the conversation, "My husband gives me all his earnings, and sometimes it is not enough, so I make up the rest and manage the household, shop around, you know. Sometimes we have money to have fruits, other times we don't. I sit together with my husband and we plan our money. He sometimes travels far to buy cheap food when he has time, or we make do with what we have."

We ended the formal interview and had tea and the mood was upbeat. The host was most generous and, even though we had paid for the place, she had provided us with lavish snacks. The focus group took about two hours, but once the tape recorder was switched off, everyone became a lot more relaxed and a fascinating story unfolded.

Mehry K., who was in charge of the house, spoke about her life. She did not start her life being in power. When she married her husband, she had no power, and not being able to bear any children, her husband married a second wife, which made her life miserable, as if he were forcing her to get a divorce.

> He used to beat me up, insult me, and took me to court. But I refused to give in, and I said to the judge, "I am not leaving my husband, I love him, and this is my house." Since he could not force me to divorce him, he turned my life into hell. My brother helped me to get an operation to deal with infertility. I then took more fertility treatment and my mother sold her most expensive jewelry to pay for all the medical costs. Then I went on pilgrimage to Mashhad, and it was there where I found out that I was pregnant. I came back only to find out that my cowife had left my husband. She had promised herself to leave my husband if I became pregnant, as she did not want to stand in the way of a marriage for which I was fighting such a hard battle. She left wishing me luck and happiness and later divorced and married a man who was catering at the Imam Reza Shrine. She said that this was a promise to Imam Reza; she wanted me to become pregnant and was miserable knowing that I was suffering and never wanted to be the cause of it . . . I then became a mother of two children and continued my education. Today my son shows my secondary diploma and says, "My father is illiterate and my mother has secondary diploma." He is proud of me. I have written my life story and gave it as a gift to a friend. My husband was very disappointed, but my son is behind me and supports me. It was such a shame that my father married me to this man in the first place. I had lots of talents and had much better suitors. But because my husband's name was the same as my grandfather's, they married me to him. What a mistake it was then. But now I have turned my life around and rule the house and will not allow my daughter to go through what I went through.

Sarah also shared a love story:

> I fell in love with my husband. I had rich suitors, men who owned half the bazaar, but I was in love with my husband. We met at one of the religious gatherings for Imam Hussein. I saw him among the mourners of Imam Hussein and he saw me; we promised to marry each other. My husband calls me a gift from Imam Hussein. We have endured great hardship together, but I am still in love with him. We have to move every year because we do not own a house. There is never enough money, but love is not short.

Do Women Choose the Work They Do?

The question of choice and paid employment is complex and multifaceted. Together with Jennifer Olmsted, we have problematized the issue in another paper, which is forthcoming. Here, to end this chapter, I wish to present another cross-tabulation between reasons for occupational choice and line of activity—one that perhaps may bring insight about earning and income. The result showed that working for others (in low-paid, formal jobs) seemed to have the highest personal interest. Although it is difficult to conclude that women really enjoy low-paid jobs, it might be that they want stability of income.

Those working as hairdressers indicated that the reason for choosing their job was their skills. Those who whose occupation was arts and crafts also reported (though less than hairdressers) that they choose their jobs because of their skills. Generally these low-paid jobs do not require a great deal of skills.

Vendors, saleswomen, food processors, massage therapists, and home caregivers reported that they are engaged in these jobs because of easy access, which confirms some of what we discussed earlier as typical reasons for a growing number of women in the informal sector.

Interestingly, many reported that social networking played a major role as an incentive for their work. This confirms earlier discussion about the importance of social networks. Clearly, many women see access to social networks as a great asset for them. This is indeed interesting and shows that women tend to strengthen their social networks through paid work and as micro-entrepreneurs. This behavior resonates well with our earlier discussion of social networks and community ties and, as we see here, how women empower themselves through their community network. Basically, to end this chapter, social networks and community ties as well as extended family networks and their relation to microenterprise and income-generating activities seem to come together in ways that enhance women's role in society. This is worth highlighting, as economic sanctions, which were imposed after this research was carried out, have come to affect Iranians of low-income households in general and women in particular. We will return to this topic in the conclusion.

Chapter 5

Low-Income Male Workers and Micro-Entrepreneurs

Comparing the Male and Female Samples

In the last chapter I discussed the results from my fieldwork on women. In this chapter, my focus will be a comparison between men and women in an attempt to develop a gender analysis of the informal sector. In order to examine the role of men in this sector, I adopt the same methodology used to study women. I worked with the same research assistants, but in some cases it was imperative to have a male interviewer, as was the case with construction workers who cannot be interviewed during the day but have to be interviewed at night at the work site—a no-female zone. Moreover, on the question of domestic violence, as we shall see later, men refused to give an answer to female interviewers or often avoided the question; therefore it was important to have a male interviewer.

For comparative purposes, I replicated the sample size and scope used for women. However, it was not possible to have in-depth interviews with low-income men. This is perhaps not as problematic as it may sound, because much of the research done previously emphasized men's role in the informal economy and overlooked the role of women.

The Sample

The same method was used to find men in the informal sector, and personal contacts were a point of entry depending on the type of profession. For example, the husband of my friend's cleaning lady was informally employed as a private night guard; janitors of apartment buildings were easy to approach as well. Interviewing informal taxi drivers was not very difficult either, as a simple ride through the city, after having asked the driver not to take other passengers by offering a higher fare (equivalent of four other passengers), allowed interviews to be conducted. In these cases one has to open the lines of communication, and it was quite common that the interviewees answered many questions. I always mentioned that I would be using the information for my research and asked for their consent. These interviews sometimes followed a different pattern than questionnaires, because I was reluctant to interrupt their answers and often an interesting outcome would surface. The most difficult workers for me were construction workers, many of whom are Afghans. As shown in Table 5.1, the range of informal jobs included underground workers (sweatshop workers), construction workers, vendors, men in transport (informal taxis, motorcycle delivery men, pizza- or other food-delivery service), cleaners, janitors, and others, such as private guards, handymen, and also men who are in the grey economy (for instance, men who work informally installing satellite dishes, which are by law illegal).

In terms of the men's age and in comparison with women, both sexes in our sample were overrepresented in the age range of 31 to 40 years, with 38.9 percent of the male sample being in this age group. Another 28.9 percent of the sample men were between the ages of 41 and 50 (very close to the data on women), while 4.4 percent were between the ages of 51 and 60, and only 2.2 percent were either

Table 5.1 Occupation

Line of activity	Frequency	Percentage
Underground worker	14	15.6
Construction worker	14	15.6
Vendor	12	13.3
Transport (motorcycle)	3	3.3
Driver, informal taxi	16	17.8
Cleaner	10	11.1
Janitor	11	12.2
Others	10	11.1
Total	90	100.0

below 20 years of age or over 60. This was in contrast with our women sample, as 9.9 percent were under 20 or over 60. Those between the ages of 21 and 30 made up 23.3 percent of the male sample but 26.6 percent of our female sample. The majority of men in our cases—76.7 percent—were married, 19.76 percent were single, and the remaining 4.5 percent were divorced or widowed.

As far as education was concerned, 6.7 percent were illiterate, 21.1 percent had primary education, 20 percent had middle school (*rahnamai*), and 44.4 percent had secondary education. These figures correspond with what was found among the female sample. Among the men, 7.8 percent had some college education. This is interesting because it demonstrates that even men with tertiary education can be employed in low-paid, informal-sector jobs. Such jobs also may explain why men may not wish to continue their university education and why the college dropout rate has been reported to be high among men. When these men were asked why they did not continue with their education, 36.7 percent responded that it was due to lack of opportunity. Ironically and contrary to what one expects, only 20 percent reported to have dropped out because of economic necessity, although when one adds those who stated their lack of access to education due to family poverty (23.3 percent), it would seem that family economic circumstances play an important role. Another 5.6 percent of men stated that, because of family pressure, they had stopped their education (this could be explained by the persistence of more traditional views on sons as potential income earners and contributors to household income). Similarly, 14.4 percent did not continue their education due to military service. This

Table 5.2 Distribution of educational attainments in male and female samples and subsamples (percentages of total of each sample)

	Total sample		Wage viewed as adequate subsample	
	Men	*Women*	*Men*	*Women*
Illiterate	6.7	7.7	7.1	9.1
Primary	21.1	12.1	28.6	9.1
Middle school	20.0	18.7	0.0	27.3
Secondary	44.4	49.5	50.0	48.5
Tertiary	7.8	12.1	14.3	6.1
Total	100.0	100.0	100.0	100.0

parallel shows that, like women, some men also face challenges in continuing their education.

A cross-tabulation between educational attainment and perception of wages as adequate had an interesting result. Among the illiterate, males and females who were employed informally had close percentages (6.7 and 7.7, respectively); the samples regarded wages as being primarily inadequate among those who were illiterate; this applied to men as well women (7.1 percent among men compared with 9.1 percent among women). The percentage of those with primary education among the male sample was higher (21.1 percent compared with 12.1 percent among women). However, men with primary education tended to be more satisfied with their income than was the case with women (28.6 percent of men compared with 9.1 percent of women). The balance shifted when those with middle school education were compared, as no men viewed their income as adequate, while 27.3 percent of women with middle school were satisfied with their wages. However, when secondary school education was considered, both men and women were fairly satisfied with their wages (50 percent of men compared with 48.5 percent of women). This satisfaction possibly could be due to the nature of the work that men and women with secondary school diplomas obtain—work that puts them into a distinctly higher-earning bracket. This can be explored further by looking at a cross-tabulation between wages. In Table 5.3, close to a third of women earn less than $5 USD a day, and half of them earn $6–$10 a day, while no men earn less than $5 a day, and close to one-third earn $6–$10. However, 38.9 percent of men earn $11–$15 a day and one-third earns $16–$20 per day; the corresponding figures for women are 15.4 percent and 4 percent. The result of the sample seems to confirm that women generally earn much less than men. What is noteworthy here is that only half those men who earned $16–$20 per day viewed their wages as adequate. In the case of the female sample, 33.3 percent of those earning less than $5 per day and 39.4 percent of those earning $6–$10 per day reported their earnings as adequate. Generally, it seems that women report their earnings as adequate despite the fact that their earnings are much lower than those in the male sample. This confirms general findings on women in the development literature, where it is found that women's earnings are less than are those of men, and generally women tend more than men to receive lower wages and work in low-paid jobs, particularly in the informal sector (as discussed in Chapter 3). Women viewing their earnings as

Table 5.3 Distribution of daily incomes in male and female samples and subsamples (percentages of total of each sample)

	Total sample		Wage viewed as adequate subsample	
Income range in US dollars	*Men*	*Women*	*Men*	*Women*
$0–$5	0.0	29.7	0.0	33.3
$6–$10	30.0	50.5	28.6	39.4
$11–$15	38.9	15.4	21.4	21.2
$16–$20	31.1	4.4	50.0	6.1
Total	100.0	100.0	100.0	100.0

adequate may be due to the persistence of the male-breadwinner/female-homemaker model.

The Male-Breadwinner Model

In several different research projects that I have carried out on female employment, many women have been either de facto breadwinners for their family or essential contributors to the household. Nonetheless, the ideal model of the male breadwinner continues to persist. This is particularly true of men who take pride in their perceived role as an ideal masculine symbol. Men earn more and, at least among those interviewed, view themselves as responsible for providing for their families. This comes with a price typical of the male-breadwinner model: men are in the position of taking charge over household decisions and, in some cases, of restricting women's roles.

Some occupations allowed for in-depth interviews, and these included vendors. For these interviews I worked with a research assistant who had great skills in fieldwork and communication with interviewees. Moreover, I did not have official permission for research, and my research assistant could easily pretend she was gathering data for her thesis. Although this may violate research codes of conduct, there was no possibility of obtaining permission from authorities, and attracting attention in the street in the case of vendors could be dangerous for a foreign-based academic. My assistant played the role of student and I played the role of an aunt who accompanied her niece to provide protection from potential male harassment while she wandered around the streets working on her thesis.

The first vendor was a shy and timid young man from Mashhad. I asked him why he was not married. His response was, "How can I afford to marry on such low salary? A man must be able to provide a good life for his wife." He sold sunglasses in the summer and socks and gloves in the winter. Another vendor, Amir, sold many different types of goods and was a man who looked much older than his age. I thought he was in his early sixties, but he showed me his ID and said, "I am young but have gone through a hard life; you think I am an old man." While my research assistant was filling the questionnaire, a couple of men gathered around us, but I dared not to ask why they were hanging out. I asked Amir if he was always a vendor. He replied,

> No, Ms. I am a carpenter, I lived in Ardebil and because our school had no running water and electricity I protested against the shah. I was only 14 and they put me in jail. My uncle was able to get me released, and after that I joined the revolution and went to the front line during the war [with Iraq] and worked as a carpenter. I joined the Jihad for Reconstruction and helped build homes for those whose home had been destroyed because of the bombings [by Iraq in the 1980–88 war]. We built homes for the families of those whose husbands/sons/fathers had been lost in war and were homeless.

"So you are a *janbaz* [war veteran]?" I asked him. "What are you talking about Ms? I hate them [the government]. They gave me nothing. They only want to fill their own pockets, and I got no free house, no nothing. Do see my nose, yes it is broken, because I fought with the city officials who do not allow me to sell my stuff; thieves, thieves, bullies they are, but I fight back."

When he was asked a question about whether he would accept wife working outside the home, his response was passionate. "I work and as long as I live I will work, I am not going to be a deadbeat husband, and I am a man and have to provide for my family." He then looked around the street and said, "Look at them, look how they dress, full of makeup and flirting with men everywhere. There is no decency around. I am not going to allow my daughter even to go to university. Anyway, my wife has young children and she needs her time with her family. She doesn't have time to work." When I asked him about how he spends his income, his response was that he gives it all to his wife.

A conversation with a male colleague who had gone to visit one of his friends, an ex-communist who had complained about all the rights women have earned under the Islamic government, came to mind. When my colleague recounted the story, we were shocked to hear an educated, ex-leftwing secular man openly criticizing recent legal changes: "The Islamic Republic has given too much power to these women." He was a lawyer and a factory owner. He documented legal changes in favor of women and had presented it to my colleague. It is clear that this middle-class, secular man would never disclose his views on the matter to a Western-educated woman like me, but he was comfortable enough to share them with an old male friend despite his also being a Western-educated, foreign-based academic. We shall return to this viewpoint later on in this chapter, but the reason I was reminded of the conversation here was that Amir the carpenter did not want his daughter to go to university or his wife to work because of what he saw as women's inappropriate attire and behavior in public, despite the compulsory dress code, and he commented that women were wearing too much makeup (which incidentally made me conscious of my own appearance, even though I try hard to blend in and appear in an modest outfit common for women to wear in places like my research location).

Among the major objections that the educated, middle-class, secular factory owner had presented my colleague was, "Look, a man must provide for his wife but if a woman earns any money this belongs to her and the husband is not allowed to ask her to spend it on household money." This theme came up in the interviews with women in Chapter 4, and we can see that although some women may benefit from keeping all their earnings, others are not necessarily able to gain at all and end up paying for the household expenses, contrary to what the secular factory owner believed.

I asked the vendor, Amir, what would happen if his wife wanted to work. He replied, "How can I allow her to work, have you seen the way women come to the streets [meaning their *hejab*]?" Since both of us had on a little makeup and fairly colorful clothes, he just shook his head knowing that we were not going to sympathize with him and would likely scorn his remark.

Another interview was with an Afghan shoe repairman. He had had only eight years of schooling and had to flee to Iran as a Shi'a, after the Sunni Pashtuns began persecuting the Shi'a Hazara Afghans. He had started working in Iran as an agricultural laborer but had suffered a back injury, which required an operation. He also rolled up his trousers and showed me his limp leg due to another job-related injury. Such injuries are typical of hard male labor in low-income jobs, and we shall return to this topic when we examine informal work hazards. He said, "Now I work as shoe repairman." I asked him what he does with his sewing machine and other equipment when the city officials start rampaging against vendors. "It is simple, we all run to the next street and hide until they are gone." Unlike women in the Metro, which is a closed space, male vendors or street vendors in general have a much easier time running away, which prevents them from having their inventory confiscated. As mentioned before, there are no male vendors in the Metro, only female vendors, and this might be because the Metro is free from street harassment and women feel more comfortable (although during the rush hour, the Metro becomes an impossible space for even ordinary travelers, which is typical of megacities, because of the presence of vendors).

Every interview with vendors attracted a number of observers who viewed our work with curiosity and were entertained. A middle-aged women stood and listened to the entire interview with the street shoemaker, and when she learned about his daily income, she was very disappointed and told us, "My daughter has a graduate degree in English and she works from 8:30 until 5:00 and earns only $400." This was after she heard that the shoemaker earns between $10 and $16 a day. It is true that office work for educated females in the private sector is extremely low paid, and even though it is in the formal sector, it remains on a contract basis and without worker's protection. This is an important issue—which has been touched on in my previous book, *Veiled Employment*—in the discussion about the dilemma of high unemployment among young educated females. It is also discussed in a forthcoming World Bank–funded paper on female entrepreneurs, a project coauthored with Jennifer Olmsted and Hadi Salehi-Esfahani (forthcoming).

The middle-aged passerby told us that the Afghan man is much respected in the neighborhood because he is a competent shoe repairman and, as result, has a lot of customers and has been working in that street corner for many years.

A young male was working part-time as a vendor (he worked in some other jobs but we could not really press much for an answer as we were interrupting his business. Sometimes it would take five to ten minutes to ask just one question because the vendor was selling, and we had to wait for his free time. This was a major problem, because some vendors used their free time to advertise their merchandize verbally). This young man worked only in the evenings, when shoppers come out for a walk around a minimall and a number of shops in the area. He worked from 8:00 in the morning until 5:00 in the evening at his first job and then from 5:00 to 10:00 at night. While he was happy for his wife to be a university student, he himself had had to leave university to support his wife, mother, and sister. This was true of some other vendors, who also supported their extended family members, such as elderly parents, a sister, or a younger brother. Family ties remain strong, and the extended family network relies on the income of those who are capable of working. I asked the young man what would happen after his wife had finished her studies: Would he ask her to work or would she herself want to work outside? He said, "Why would she want to do that? I will provide for her and she can be comfortable." It would have been almost impossible to put that to a test and ask his wife if she would prefer to stay home or work for pay. In my personal experience, some woman are happy to stay home rather than work at low-paid jobs, as we came to see in the results of the interviews among women. However, some women have little choice, because their husbands do not give them enough housekeeping money.

A young man who had left university pointed out that he had to provide for his wife, brothers, and sisters. "Going to university has no future," he argued. Then he added that because there are many university graduates with no jobs, it is better to go straight to work and earn an income. He was against his wife working outside the home, saying that when he works from 8:00 in the morning until 11:00 at night, he wants "to come home to some peace and rest and does not want to have to share housework and pick up after a working wife."

An informal driver with whom we spoke said, "Women have a lot of education and do any work for much less money, and they have driven office jobs' pay low." The abundance of university graduates who are young females and who are ready to take low-paid formal jobs has affected the male labor market, and some are angry about it. Instead of blaming the employer, they blame women, and some blame the government for giving so much "freedom to women." We have discussed this point before, and we will read more remarks about this frustration at the end of this chapter. This is reminiscent of rising violence against women in Maquiladoras, Mexico, where women have access to low-paid jobs and men do not, causing men to place the blame on women for the lack of employment opportunities (Pantaleo 2006).

One of the questions we asked men concerned helping their wives with housework chores. Most men responded that they work such long hours that they do not have time to help their wives. This response seems to be based on the assumption that working women have shorter work-for-pay hours. However, when we compared the number of hours between the two samples, 47.8 percent in the male sample worked between seven and nine hours a day compared with

46.2 percent of the women. The difference was marginal, but among those who worked more than ten hours a day, there was a significant difference, as 41.1 percent of the men worked long hours compared with only 26.4 percent of the women. Both samples were from low-paid jobs, but there is a problem with this kind of comparison when it comes to the number of hours of work, since some of those women were heads of households, and they had no choice other than to work long hours. Since we had no access to the wives of those men, we could not know if they worked (most seemed not to), and if they did, what the average number of hours would be. There was no way to tell whether women work fewer or the same number of hours as men, although generally it is conceivable that women tend to work less hours than men due to the prevalence of the male-breadwinner model. In effect, since the stereotypes about male-female relationships in marriage is that men are providers and women are homemakers, the entire social structure is geared toward a lesser number of necessary hours for women outside the home than for men. This, however, does not mean women work less; it simply means that women have shorter hours working for pay, and their unpaid and reproductive work remain the same.

Despite prevailing attitudes about gender roles, a relatively high number of men—54.8 percent—responded that they help their wives with the housework. When we had asked in the female sample whether their husbands helped with housework, the figures were not widely different, as 45.1 percent reported that their husbands did help. However, it remains to be seen how often and to what extent men helped their working wives. Most of the men interviewed worked either seven to nine hours or more than ten hours a day, and if one adds travel time to working hours, there is not much time for them to do anything else.

Table 5.4 Distribution of hours of work in male and female samples (percentages of total of each sample)

Hours of work	Men	Women
1–3	1.1	2.2
4–6	10.0	25.3
7–9	47.8	46.2
10+	41.1	26.4
Total	100.0	100.0

A middle-aged informal driver who drives without a license (there are some men and I have seen one woman) told me that, due to rising gas prices in accordance with reductions in fuel subsidies, he now is working at three jobs to support his family. With a secondary school diploma and a diploma as a chef, he works from dawn to dusk at three jobs: as a caterer, a building inspector, and part time as a *mosafer kesh* [informal driver]. He is happy to work three jobs, but he does not want his wife to work: "My wife is 47 years old [a year older than the driver] and she needs to rest. She is a good wife; she always is economizing and never wants me to spend a lot of money."

In contrast, another taxi driver indicated that he was very happy for his wife to work: "My wife enjoyed her job as a teacher, but she lost her job because someone reported that she was shaking hands in public with a strange man. He was her step-brother, but she was never able to counter the tarnishing of her reputation [*sic*] and lost her job." He was content with his wife working, but she chose not to look for another job and stayed at home. He said, "It is difficult for women to work. Here we have a female taxi driver, and when something goes wrong, she has to go to a mechanic who charges her more than us because we can fix part of the problem ourselves or do it all ourselves and not bother with a mechanic at all. It is much tougher for women taxi drivers and their profit is less because they have to use mechanics for every little thing."[1]

Several of our interviewees expressed concerns about their wives working outside the home because of the possibility of them having an affair with other men. Living in Tehran, one does know that some married men and women engage in affairs. This is not to legitimize male objection to women's right to paid work, because there are obviously some married women who do not work and have affairs. Generally, however, the idea of working outside and having an affair seems to be a way men express their objection to women's access to paid employment.

Access to Employment, Job Satisfaction, and Work Hazards

In Chapter 4, a great deal of emphasis was placed on access to employment and reasons for choosing particular jobs. Clearly, this is a more important factor for women than it is for men, since men are supposed to be the breadwinners and they are expected to take it on themselves to find work, whatever the job. Therefore, in this section, little emphasis is placed on what factors were at work when discussing access to employment. Close to half of the men did not possess any skills for their jobs (46.75) compared with a third of women (33 percent). But an interesting distinction between men and women was that, in order for many women to find employment, they had to have some kind of diploma or license (37.4 percent), whereas qualifications were less important for men (17.8 percent). This confirms that women have to have more skills and more education, not only for high-paid jobs, but also for low-paid employment in the informal sector.

Generally, however, men worldwide tend to be engaged in high-risk informal employment. Among our sample, a CD vendor who earned more than $20 a day said, "I earn good money but it is dangerous." I asked him if it is more dangerous that other types of vending, and he responded that some of the CDs and films he sells are not legal, but that is why he makes money. He was highly reluctant to share information, but as we were two women with fairly loose *hejab*, he eventually trusted us and agreed to an interview. Some from our sample were from the construction sector with its obvious occupational hazards, but it was difficult to interview them fully.

Some men complained about having to spend part of their earnings on treatment for physical pain caused by their work and their high medical costs. This was not a source of complaint about earnings when women were interviewed, but men can typically work in jobs that are more physically demanding than is the case with women.

Construction work is a dangerous profession, but as explained earlier, it was difficult for me to interview construction workers and to get firsthand knowledge of their problems. The occupation has many Afghan workers, who mainly have no work permits and who are not citizens. It may be that the situation of Afghan workers will deteriorate further because of government cutbacks on subsidies and also because of agreements between Iran and Afghanistan that effectively mean Afghan migrant workers will not be granted Iranian citizenship. With an increase in the price of food, water, and fuel such as gas and electricity, Afghan male workers will suffer from a reduction in their real income. Additionally, it is not clear what will happen to the industry with the new household bonus program comes into force, as it does not include the foreign nationals, mostly Afghan migrant workers, who have a heavy presence in construction.

Since we had asked our female sample about their job satisfaction, we asked our male sample the same questions. Notably, more men reported no job satisfaction than was the case with women: 17.8 percent of men compared with 7.7 percent of women. These figures were similar for those who reported that their work does not provide much satisfaction: again 17.8 percent of men and 6.6 percent of women. Men seemed to be more dissatisfied with their jobs, as 22.2 percent of men and 11 percent of women had a little satisfaction from their work. Close to half of women reported average satisfaction from their job, 47.3 percent, compared with only 33.3 percent of men. The percentage of women with relatively high and very high satisfaction was much greater than that of men: 26 percent among women compared with only 8.9 among men. Clearly, between the two samples women expressed more job satisfaction than men. This is an important factor, as it may explain some male behavior. For example, men tend to work longer hours, in more physically dangerous occupations, and have less job satisfaction, and this may lead to an overall low quality of life, which might make them prone to drug abuse and domestic violence, both of which should be viewed as social problems.

Economic Hardship, Masculinity in Crisis, and Domestic Violence

For many men, especially among the low-income households, the lack of ability to make a decent living and the fact that many of them are unable to provide for their families means the ideal of the male breadwinner is in crisis. As one of my informants said, "There used to be a time when one person worked, the entire family was fed. Now everyone works so that one can be fed." Life has changed; economic problems, high inflation, the rise of consumer society, and more recently biting sanctions have made it imperative for many men to work long hours without being able to cover the cost of their families. This has brought with it insecurities about men, which sometimes can translate into domestic violence.

Since many of the interviewees who were female raised the issue of violence, an extra question about domestic violence was included in the male questionnaires. In fact, there was a carefully worded question on the questionnaire: "Do you think physical punishment is necessary to secure marriage?" We posed the question to 13 interviewee street vendors as a test. Among the 13, only one admitted to having abused his wife. (Our assumption is that men do not necessarily admit this, since it is socially unacceptable for men to say publically that they abuse their wives. This may be true of North America as well, except for men who appear on the *Dr. Phil* show to say how sorry they are.)

The only man admitting to having beaten his wife was the Afghan shoe repairman. He was the only Afghan I interviewed directly, and he told me that at one time he had this bad habit but now he no longer beats his wife. There is a vast literature on the issue of domestic violence throughout the world, and during our fieldwork there were complaints about men by some of the women we interviewed (especially in focus groups). Any intervention on the part of national or international organizations needs to take into account a gender perspective, looking at men's as well as women's views, and how their lives are transformed and affected by particular social and economic changes.

On the questionnaire response, very few respondents admitted to beating up their wives, but if any did, a highly sophisticated male interviewer assisted with the responses. However, even in those cases, men never used the words *wife beating*; instead they used *kotakkary* [physical fight between two people]. It is entirely possible that some women fight back physically, but even in such cases, men have an obvious physical advantage. The law has no punishment for battery of one's wife, and men can easily engage in domestic violence without any legal or, in some cases, social retribution. It is for this reason perhaps that recently there have been more instances of women killing their husbands. A film based on a real case of domestic violence became a box-office success. In *Gharmez* [Red], popular actress Hedieh Tehrani portrays a woman who is beaten up and psychologically tortured by her husband, and her sister-in-law is complicit in the beatings and torture. The abused wife is not able to obtain a divorce, and the story ends with Tehrani preparing herself to murder her husband—an act she manages to carry out.

In a telling instance on the taboo of discussing domestic violence, during an interview conducted by my female research assistant, pretending that she was my niece gathering data for her thesis, we asked a fairly young man working at a newsstand about wife beating. When the respondent paused, I interrupted and said, "Sometimes it is necessary to give a lesson. Look at my niece: when she was younger I had to beat her up; she was naughty and I had to teach her to behave." I was at the door of the newsstand and behind me there was a man sitting down by the door, and he said, "Don't listen to these two women. She is not her aunt but is her professor, and they want to know if you are a wife beater; they are two feminists." I was frozen, and my research assistant, who always has something intelligent to say on such occasions, also became speechless for a moment, but then she quickly moved to the next question.

On the issue of drug abuse, we asked, "If you are attending an all-male gathering and there are some drugs that everyone is using, will you accept an offer or reject it?" No one admitted to drug abuse either, and perhaps one should not be surprised, because, unlike wife beating, which is socially unacceptable even if not legally subject to punishment, drug abuse is viewed as a crime. Unfortunately, no documentation could take place on the subject. In any event, as noted before, the black economy is an independent field of inquiry and needs a separate book itself.

The first ten interviews proved that the questions on domestic violence and drug abuse will not bring useful answers, and it seemed futile to ask them. Most of our respondents told us that woman rule the house and women manage their relationships, not men.

There is a body of literature on the issue of men and the masculinity crisis, emphasizing the importance of understanding and concentrating on men from a development policy perspective. Sylvia Chant and Mathew Gutmann emphasize the importance of paying attention to men and masculinities, not just in gender and development literature, but in the media as well. They point out in the introduction to their paper that there was a great deal of attention on gender and development, and much of the focus was entirely, if not exclusively, on women (Chant and Gutmann 2001). It is true that women are still in more vulnerable circumstances in comparison with men, but increasingly, men—especially young men and low-income men—are in a similar situation and suffer similar vulnerability. This is, incidentally, not limited to the developing world, as throughout the world women are outperforming men in different domains such as education and work.[2] This has created a crisis for traditional perspectives on masculinity (Hearn 1998, 1998b; Jackson 2001; Chant and McIlwaine 2008; Escobar Latapi 1998; Güendel and González 1998). Men's economic circumstances have deteriorated with the mass entry of female labor into the general labor force and the tendency of women, especially those with a higher education, to work harder and for less income. This has been reflected in many of the interviews we conducted. This affects male identity and their masculinity as fathers, brothers, and husbands. It has a direct impact on marital relations, and it can work for or against both men and women. The topic is a global crisis, and it has been taken up seriously by many academics (Moore 1994; Williams 1998). What is interesting is that the debate within the development literature is raised among female scholars.

Moreover, it can be argued that the concern over the vulnerable male is not entirely new, stemming from the early days of the second-wave feminist movement and the work of Bell Hooks, who writes critically of the notion of equality within a context of deprivation of African American men. For her, to fight for gender equality among poor African American men is irrelevant and meaningless.

In the context of the developing world, Sylvia Chant emphasizes in her book the significance of the erosion of the role of men as providers and its link to rises in domestic violence and crime, and in the case of Iran, one may add drug abuse. The increase in access to employment and education for women is a trend that coincides with a rise in violence and crime among men (Sweetman 1997). At a February 2013 conference organized by the United States Institute for Peace on the topic of rape, women's rights activists, policy makers, and international organizations placed emphasis not just on women as victims but also on men in conflict zones and how the problem is a social one.[3]

EXPENDITURE POWER AND OWNERSHIP

One of the interesting points that had been raised is that some women have reported that their spouse does not reveal his real income. In the literature, it has been argued that women tend to spend their income on their family, while men have a tendency to spend their income more on themselves. The question is also important in view of the erosion of the male-breadwinner/female-homemaker model, despite the fact that the men interviewed reported that they still feel responsible for providing for their families (Blumberg 1998; Bahramitash 2005). This, however, should be complemented with data on male versus female expenditure.

Table 5.5 shows that 48.9 percent of men spend a major part of their income on a down payment or rent, while the corresponding

Table 5.5 Income, expenditure and gender (percentages of total of each sample saying yes for each item)

Do you spend a major part of your income on	Men	Women
rent or down payment?	48.9	34.1
children's expenses?	26.7	59.3
supplementing housekeeping expenses?	74.4	79.1
purchase of household goods?	12.2	47.3
contributing to household savings?	8.9	23.1
paying off loans you received for purchasing goods?	25.6	36.3

figure for women is 34.1 percent. When children's expenses are reviewed, however, there is a complete reversal, as 26.7 percent of men report contributing toward children's expenses, while more than half of women (59.3 percent) reported contributing to children's expenses. The results from the two samples are an interesting challenge to the breadwinner stereotypes. Both men and women contribute to housekeeping expenditure: 74.4 percent of men and 79.1 of women. It is true that the two samples are different, and only working females have been interviewed. Nonetheless, there is no doubt that the women who work no longer (if they ever did) work to pay for their own expenses. Women also reported that their contribution toward household goods and paying off loans is higher than men in the sample (47.3 percent and 35.3 percent, respectively).

The research also focused on ownership, and it was interesting that more than half of both samples did not possess any property. When there was ownership or rental, men reported more ownership, 22.2 percent, compared with 8.8 percent for women. Among the samples, 13.3 percent of men and 13.1 percent of women reported that they rely on their parents for shelter, as illustrated in Table 5.6.

Decision Making in the Household: Male versus Female Samples

What is perhaps the most important aspect of employment and income is the degree to which earning an income leads to having power over decision making. In Table 5.7, we see to what extent Ali's response is true when he said, "Of course, I give her everything.

Table 5.6 Property ownership and renting: male versus female samples (percentages of total of each sample)

In whose name is your house purchased or rented?	Men	Women
Does not possess any	56.7	57.1
Myself	22.2	8.8
My spouse	7.8	13.2
Shared	0.0	6.6
Children	0.0	1.1
Parents	13.3	13.2
Total	100.0	100.0

Table 5.7 Decision making in the household: male versus female samples (percentages of total of each sample)

Who makes decisions over the main household expenditures?	Men	Women
Myself	20.0	28.6
My spouse	28.9	5.5
Consulting with my spouse	30.0	42.9
Consulting with my parents	2.2	0.0
Others	0.0	2.2
Not relevant	0.0	1.1
No response	18.9	19.8
Total	100.0	100.0

She is the queen of the house." The result seems to be highly significant, since women, more than the men of the sample, reported that they are in charge of decision making: 28.6 of women compared with 20 percent of men. More men stated that their wives make the financial decisions, at 29.9 percent, than is the case with women, at 5.5 percent. However, more women reported that they consult with their husband (42.9 percent) than men reported consulting with their wives (30 percent). It seems that working women tend to make more decisions on their own or in consultation with their husbands than is the case with men and their spouses. The findings suggest that women's work does turn into decision-making power over household expenditure.

Social Network and Access to Credit

In the last chapter, when we examined women's access to credit, it was argued that due to the lack of access for women to formal credit and banks, rotating credit and saving associations (ROCSAs) were highly prevalent among women. Men do not engage in ROCSAs, as these clubs are restricted to their female relatives. Instead, when asked if they need credit, 46.7 percent of men reported that they rely on their own savings. The corresponding figure for women was 35.2 percent (many of whom also belong to ROCSAs). More men than women reported that they would borrow from their spouse: 17.8

percent of men compared with 5.5 percent of women. More women reported borrowing from their mothers: 15.4 percent of women compared with 7.8 percent of men (traditionally sons are supposed to take care of their mothers, and this could explain why fewer men borrow from their mothers). Both men and women borrowed from their fathers: 18.9 percent of men and 14.3 percent of women. Both men and women also borrowed from relatives: 29.9 percent of men and 25.3 percent of women. It is interesting that more men than women borrowed from friends: 25.6 percent of men compared with 5.5 percent of women. This is important and is an entry point into a discussion of how the social network operates for men. More men than women seek loans from banks: 14.4 percent of men compared with 4.4 percent of women. However, women seemed to be more at ease in approaching charity organizations: 7.7 percent of women compared with 3.3 percent of men.

Among men, 44.3 percent reported that their job depended on their social network, and it is clear that some specific types of jobs, such as performing custodial (janitor) or cleaning services, rely on the social network. The social network can also assist in other ways. One taxi driver (mentioned previously), who also worked as a building inspector, said, "I find jobs because people know me and know of my work. When there is a job, they call me." He also worked as a caterer, and this job relied heavily on his social network: "When there is a contract, my friends tell me, and they also give suggestions about the price I should offer."

In Chapter 4, some of the focus groups' documentation was presented. I wish to end this chapter with one focus group. In the case of men, it was difficult to organize a focus group. At one point, I had asked the local taxi company to organize a focus group, which they were happily willing to do, but from the start of this project the aim was not to attract any attention. The research has in the case of men been handicapped by gender segregation and by my own gender. Following is one focus group, whose results might have been tainted by my very inquisitive presence. There are men of low income who feel may hostile toward an accomplished middle-class, educated woman who has come to "study" them. Some of the responses may be a protest against my "observing" them and turning them into subjects! This is not to deny that my own subjectivity as a female has not interfered with data gathering.

Table 5.8 Sources of money (percentages of total of each sample saying yes for each source)

If you need money, which sources do you use?	Men	Women
My own savings	46.7	35.2
My spouse's savings	17.8	5.5
Ask for a loan from my mother	7.8	15.4
Ask for a loan from my father	18.9	14.3
Ask for a loan from relatives	28.9	25.3
Ask for a loan from friends	25.6	5.5
Ask for a loan from my employer	10.0	3.3
Seek a loan from a bank	14.4	4.4
Seek a loan from a charity organization	3.3	7.7
Seek a loan from an interest-free financial institution (*gharz-ol hassaneh*)	5.6	7.7

Street Corner Focus Group

At a busy corner in Tajrish Square, my research assistant and I interviewed three taxi drivers about the breadwinner model, work, and wife disobedience. None of the three thought that their wives should work. One of them was married to a woman who could translate from English into Persian, but even that was not allowed, even if it were to take place at home. One man stated, "You can't trust women. As soon as they have a bit of money, they stand up to you and don't listen to you. For example, we have here a female taxi driver, and she is the worst. She has a foul mouth and swears at us and others; none of us swear as much as she does."

I asked them what a woman could do if she needs money—for example, if she is the head of a household. "She should get married," one of the driver's responded. Then another driver said, "You know, Mum, this government is prowomen, they support women, and they are behind them. If there was a fight between you and me, and we went to a police officer, I would be the one who gets into trouble, not you. The authorities are always on their side and not on ours."

We had been trying very hard to get at least one man to admit to wife beating, and we finally did. "What happens if your wife does not listen to what you say?" I asked them. One of them with a very strong Azeri accent said, "What do you mean? I don't allow my wife to leave the house without my permission." I was a little shocked and asked, "So what happens if she does?" "I will divorce her," he responded. I suggested he may not be able to divorce her, because, as they just said, the government supports women and he has to tolerate her behavior, so what will he do? "I will kill her!" he said. My expression of shock was not masked any longer, and another driver with an Azeri accent said, "Mrs., he is from Ardebil. You know, they have to sound very macho." This implied that even his friends did not believe he would.

To change the subject, I asked about their income and how it was after rising gas prices. They all complained, but when I asked if they would prefer a public job, all three said, "God no. We prefer to work for ourselves and don't want to have anything to do with the government." This was a different response from another taxi driver who wished he had a public-service job with a steady income.

Later that evening I was having dinner with my close friend, Farkhondeh Aghai, who is a writer, a sociologist by training, and a longtime senior analyst at the Central Bank of Iran. I shared with her the story of the evening and how disturbed I was to have interviewed a potential wife murderer. She said, "I am not surprised. He is from Ardebil, and men from Ardebil feel they have to say these things that sound macho. But much of what they say is just words. I have met a number of them who are very good husbands and do more than other men at home for their wives. It is the rhetoric of machismo rather than the actual practice." I then thought of a very close relative of mine who had married a man from Ardebil; she had an affair with a man in the same apartment building, and this only caused a fight. I told my friend about the incident from my own personal experience, and how the husband was always talking macho but in actual reality lived with his wife who betrayed him. It is indeed difficult to know if the taxi driver meant what he said, or if it is, as my friend and my own experience indicates, that with men from Ardabil, macho talk is just talk.

It seems that some interviewees felt the urge to repeat what the dominant culture of their communities expect of them, even though it may be entirely possible that this is against their own sense of justice and they will not engage in behavior that is violent. Although, it is equally possible that some of them by nature may be disposed to engage in violent action, since violence against women is a worldwide problem. The image of a real man is one who is tough and uncompromising and perhaps bad tempered, whereas some men actually may be by nature soft, not domineering, and inclined to keep matters at the level of words and not action. Nonetheless, it is highly important to have the legal system behind those who may need protection against domestic abuse.

Conclusion

Some Insight for Forward-Looking Initiatives

Fighting Poverty and Unemployment, Social Economy, Unionization, and Social Entrepreneurship

This chapter ends the book with some insight into how the issue of economic empowerment can be approached without the destruction of the social economy. In both chapters based on the fieldwork, we witnessed how social networks are important for finding the means of earning an income. This was more critical for women as community stakeholders (women as pillars of the extended family network and the immediate community). In my forthcoming publication with Jennifer Olmsted, we have looked into the ways low-income women are an indispensable part of the social safety net. This theme is implicit rather than explicit in this book. Here, however, some in-depth interviews will be included to shed light on how social economy, and more specifically social entrepreneurship, is an important building block for improving the lives of millions of Iranians.

Before addressing the topic, I wish to add that since the first draft of this book was completed, Iran's economic situation has worsened significantly. Some of this has been due to national economic planning, while the imposition of so-called smart sanctions on Iran (they are called smart because they supposedly target Iran's nuclear program) in January 2012 has led to devaluation of the Iranian rial, reaching around 40,000 to $1—nearly a 40 percent increase in six months. In November 2012, the rial lost half its value in a single week.[1] Ironically, the highest devaluation occurred around the time that the conference for the Non-Aligned Movement (NAM) took place in Tehran. The outcome of the conference made Iran the leading member of the movement, which includes 120 member nations and 17 observer states. NAM had voted for Iran to lead the movement until 2015. While Western countries are imposing sanctions, the NAM countries, whose mandate is to be independent of the world's power blocs, have voted for Iran to become their leader for the next three years. Nevertheless, the power of Western countries and their severe grip over international financial transactions are harming Iran's economy, and those who are the most vulnerable—the low-income families—are the collateral damage.

Here, case studies are included that highlight how different individuals have found ways of transforming social conditions for the low-income households. The chapter starts with a case study of a social economy and antipoverty initiative founded by a woman from a low-income household, who not only pulled herself out of poverty but also created a network that provides a safety net for other women of low-income households. As discussed in the Introduction, the social economy plays a role in antipoverty programs. In this case, an Islamist woman is interviewed. There is a tendency among those living in low-income neighborhoods to be religious, and her case is not an accident, as it does reflect the majority of those in a similar situation. Incidentally, it is very intriguing to write about this initiative as a scholar who has spent much of her academic career in Quebec, where traditionally the Catholic Church has been the pillar of the province's social economy. The roots of Quebec's social economy date back to the time when the Church had a strong hold over the province before the 1960s (Linteau 1983; Mendell 2002; Seljak 2006) and the Quiet Revolution, which transformed the province from a religious society to a secular one (one that rebelled against its religious elite; Behiels 1985; Quarter 1992; Quarter, Mook, and Armstrong 2009).[2]

This case is followed with an example of state support for the social economy in a discussion of the Bonyad Mostaszafin [Foundation for the Disempowered] and its antipoverty programs. By the way, this also applies to the Canadian state, which has embraced the social economy on a large scale to generate employment and to strengthen and build a social safety net to fight poverty. Next, this chapter will examine the unionization of the arts-and-crafts cooperatives, which was initiated by a young woman. This is an excellent example of bringing protection to artists who have microenterprises in the informal sector. This is followed by an example of another young woman who founded a factory in one of the poorest and most traditional communities. She uses state funds and channels them into a factory primarily geared to generating profit, but with a focus on challenging gender stereotypes.

We then relate another example of social entrepreneurship focused on rural areas and small cities founded by a man who came from a village, migrated to Tehran and to the United States, and then returned to Iran to start his business. His social entrepreneurship became the basis of his success. He is now creating a model for development in the village of his birth. In this model he creates employment, supports entrepreneurship and small business, ventures into environmental protection projects, and seeks to build ecotourism using local and indigenous habitats, knowledge, and history. The chapter ends with a pertinent example of how social economy, social entrepreneurship, and formalization of the informal sector can come together in an anti-poverty program: the story of how female heads of households and their male dependents (including young men) formed the Seddighin Foundation.

SOCIAL ECONOMY AND RELIGION

I learned about Mrs. D during an interview with Mrs. Rezai, the founder of a nationwide arts-and-crafts cooperative union. During the interview, Mrs. Rezai continually referred to people's groups and popular groups, and I was compelled to keep pressing for a definition. It was through an example she gave that I came to understand that by people's and popular groups she was referring to the social economy. Mrs. Rezai referred me to Mrs. D, who, as we shall see, is a clear example of someone who is active in the social economy and also comes from a deeply religious background. When I finally got to meet Mrs. D, I learned that her father had migrated to Tehran in the 1950s from the small northwestern city of Ardabil, a religiously conservative place in Central Azerbaijan province, which borders East Azerbaijan on the south and west, Gilan province to the east, and the (former Soviet) Republic of Azerbaijan on the north. She told me that she had been religious since she was a child:

> I have always felt a strong force, the force of God behind my life, and was an admirer and servant to Imam Hosein and Our Lady Fatima Zahra [revered sister of Imam Hosein]. During Moharram[3] I would be lost to the world in dedicated prayer to the Imam and my lady. I would not even comb my hair, and from dawn to dust I would work until I would drop, making and preparing food for the Imam mourners, and I gave all my time to the point of total exhaustion. My love and passion

> for the two saints is overwhelming and fills me with the richest feelings. I was physically punished so many times for not coming home on time, because on the day of Ashura I would be wandering around, following the mourners and getting involved in volunteer work for Imam Hosein. Then I would go home late, and my parents, who were worried sick, would be mad and punish me. This would go on for days and days during the month [of Moharram]. I just had no control over myself, and I would cry, serve, and follow the *dasteh* line [organized group of mourners]. The Karbala massacre [the battle between Imam Hosein and the army of the Umayyad Caliph during which the Imam and all 72 of his followers were killed on the tenth day (Ashura) of Moharram, 680 CE] was the tragedy of my life. When the tragedy was recited or enacted, I would not understand myself and lose control. My life has been tied and entangled with Ashura.

Mrs. D completed primary school but did not attend middle or secondary school. Her family arranged for her to marry a man from Ardabil. Her marriage started with great economic hardship, and she eventually gave birth to nine children, while living in one room. But she said, "God is great and our life had *barakat* [blessings]. I would cook a small pot but no one was ever hungry in my house. Because of our devotion and dedication to the holy Imam and my lady, *barakat* was part of our life no matter how much money we did or did not have." When I asked her if her husband was a good one, she quoted a Qur'anic verse, which she interpreted as "cherish your men as they are superior to you." I pressed for an answer and finally she said, "We have differences of opinion, but I believe that men must be happy in their married life." I did not insist on obtaining more information about her husband.

After several years, Mrs. D said the family moved into a house where other members of her own extended family lived. "While I lived with my extended family, I slowly started to realize that our household was not managed properly and I had to make changes. I started to educate myself in the Qur'an and jurisprudence, and my husband had no objection. Through educating myself, I became a Qur'an teacher and later on became a female preacher." Her daughter was educated in a religious university (*hozeh*) and became a certified preacher. Although Mrs. D is uncertified, she nonetheless is a highly popular preacher. From what she chose to share with me, it seemed that she was earning much of the household income after becoming a preacher. "I was feeding 11 people," she kept repeating. "At 8:00 in the morning when my pupils were due to arrive, everyone was fed, my house was clean, and my lunch was in the oven."

Her charismatic preaching had slowly brought a small fortune, which enabled her to buy a house. "I made a vow to turn the basement of the house into a *Hoseinieh* [a house belonging to Imam Hosein] if I managed to buy the house. With the help of God, the money to purchase the house came my way, and we bought this house." The house had a small yard and a large basement, which Mrs. D had turned into a *Hoseinieh*, a place entirely dedicated to preaching. She does go to other peoples' homes to preach when there are *sofrehs* or *molodis* (all-female prayer gatherings; food is severed at *sofrehs*, while *molodis*, which commemorate the birthday of a saint, are celebratory occasions that in many cases have musicians and singers), but she mainly organizes religious occasions in her own *Hoseinieh*, where close to 400 women can gather.

She is engaged in a range of activities. She has a box to which everyone contributes one or two dollars; this is similar to but different from other rotating credit clubs. In this saving club, people join entirely on the basis of their good faith and a belief that giving interest-free loans is an act of devotion aiming to bring *barakat* to one's life. Every one contributes one or two dollars, and she has about four thousand dollars, which is used to give small loans to those in need. "From those on the basis of their ability to those on the basis of their need" is the way her fund operates. Since the community is closely knit, everyone knows of one another's problems. While there, I met a woman whose husband had become a drug addict, and she had to live in a garage that was provided by friends and work in a hospital as a cleaner. I asked if she would agree to be interviewed as part of my sample. She did, but she told me that she also works as a maid and requested that I keep this information private, even from Mrs. D. It was an interesting case of the role of a social network: It is positive as well as negative, in this case bringing shame to a woman for performing low-status jobs.

Mrs. D often gives these loans to those who face a crisis. People in the neighborhood know one another, and when something happens to one person, the information travels quickly, and Mrs. D is on the phone to say, "It is your turn to use your loan" to the woman who has just faced the financial crisis. This is done without the direct knowledge of the receiver that she is in effect receiving charity. An observant Muslim who gives charity must remain anonymous so that the dignity of the receiver is preserved. For this reason, the emergency charity is given in the form of a loan and under the pretense that there was a lottery and the recipient's name won. If the recipient cannot repay the loan and defaults, Mrs. D asks someone else to make her repayment or manages it herself to keep the flow of cash.

The other half of her collection goes toward the reconstruction of holy Shi'a sites that were destroyed in Najaf, Karbala, and Samarra, Iraq. On her table there were tickets to be sold for the Shi'a sites in Iraq. I asked whether she receives any government help or contributes to government efforts, and she replied that she refuses to be part of the government and does not ask for any funds for her *Hoseinieh* or her Mosque-reconstruction effort. "I only ask from God. There are many rich organizations which want to help us, even government organizations, but I refuse, and all we have and need is brought to us." She has maintained her independence and the self-sufficiency of her network by refusing to accept financial assistance from outside.

Besides providing loans, Mrs. D holds bazaars and uses the profit from sales for her loan operation. She practices traditional medicine and has part of the *Hoseinieh* dedicated to selling herbal medicines, the profit of which again goes to her redistribution fund. Besides that, she works as a marriage counselor. I asked her about women who had problems with their husbands, such as drug addiction and domestic abuse. "I try to talk to the wife and help to relieve her stress, but sometimes men have to learn to change their attitudes." Although I pressed her for what she meant and what might motivate those men who did not listen to their wives, she declined an answer. It is possible that belonging to her group could be empowering to some women. In a closely knit community bounded by poverty and ethnicity (mainly Azeri), any bad behavior on the part of a wife would circulate rapidly, bringing shame to the husband. Further, it is often common that relatives of a woman can be supportive of her in cases of a husband's severe behavior and may intervene. This is not to say that the standards of bad behavior and physical punishment are necessarily high. It may be that a large degree of domestic abuse is tolerated before anyone's objection or shame is raised.

To end this interview on a word of caution to the reader, it is not always the case that these women lack power in their community, but power also can generate clientelism. This was revealed to me when I conducted an interview with one woman who participated in Mrs. D's celebration of the birthday of the Twelfth Imam, or Mahdi (the awaited messiah for Shi'a Muslims). The woman did not wish to convey information in front of Mrs. D and requested that the interview be conducted in private. This was when, not surprisingly, I discovered that some women had reservations about the nature of the charitable work offered by the *Hoseinieh*. This was confirmed further with other research. In some cases, assistance can come with strings attached. The fact that one of the interviewees wanted to talk to me in private suggested that she wanted to reveal things that could put her out of favor with Mrs. D, who does enjoy community power.

State-Funded Social Economy through Bonyad Mostazafin

Generally the literature produced in English on Iran's various charitable foundations has a tendency to associate them with corruption, mismanagement, and lack of useful function (Roy 1994; Fairbanks 2005; US State Department 2006). Nonetheless, a review of the foundations' own publications in Persian documents their support for a diverse range of projects to help low-income families. In order to get an independent perspective on some of their operations and projects, I interviewed Mr. Jarrahi, who was the director for Development and Services in the country's largest foundation, the Bonyad Mostazafin[4] [Foundation for the Poor]. Jarrahi, a graduate of the London School of Economics, was involved in the antipoverty programs of the foundation and explained its current plans: "As you know, the primary objective of the foundation is being involved in poverty alleviation initiatives in an indirect way. As part of our efforts, we have tried to fund employment-generating activities in megaprojects, such as large-scale agricultural and industrial initiatives that lead to efficient production as well as employment generation. As an example, we have been funding one of the largest ranches in the country as well as major soft drink companies."[5]

Mr. Jarrahi was especially concerned with the issue of communications and explained how in his own domain he has been involved actively in mobile phone service. He reminded me of a the state of mobile phones four years ago, when mobile phones were highly expensive and only the high or middle class were able to purchase one. He said that he started to focus on mobile phones after reading about a young man who had killed his mother in Borazjan (a small city in the south of Iran) because she refused to give him money to buy a mobile phone. The young man may have wanted a cell phone for status and prestige, and at the time, the high cost of cell phones restricted them only to those in the top income brackets. As he thought about this, he got the idea "to invest in an information system with a social approach and to bring access to mobile phones to those at the bottom of the social ladder. World statistics indicate that increasing access to mobile phones increases people's income by 10 percent, especially among those who are from low-income households."

Mr. Jarrahi then gave me an example from India, where many people do not have a house and sleep on the street, but where as part of the Indian government's poverty-alleviation program, such people are provided with inexpensive mobile phones to increase their incomes: "A newspaper delivery man can use his mobile phone to organize his day around distributing newspapers in an efficient, time-saving manner and thereby increase his income. Moreover, it is illustrated that overall GNP increases 1.2 percent when access to mobile phones increases." He added, "The project was submitted to the parliament and was rejected for funding. Mass lobbying had to be used and it took two years finally to convince the parliament that, with inexpensive, easily accessible mobile phones, the poor would benefit."

Mr. Jarrahi said that, in Iran, "today we have 110 million phones, many of them belonging to lower income and the poor. We still have to work on this project because the cost of mobiles in villages is still high." He further explained that "increasing access to mobile phones for the poor is the first step for another project, which is designed to bring banking to the poor." In a graph, he showed me how the rich and middle class use the banking system, but the lower-middle class is underbanked and the poor are unbanked. Then he handed me a leaflet on the topic of how the poor can be empowered by increasing easily accessible banking through mobile phones. He continued,

> In India, Kenya, and even Afghanistan, some women use mobile phones to set up a bank. Through this system all a person needs to set up a mobile phone bank is a table to set up a business and sit behind it with a mobile phone. This is how we plan to bring banking to the unbanked. This project not only will help the poor, but it also contributes to the national economy. Currently from the time money is given [in form of salary], it takes 14 days for the money to return to the bank in the form of deposit or savings. Easy access to the bank will shorten the circle and increase banking reserves, which in turn will increase banking capacity in generating income for investment in national or private projects.

His next plan is to extend the use of mobile phone for health purposes. "We realize that our national health-care system faces short comings. Mobile phones can be a vehicle to increase access to doctors and nurses through special communications methods with health clinics and health-care providers. This is another benefit of mobile phone expansion." He was very passionate about the issue of access of the poor to the health-care system, and together with seven others he had set up a nongovernmental organization (NGO) to address lack of access to affordable health care for those with kidney disease. They found an old public hospital, which was depreciating rapidly, and asked to take over part of the facilities and engage it in a nonprofit project. Today the Shahid Labfinejad Hospital is the largest and most efficient hospital for those with kidney disease, and no one is turned down because he or she has no financial means.

Working with, against, and through the Government: Founder of Trade Union for Arts and Crafts Cooperatives

Mrs. Rezai received me in her office in a lower-middle-class neighborhood close to Haft Hooz. A woman of 37, she was ready to share with me many years of hard work and passion to create a nationwide trade union for artists, craftsmen, and women cooperatives. Born into a middle-class family, she attended law school where she chose to study Islamic law and jurisprudence, which she found to be most important for her work as a social activist. She told us, "I think a woman is only limited as she sees herself. I have taken up the impossible to prove that there are no limits to what a woman can do." While a law student, she worked as a volunteer for the Kahrizak Foundation, run by Mrs. Bahadorzadeh, who tirelessly works to bring the best technology and provide highest quality care for the elderly poor. Rezai said that she felt inspired and energized by Mrs. Bahadorzadeh's work, and she spent seven years at Kahrizak, working primarily as a volunteer but later as paid staff. It was there that she found the joy and gratitude of working in a nonprofit organization: "I think woman tend to be caring for organizations and are interested in sustainability, while men tend to be more for profit even if it is for short term."

Since 1998, she has worked as a social activist through local and neighborhood organizations focusing on students and the youth. Together with seven other students, her friends from law school, and childhood friends, she started a collective that works on a volunteer basis to give assistance to students in financial need by using their skills to find and generate employment. The collective was active in identifying the type of jobs students could find, such as giving private lessons, producing arts and crafts, catering, and so on. Since the collective was made up of volunteers with different backgrounds, it could provide different types of advice from business management to legal advice to social work. Later the collective took special training courses to be able to work as a mobile vocational training center. They took courses in computers, carpet weaving, Klim making, Jajim making, calligraphy, wedding planning, ceramics, and painting on ceramics and other types of arts and crafts, and even singing and playing musical instruments. The collective continued to provide different skills to young people and students in order to be able to generate an income.

This expansion of teachable skills coincided with a government policy in 2000 to give small loans to enable self-employment and encourage small businesses. Rezai applied for a small loan from the Ministry of Work and Social Welfare. It also happened that she had relatives in high-ranking positions in the ministry, and they advised her not to apply for a small self-employment loan but rather to become a cooperative (since with seven members it is possible to form a cooperative) and therefore apply for a cooperative loan. Thus the collective become the first all-female cooperative in carpentry woodwork. Since it was all female, the cooperative was harassed for wanting to be a feminist organization.

The cooperative started a website and sent out calls for participation to other local groups, which were organized through religious gatherings and independent of the state, such as neighborhood groups sometimes based on ethnicity, such as the Azeris. In fact, Rezai worked closely with Mrs. D. As a mobile cooperative, they provided volunteer training for different municipalities between 2002 and 2005. Their focus was vocational training at municipal centers. I asked her if she worked with the municipal government. "I never worked for the municipal government and always wanted to be an independent entity," she responded. But the work of cooperative became popular and its constituency grew. At that point the cooperative was active in giving training in 48 different branches of arts and crafts, and its staff started to grow. While working with those who had graduated, she witnessed that artists and craftsmen often were exploited. The government provided no protection, and there was no unionization of artists and craftsmen. She focused on her own cooperative production and contacted a major distributor of *mogharagh*, an Iranian type of woodwork. She found a major distributor who wanted to hire her and was delighted also to have found an educated and highly skilled woman to work for him. The man told her that he would provide her with all the material and that he would do the finishing paint; she was to produce only the woodwork. Rezai turned her garage into a workshop and called on her friends, who in less than a week had produced 500 pieces, each of which is sold for close to $30. However, what she was paid was 50 cents per piece. When she asked for a contract, the distributor refused. This provided her with documentation of the exploitation of woodworkers in her own case, and then she continued to gather statistical information in order to show that a high percentage of woodworkers were exploited. She took the complaint to the Ministry of Cooperatives and lobbied for a call to action to unionize wood workers. The ministry reluctantly responded by calling for a nationwide handicraft cooperatives' union in 2005. Major cooperative representatives were called on to come to the capital to discuss the matter with the ministry. Calls to organize a committee were distributed three times until finally a meeting took place. Rezai recalled that meeting:

> The hall was filled with 50 men and I was the only woman and much younger than most. The ministry pressed for volunteers to take up the job of starting a nationwide union. One by one all men declined until I was the only one left who had not refused the job. I announced that I would, since there were no other options. I became responsible for creating a nationwide union for arts and handicrafts, and to carry out what the previous Queen, Farah Pahlavi, had wished in the year I was born. Queen Farah took the motion of unionizing artists and craftsmen to the parliament, but it was not acted on because of the political turmoil that led to the 1979 Revolution.

Rezai said that she found the position challenging to manage, but her background in law was useful to her now:

> It was a daunting task. I had to travel throughout the country, negotiate with all major cooperatives and bring them all on board to form a union and work as a unionized entity. All the middle-men mafia groups and those who made fortunes at the expense of low-paid jobs challenged this unionization. But being a lawyer was a major asset and enabled me to mobilize support for the initiative. Once the nationwide union was formed and my office became its headquarters, I saw the mission as accomplished and felt it was time for me to take a break.

She had undertaken the job even though she still worked as an artisan and ran her own small company to generate an income while continuing her volunteer work for the cooperative. She said,

> I worked around the clock, and the ministry was aware of my work. At one point the ministry announced that my ticket was ready to go to Baku to showcase the products of the Iranian arts and crafts cooperative at an international exhibition. I had no choice, as I had promised to deliver. By the end of the trip, my cell phone costs were close to $800, which I asked the ministry to pay. I had promised the ministry to

> deliver a union, and I had fulfilled my promise against all odds. Once I finished the job, I felt like a runner who had reached the end of the line and collapsed out of the exhaustion, an exhaustion that took its toll. To recover, I went on a pilgrimage to Iraq to find my soul, a soul I had lost in the everyday hard work of negotiating for workers' rights.

The pilgrimage to Iraq turned out to be pivotal for Rezai, and she explained how she became involved in the restoration of Shi'a holy sites:

> A soul-searching pilgrim found another mission. The bombing of some of the Shi'a holy sites had mobilized resources to reconstruct those sites and enhance their artistic aspects. I took on the task of reconstructing the Shi'a sites in Najaf, Karbala, and Samarra. In Samarra, the situation was very dangerous, as Wahhabis [extremist, anti-Shi'a Sunni Muslims] had placed a bounty of $750 on each Shi'a head. But the joy [of restoring the damaged religious sites] was indeed immense, and I found the task of embellishing those shrines most satisfying and rejuvenating.
>
> I returned to my work with my cooperative and vocational training in municipalities. By then, I had earned a reputation for carrying out impossible tasks. The head of the Ardabil Woman's Center at the Ministry of National Affairs invited me to organize an exhibition and conference on the arts and crafts of Ardabil women. This would be a one-day conference to showcase the capabilities of women in this province.

Ardabil, as mentioned before, is a conservative city as far as gender roles are concerned. Rezai is Persian-speaking, while the majority of people in Ardabil speak Azeri Turkish. Although the Ministry of National Affair's Women's Center had invited her to speak, this did not mean that the rest of the ministry or other government officials would endorse the initiative. "The problem with Ardabil is beyond religion, and the province is culturally against women's public participation," noted Rezai. Although the Women's Center was behind the initiative, she had to earn the support of the provincial governor (*ostandari*) and of the religious leader of the Friday prayers. She elaborated,

> It was indeed interesting that in private both the governor of the province and Ayatollah Amoli were in favor, but they kept their distance in public, and the situation became extremely difficult as the countdown to the exhibition started. The night before the exhibition was due to take place, I was told to conceal it. This was not going to

happen, I told myself. It was time to call on every single person who could help. Together with those from the Woman's Center, we called women police, women athletes, and women sports clubs to mobilize, as well as all the friends and allies I had managed to muster. [Incidentally, Ardabil women are winners of running medals in international sports competitions but never attend as an Ardabil team; rather, they attend as members of other provincial teams so as not to provoke their fellow provincial males.] My man,[6] who happened to be an Ardabil native, was a major asset and often would come to negotiate with other men to convince them that the exhibition should go ahead. The exhibition did take place and became the first occasion during which 2,500 women came together, while music was playing, to see and to show what they are capable of doing as artists and craftswomen. It was the first nonreligious gathering to bring such large number of women together. The occasion ultimately became a success, and the ayatollah endorsed it, as well as province's governor. Then the Presidential Office called me to come to Tehran. There were complaints that this Persian-speaking woman wanted to corrupt Ardabil women. Now I am being asked to be in charge of similar initiatives in Tehran! But I am contemplating. I always have avoided politicization and factionalization. I do not wish to be associated with any particular official, whether he be a president or not. I believe in what I do, and I keep politics as far from it as possible so that once the officials change, the work remains. Because I am a lawyer, my approach is to define a job, to keep it to its legal and clearly defined parameters, and to that I avoid establishing networks based on political allegiances. I maintain the continuity and transparency of the work I do.

When I asked Rezai whether she was still active with the cooperative union, she smiled and nodded her head: "Yes, I am back to where I left off. A full circle has brought me back."

Setting up a Factory: Breaking Female Stereotypes

Farahnaz Mozafari, 32, was born in Gemishan, Golestan Province (eastern end of the Caspian coastal plain), and owns a factory that produces ropes. She is also a member of the managing board of Empowered Women of Golestan Province, a nongovernmental organization. In 1999, she won an award and was distinguished as an elite professional woman of the country. I met her at a conference of the Persian Gender Network in Washington, DC, and her story was moving. A soft and quiet-looking woman who dressed very simply, one would not guess she was a factory owner and winner of several awards for her service to the community as a social entrepreneur.

Her success, however, had not come about easily, as she indicated in our recent email exchange, and she is still under pressure. Her grandfather was a merchant who imported and exported to and from the former Soviet Union. "I was inspired by my grandfather to become an entrepreneur and sought a loan to set up a factory business." She admits that she had to struggle with her family, but added that she believes in life's challenges: "If one earns something easily, then one loses it just as easily."

She had to challenge not only her family but also her local culture, which is predominately Sunni Muslim and ethnically Turkmen. The Turkmen opposed bank loans because of their interest rates, as they regarded interest as *haram* (religiously forbidden). The Turkmen tribes of Golestan have a long history of antagonism toward women's public roles, and Mozafari said she knew that it was not going to be an easy task to be accepted as a woman entrepreneur. However, she managed to convince her father to allocate some financial resources, then applied for a small business bank loan, and received $44,000. She not only had taken out a loan, but it was the largest loan anyone locally had applied for, and she had received it because of government policy during the Khatami presidency (1997–2005) to support small businesses.

As though borrowing and setting up a factory was not enough, she became the first woman to drive to her work. For all this, there was a price to pay. The local people boycotted her product and actually paid a higher price for lower quality rope. This boycott almost drove her into bankruptcy. However, she came up with a plan to sell her product in the neighboring province of Mazandaran under a different brand name. This proved to be a success, as her rope was highly competitive and much less expensive than the alternatives in the market. Soon even people from Golestan province bought her product, unaware that it was rope from her factory that they were purchasing. Once she had dominance in the market, she started to mix her old brand with the new one, and since customers were already satisfied with her product, she kept a large share of the market. Thus people of Golestan came to terms with the first female factory owner, as she had already captured the market in the neighboring provinces.

Her driving was no longer a problem. On the contrary, it had caught on in the entire community, and today more than half the women in Golestan have driver's licenses. Female-only driving schools even have mushroomed. Mozarfari, in fact, has become a role model, and national television broadcasters have produced four documentaries on her work.[7] Her joy, as she shared with me, is that she has brought employment to her people and is proud to be able to export her product outside of Iran and to the markets north of Iran.

Social Entrepreneur: A Male Example

Ali Asghar Jahangiri was born in 1945 in Kandelous, a village in northern Iran, and spent part of his childhood there.[8] He later moved to Tehran to continue his education and graduated from Ami Kabir Polytechnic University with a degree in textile production. Then he went to London, where he obtained a graduate degree in sociology. After London, he moved to the United States, where he worked for several years with an oil company. In his memoir he writes that he was unhappy being away from Iran and eventually decided to return home. Since returning, his main efforts have revolved around rebuilding his village and helping its residents. He has set up the Kandelous Help Foundation, a nonprofit organization with the aim of rebuilding Kandelous and the seven other villages in the Kojour area. Through his efforts, all the villages now have electricity and extensive infrastructure, including strong communications, numerous schools, and hospitals.

Jahangiri's goal in rebuilding Kandelous has been to turn the village into a model community by preserving its natural habitat and using its natural resources for herbal medicine. He has set up herbal medicine farms where families who work are paid a high wage. Herbs also are used for herbal drinks, cigarettes without nicotine, beauty products, and a whole array of different products that are all natural and produced in an environmentally healthy way. In addition, he has created in Kandelous the Jahangiri Cultural Complex, which includes a museum to preserve the cultural folklore of people in the Kojour area. A small hotel has also been set up for eco- and cultural tourism.

Perhaps Jahangiri's most important contribution is his mission to create jobs. He has created a web-based support group with chat rooms where students and those who want to start small businesses can enter into a discussion. He has made a commitment to provide free advice and consultation to young people to start microenterprises in small towns and villages. In fact, I found myself searching for his office in Tehran's busy Hafteh-e Tir Square when I saw a young man carrying a huge bouquet of flowers and who was walking in the same direction as I. This young man looked like someone coming from a small city. We arrived at the office and took the elevator together, and I was thinking to myself: He looks like someone coming from a small town; he must be one of Jahangiri's success stories. Indeed, I was right: Jahangiri had helped him to start a microenterprise, and the young man had come there to thank him. Such help has helped to make Jahangiri very popular in the business community, and he now teaches many courses on the topic of entrepreneurship and microenterprises. Since these courses typically are poorly paid, no doubt his incentive to teach is not the meager cash remuneration but rather the information it provides for young students.

Tehran's First Conference on Social Entrepreneurship: The Seddighin Foundation

The Women Managers and Entrepreneurs Association (WMEA) organized this conference in 2004 to bring together a group of female entrepreneurs to focus on issues related to enhancement of female entrepreneurs and employment for women. WMEA has held several other conferences, including one on the topic of social entrepreneurship. That conference's proceedings include a history and overview of social entrepreneurship and present a number of selected social entrepreneurs. In its review of the historical roots of antipoverty community programs, the conference proceedings mention examples from the city of Tabriz, the capital of East Azerbaijan province. Historically the city has had a strong communal social network, particularly during the process of social transition from an agricultural to an industrial economy, which was accompanied by the decline of the agricultural economy and migration to Tabriz and other large cities. The conference proceedings state that "a city of 2 million inhabitants, including 400,000 ghetto settlers" (2004), had set up an extremely strong social safety net, which has managed to deal with the homeless and the destitute as well as reduce theft and other social problems.

This is an example of highly successful social economy, undoubtedly based on religious institutions, such as the Nobar Charity Foundation established in 1964. Today this foundation mobilizes 1,600 donors, some of whom not only live outside of the city but have even moved to larger cities or migrated from Iran and yet continue to be affiliated and contribute to the charitable organization. The conference proceedings also point out that antipoverty efforts in the form of charitable and noncharitable organizations have evolved in their forms and target groups. For instance, there are now organizations that are focused on environmental issues, such as the Women's Association to Fight for the Environment established by Mahlagha Mallah. Such organizations have grown in parallel with governmental and nationwide programs, such as Imam Khomeini Relief Committee.

The Seddighin Foundation is an interesting case among the selected social entrepreneurs. The conference proceedings included an interview with its founder, Ms. Bonyanian, and there is some more information on its website.[9] The foundation, which started its activities as an NGO during the Khatami era, has focused on Bonyanian's efforts with female-headed households (FHHs). Seddighin's main aim is economic empowerment and support of low-income FHHs. The foundation does not focus entirely on economic empowerment and income-generating activities but also includes social support. For instance, it provides legal aid for women in an effort make sure that they are aware of their legal rights and entitlements in different domains, from labor rights to civil rights to family rights. In addition, Seddighin aims to empower FHHs, promote self-confidence, and encourage individual initiatives to enhance FHHs' socioeconomic status. As an example, it provides educational and vocational skills-enhancing services. These services are complemented by programs such as cultural and entertainment activities to give encouragement and support, and to alleviate the psychological burden on their members.

Seddighin believes in engaging the state and its various social assistance programs. This is an important point, since the growing social economy may be one way of releasing the state from its responsibility to provide social welfare, and it is critical not to lose sight of the fact that the state must be held responsible for its social programs for its citizens. However, the foundation does not rely only on state funding but attempts to build its own financial resources. Thus the organization has sought to break away from the traditional charitable approach and move toward sustainable self-help programs by channeling charitable donations to programs that can give a head start to FHHs, build on their self-confidence and self-belief, and encouraging them to gain economic independence. Through its various fund-raising programs, the organization has managed to create its own sources of funding.

The Seddighin Foundation currently has 250 households in its various programs, with the total number of individuals at 750. The organization has ventured into several businesses, such as opening a reception hall called *talar abrisham* (Silk Hall), with catering services. The organization has sought to provide catering on the basis of signed contracts to provide lunch for large governmental and nongovernmental offices such as the Iran Handicraft Factory, Leasing Car, and the Mostazafin Foundation; it delivers 2,400 meals a day from a location provided by *Behzisty* (the Office of Welfare). It has also set up a clothing workshop for piecework production of trousers, work clothes, and Islamic outerwear (*manteaux*, long coats that are an alternative to the *chador*). The production line is called Piratan, and it is an all-female initiative, with production taking place in a large hall. In addition, it accepts interns and welcomes training for young women and dependents of FHHs. Recently it has branched into another locale in the Kosar complex of Sharh-e Ray (an industrial area on the eastern edge of Tehran). The Office for Women of the Office of the Mayor of Tehran also has offices in Kosar and may provide some assistance to the new Seddighin branch.

Seddighin has managed to set up a limited-liability company, Pajohesh Gostar, which channels all its profits into the account through which its various programs are funded. The company works under the Ministry of Labour laws and makes a point of following strong labor-protection measures, such as full insurance coverage. The company is engaged in a variety of services, such as catering, cleaning, and nursing. It has a policy to enter into joint ventures for profit-making projects, and it uses its income to invest in its social-entrepreneurial projects. The foundation recently has employed men from FHHs, and unemployed sons of women heads of households increasingly are becoming part of the target group. This is particularly critical, as unemployment has become a problem for the country.

This book ends with this example because this organization is an important model of how to provide employment and economic empowerment, and it shows how the informal sector can be formalized in the social-economic domain. It is a forward-looking organization with labor-protection laws and insurance that goes beyond simple economic empowerment, and it is being inventive in projects that can become self-sustaining. It has branched out into other types of services: legal aid, vocational training, and creating a community of FHHs who can work as a collective in various microenterprises. No doubt the social network and its social capital are vital to the informal sector, and its presence must be documented and understood. However, this can feed into the formation of organizations that can turn into venues that formalize the informal sector with labor protections and secure employment. This foundation goes beyond simple economic empowerment and into social empowerment and solidarity building.

Appendix

Table A.1 Distribution of individuals 16 and older by economic sectors, job types, and gender in 1986 (by percentage)

	Men			Women			Total		
	Urban	*Rural*	*All*	*Urban*	*Rural*	*All*	*Urban*	*Rural*	*All*
Sector									
16+ First self-employed (5 sectors)	100	100	100	100	100	100	100	100	100
16+ Self-employed (agriculture)	14.8	80.0	59.3	20.3	62.3	56.6	15.4	75.2	58.7
16+ Self-employed (mining and industry)	15.2	3.6	7.3	61.0	36.0	39.4	20.4	12.4	14.6
16+ Self-employed (utilities)	0.0	0.0	0.0	0.0	0.0	0.0	0.0	0.0	0.0
16+ Self-employed (construction)	5.1	0.7	2.1	0.0	0.0	0.0	4.5	0.5	1.6
16+ Self-employed (services)	64.9	15.7	31.4	18.6	1.6	3.9	59.7	11.9	25.1
16+ First wage and salary (5 sectors)	100	100	100	100	100	100	100	100	100
16+ Wage and salary (agriculture)	3.2	14.3	8.3	4.2	37.1	14.2	3.3	15.9	8.9
16+ Wage and salary (mining and industry)	26.0	11.0	19.0	11.7	25.0	15.7	24.2	11.9	18.7

	Men			Women			Total		
	Urban	*Rural*	*All*	*Urban*	*Rural*	*All*	*Urban*	*Rural*	*All*
16+ Wage and salary (utilities)	2.5	0.8	1.7	1.5	0.0	1.0	2.4	0.8	1.7
16+ Wage and salary (construction)	14.9	19.0	16.8	0.4	0.9	0.5	13.1	17.8	15.2
16+ Wage and salary (services)	53.5	54.9	54.1	82.3	37.1	68.5	57.1	53.6	55.6
16+ First self-employed and wage and salary (5 sectors)	100	100	100	100	100	100	100	100	100
16+ Self-employed and wage and salary (agriculture)	8.1	56.9	36.6	10.5	59.9	46.8	8.4	57.5	38.4
16+ Self-employed and wage and salary (mining and industry)	21.4	6.2	12.5	31.1	35.0	33.9	22.6	12.3	16.3
16+ Self-employed and wage and salary (utilities)	1.4	0.3	0.8	0.9	0.0	0.2	1.4	0.2	0.7
16+ Self-employed and wage and salary (construction)	10.7	7.2	8.6	0.2	0.1	0.1	9.5	5.7	7.1
16+ Self-employed and wage and salary (services)	58.3	29.5	41.5	57.2	5.0	18.9	58.2	24.3	37.5
16+ First self-employed and wage and salary (3 sectors)	100	100	100	100	100	100	100	100	100

	Men			Women			Total		
	Urban	*Rural*	*All*	*Urban*	*Rural*	*All*	*Urban*	*Rural*	*All*
16+ Self-employed and wage and salary (agriculture)	8.1	56.9	36.6	10.5	59.9	46.8	8.4	57.5	38.4
16+ Self-employed and wage and salary (industry)	33.6	13.6	21.9	32.3	35.0	34.3	33.4	18.2	24.1
16+ Self-employed and wage and salary (services)	58.3	29.5	41.5	57.2	5.0	18.9	58.2	24.3	37.5

Note: "First self-employed" implies the first job reported by the individual as being a self-employed job. Similarly, "First wage and salary" implies the first job reported by the individual as being a wage-and-salary job.

Source: 1986 Household Income and Expenditure Survey (HIES), Statistical Center of Iran.

Table A.2 Distribution of individuals 16 and older by economic sectors, job types, and gender in 1997 (by percentage)

	Men			Women			Total		
	Urban	*Rural*	*All*	*Urban*	*Rural*	*All*	*Urban*	*Rural*	*All*
Sector									
16+ First self-employed (5 sectors)	100	100	100	100	100	100	100	100	100
16+ Self-employed (agriculture)	16.7	79.6	57.7	17.9	66.5	59.5	16.8	75.9	58.1
16+ Self-employed (mining and industry)	15.2	5.4	8.8	65.7	31.5	36.4	20.8	12.8	15.2
16+ Self-employed (utilities)	0.0	0.0	0.0	0.0	0.0	0.0	0.0	0.0	0.0
16+ Self-employed (construction)	6.7	1.1	3.0	0.3	0.0	0.0	6.0	0.8	2.3

	Men			Women			Total		
	Urban	*Rural*	*All*	*Urban*	*Rural*	*All*	*Urban*	*Rural*	*All*
16+ Self-employed (services)	61.4	13.9	30.4	16.0	2.0	4.0	56.4	10.5	24.3
16+ First wage and salary (5 sectors)	100	100	100	100	100	100	100	100	100
16+ Wage and salary (agriculture)	3.2	25.1	13.4	4.4	33.9	16.5	3.4	26.1	13.8
16+ Wage and salary (mining and industry)	23.5	16.0	20.0	13.5	44.5	26.3	22.1	19.2	20.8
16+ Wage and salary (utilities)	2.0	1.2	1.6	0.3	0.0	0.2	1.8	1.0	1.4
16+ Wage and salary (construction)	18.0	30.7	23.9	0.8	1.1	0.9	15.6	27.4	21.0
16+ Wage and salary (services)	53.3	27.0	41.1	81.1	20.5	56.1	57.1	26.3	42.9
16+ First self-employed and wage and salary (5 sectors)	100	100	100	100	100	100	100	100	100
16+ Self-employed and wage and salary (agriculture)	8.7	57.4	36.0	9.1	60.7	46.1	8.7	58.1	37.9
16+ Self-employed and wage and salary (mining and industry)	20.1	9.7	14.3	31.8	33.8	33.2	21.6	15.1	17.7
16+ Self-employed and wage and salary (utilities)	1.2	0.5	0.8	0.2	0.0	0.0	1.1	0.4	0.7

	Men			Women			Total		
	Urban	*Rural*	*All*	*Urban*	*Rural*	*All*	*Urban*	*Rural*	*All*
16+ Self-employed and wage and salary (construction)	13.4	13.1	13.3	0.6	0.2	0.3	11.8	10.3	10.9
16+ Self-employed and wage and salary (services)	56.6	19.2	35.6	58.3	5.3	20.3	56.8	16.1	32.8
16+ First self-employed and wage and salary (3 sectors)	100	100	100	100	100	100	100	100	100
16+ Self-employed and wage and salary (agriculture)	8.7	57.4	36.0	9.1	60.7	46.1	8.7	58.1	37.9
16+ Self-employed and wage and salary (industry)	34.7	23.4	28.4	32.6	34.0	33.6	34.5	25.7	29.3
16+ Self-employed and wage and salary (services)	56.6	19.2	35.6	58.3	5.3	20.3	56.8	16.1	32.8

Note: "First self-employed" implies the first job reported by the individual as being a self-employed job. Similarly, "First wage and salary" implies the first job reported by the individual as being a wage-and-salary job.

Source: 1997 Household Income and Expenditure Survey (HIES), Statistical Center of Iran.

Table A.3 Distribution of individuals 16 and older by economic sectors, job types, and gender in 2009 (by percentage)

	Men			Women			Total		
	Urban	*Rural*	*All*	*Urban*	*Rural*	*All*	*Urban*	*Rural*	*All*
Sector									
16+ First Self-employed (5 sectors)	100	100	100	100	100	100	100	100	100
16+ Self-employed (Agriculture)	23.2	77.3	56.3	32.0	84.0	74.2	24.2	79.1	60.3
16+ Self-employed (Mining and Industry)	9.6	3.1	5.7	35.0	11.9	16.2	12.7	5.5	8.0
16+ Self-employed (Utilities)	0.1	0.1	0.1	0.0	0.0	0.0	0.1	0.1	0.1
16+ Self-employed (Construction)	7.2	2.1	4.1	0.1	0.0	0.0	6.4	1.5	3.2
16+ Self-employed (Services)	59.8	17.4	33.8	32.9	4.1	9.5	56.6	13.8	28.4
16+ First Wage and Salary (5 sectors)	100	100	100	100	100	100	100	100	100
16+ Wage and Salary (Agriculture)	4.6	21.5	12.7	6.1	44.8	20.2	4.8	23.4	13.6
16+ Wage and Salary (Mining and Industry)	18.5	12.7	15.7	10.5	22.5	14.9	17.5	13.5	15.6
16+ Wage and Salary (Utilities)	1.8	0.9	1.4	0.3	0.1	0.3	1.6	0.8	1.3
16+ Wage and Salary (Construction)	28.3	42.6	35.2	1.8	3.6	2.5	24.8	39.3	31.6
16+ Wage and Salary (Services)	46.8	22.3	35.0	81.3	29.1	62.2	51.3	22.9	37.9

	Men			Women			Total		
	Urban	*Rural*	*All*	*Urban*	*Rural*	*All*	*Urban*	*Rural*	*All*
16+ First Self-employed and Wage and Salary (5 sectors)	100	100	100	100	100	100	100	100	100
16+ Self-employed and Wage and Salary (Agriculture)	11.7	50.0	32.5	15.4	76.5	55.6	12.2	55.1	36.2
16+ Self-employed and Wage and Salary (Mining and Industry)	15.1	7.8	11.2	19.3	13.9	15.8	15.7	9.0	11.9
16+ Self-employed and Wage and Salary (Utilities)	1.2	0.5	0.8	0.2	0.0	0.1	1.1	0.4	0.7
16+ Self-employed and Wage and Salary (Construction)	20.2	21.9	21.1	1.2	0.7	0.9	17.8	17.8	17.8
16+ Self-employed and Wage and Salary (Services)	51.7	19.8	34.4	63.9	8.9	27.6	53.3	17.7	33.3
16+ First Self-employed and Wage and Salary (3 sectors)	100	100	100	100	100	100	100	100	100
16+ Self-employed and Wage and Salary (Agriculture)	11.7	50.0	32.5	15.4	76.5	55.6	12.2	55.1	36.2

	Men			Women			Total		
	Urban	*Rural*	*All*	*Urban*	*Rural*	*All*	*Urban*	*Rural*	*All*
16+ Self-employed and Wage and Salary (Industry)	36.5	30.2	33.1	20.7	14.7	16.7	34.5	27.2	30.4
16+ Self-employed and Wage and Salary (Services)	51.7	19.8	34.4	63.9	8.9	27.6	53.3	17.7	33.3

Note: "First self-employed" implies the first job reported by the individual as being a self-employed job. Similarly, "First wage and salary" implies the first job reported by the individual as being a wage-and-salary job.

Source: 2009 Household Income and Expenditure Survey (HIES), Statistical Center of Iran.

Notes

Introduction

1. The Bretton Woods institutions, named after the locale of the 1944 conference where they were established, are the International Monetary Fund and the International Bank for Reconstruction and Development (World Bank). The Bretton Woods system was designed to harmonize international currencies and finance and to facilitate financing of reconstruction and development.
2. Rostow was the special assistant for national security affairs to the US president during the Kennedy and Johnson administrations.
3. Interestingly the article argues that emerging economies will have less debt than what used to be the First World. Moreover, 40 percent of trade is now between countries of the Global South—that is, South-South trade.
4. There is evidence that development has not categorically affected men positively. Chant and Gutmann (2001, p. 241) point out that young men of low income are more vulnerable to insecurity and marginalization, and in Latin American and Caribbean countries—and to a lesser extent in Southeast Asia—men are lagging behind women in education, while in Africa men are less able to provide for their wives and children.
5. There have been more documentation and programs to address male-female violence but none on male-male violence. Furthermore, to assume males are violent and females are nonviolent is simplistic.

Chapter 1

1. The idea of social capital and its relationship to the market dates back to the Enlightenment in the work of David Hume, who argued that "moral sense" or "sympathy" "would emerge . . . to support new forms of economic activity" (Woolcock 1998, p. 159).
2. Economic capital is defined as any material resource available to actors (Bourdieu 1986, p. 243). Family income, individual income, financial assets, and other forms of material resources define economic capital. Yet, in Bourdieu's theorizing of the social universe, economic resources are only one form of capital for positively conditioning

reward-generating actions. Cultural capital refers to the totality of skills and knowledge possessed by the actor, such as individual education, family education, and vocational training.

3. Employment opportunities and specific mental and physical skills demonstrate the significance of cultural capital. Bourdieu further specifies three forms of cultural capital: the embodied state, the objectified state, and the institutionalized state (Bourdieu 1986, p. 247). In the embodied state, cultural capital refers to an actor's mental and physical abilities to take action. Motivation, attitude, culture, and individual cultivation are also considered part of an embodied state of cultural capital.
4. For example, see Deniz Kandiyoti (1988) and Katharine Rankin (2002). The latter argues that this is equally true of Anglo middle-class women in the West.
5. The interviewee wished her name to remain anonymous.
6. Self Employed Women's Association website, http://www.sewa.org.
7. Green Belt Movement website, http://www.greenbeltmovement.org.
8. BRAC website, http://www.brac.net.
9. "SIX-S, Burkina Faso," http://www.iisd.org/50comm/commdb/desc/d12.htm.

CHAPTER 2

1. Post-Fordism is the mode of production and associated socioeconomic system theorized to be found in most industrialized countries today. It can be contrasted with Fordism, the productive method and socioeconomic system typified by Henry Ford's automobile plants, where workers worked on a production line, performing specialized tasks repetitively.
2. Spidla supports the notion of systematic discrimination when he discusses that although the European Commission finds the Turkish Constitution satisfactory when it comes to pay equity, progress is needed in terms of parental leave, equal pay, equal access to employment, and social security.
3. Women have faced resistance from men in the formal and informal sectors in hiring, the types of jobs women are assigned, and harassment while working. Egyptian women have witnessed a devaluing of their work in the feminization of certain jobs, which allow flexibility and are not too demanding so they are able to attend to their domestic duties (Chen, Vanek, and Carr 2004, p. 60). While such jobs allow women to attend to the very real duties of home and family, they are also low-paying, dead-end jobs. They are not careers and usually have nothing to do with women's training in school. This situation is found in both the informal and formal sectors, and as Elgeziri notes, even government industry is not immune to this line of thinking (Elgeziri 2010,

p. 13). This has worked as a push factor to send women into informal work to help their families economically, while they can still perform their traditional duties.

4. Ekhbar Eshteghal, "60% Faalan Mashaghel Zirsamini Daranad/ Mashaghel Zirsamini Panahgah Bikaran," *Hamikar*, accessed August 2011, http://www.hamikar.com/fa/guest/news/news/49.
5. http://iraneconomy.blogfa.com/post-79.aspx.
6. Furthermore, and as we will see reflected many times following, Rajai argues that women's roles in the informal economy are different than men's, and women face many more unique challenges than do their male counterparts, such as lack of child care and help with household duties while maintaining their own work (Lila Rajai 2008). In fact, F. E. Moghadam encounters this very obstacle in the advancement of women's careers in her study on women working in informal white-collar occupations in Tehran. Yet this is a much larger challenge for women of low-income households.
7. For a more elaborate discussion of the lack of female networks in the business community, Global Entrepreneurship Monitor has a very rich literature.

CHAPTER 3

1. "Iran," *Encyclopedia of the Nations*, http://www.nationsencyclopedia.com/economies/Asia-and-the-Pacific/Iran.html#ixzz1QcUh7qhW.
2. http://alef.ir/1388/content/view/109534, accessed July 2011.
3. "The Feminization of Poverty," UN Division for the Advancement of Women, accessed August 2011, http://www.un.org/womenwatch/daw/followup/session/presskit/fs1.htm.

CHAPTER 4

1. Solmaz then helped me look around the neighborhood for a sweatshop that, ironically, had male piece workers, including a teenage boy. I asked if I could take a picture. They agreed but were very nervous about being reported to authorities, as the sweatshop was illegal.
2. Here it should be noted that there are official female seminaries, such as Maktab Alzahra, which give a degree and are run by and through the Qum Centre for Religious Studies. Women can earn an undergraduate degree in theology and continue to do a master's degree. This is entirely theological and out of the domain of the state. But there are women preachers who do not hold a degree and are freelancers who become accepted by the community and, in some cases, even more popular that those who hold a degree from the official Theology School run by Qum. Although Mina was the only person to speak

negatively of credit clubs, it may be important to pay close attention to who is running the club, as there are doubtlessly cases of fraud.

3. The *Basijj* was the paramilitary volunteer force during the Iran-Iraq war, but more recently they have become known as the morality police.

CHAPTER 5

1. When I returned to Canada and travelled to the United States, I was driven by an Spanish female taxi driver who gave me a long history of how she has to deal with her job and how when her car breaks down she has to do it all by herself. Her main complaint was her lack of ability to pay her hospital bills. I thought to myself how similar it is for people in low-paid jobs throughout the world.
2. One of my colleagues whose son has just started primary school is constantly worried about his son in an atmosphere that he considers geared to encourage girls' education and activities. My colleague, a professor of international development with numerous books and a women's rights advocate, is nonetheless worried about how his own son might suffer from a girl-friendly atmosphere.
3. "The Missing Peace Symposium 2013: Sexual Violence in Conflict and Post-Conflict Settings," United States Institute of Peace, http://www.usip.org/events/the-missing-peace-symposium-2013.

CONCLUSION

1. Jay Newton-Small, "U.S. Sanctions Take a Toll on Iran's Currency," *Time*, October 2, 2012, http://swampland.time.com/2012/10/02/u-s-sanctions-take-a-toll-on-irans-currency.
2. Quebec's Quiet Revolution was a time of rapid social change between 1960 and 1966. The revolution was marked by a rejection of what many thought of as the three main components of French-Canadian values—agriculturalism, antistatism, and messianism—in favor of secularism and more liberal values.
3. Moharram is a Shi'a holy month that commemorates a historical battle between Hosein ibn Ali, grandson of the Prophet Mohammad, and Yazid, the second Caliph of the Umayyad dynasty in Damascus, who ruled 680–83. In Shi'a culture, Hosein and his resistance against the Umayyad Caliph's rule is a symbol of courage and standing for social justice.
4. One of the largest foundations, Bonyad Mostazafin belonged to the shah's family prior to the revolution. Currently it operates as a welfare organization and is semipublic with reported revenues of $10 billion in 2005. "Business: A Mess; Iranian Privatisation," *The Economist* (London), July 21, 2001. See also its *Middle East Explorer* entry: http://www.middleeastexplorer.com/Iran/Bonyad.

5. The latter are generic versions of Coca Cola and other types of nonalcoholic drinks, which are produced inside the country instead of being imported from abroad.
6. This is her exact wording, "my man," and I respected her by not asking whether this meant she was married to him permanently or this was a temporary marriage, since she did not call him "my husband."
7. Interview with Farahnaz Mozaffari, accessed 2013, http://karafarini.jkmt.ir/index.php?option=com_content&task=view&id=456&Itemid=80.
8. "Kandelous Historical Village: Green and Beautiful," January 6, 2011, http://english.irib.ir/radioculture/iran/tourism/item/77156-kandelous-historical-village-green and beautiful?tmpl=component&print=1.
9. "Seddighin Charity Foundation: Female Headed Households," accessed 2012, http://www.seddighin.com.

References

Abed, E. L., and A. M. R. Chowdhury. 1997. "The Bangladesh Rural Advancement Committee: How Brac Learned to Meet Rural People's Needs through Local Action." In *Reasons for Hope: Instructive Experiences in Rural Development*, edited by Anirudh Krishna, Norman Thomas Uphoff, and Milton Jacob Esman, 41–52. West Hartford, CT: Kumarian.

Abu-Lughod, Lila. 2001. "Oriental and Middle East Feminist Studies." *Feminist Studies* 1: 101.

Ackerly, Brooke. 1997. "What's in a Design? The Effects of NGO Choices on Women's Empowerment and on Family and Social Institutions in Bangladesh." In *Getting Institutions Right for Women in Development*, edited by Anne Marie Goetz, 140. London: Zed Books.

Afshar, Haleh. 1991. *Women, Development, and Survival in the Third World.* London: Longman.

———. 1996. "Islam and Feminism: An Analysis of Political Strategies." In *Feminism and Islam*, edited by Mai Yamani, 197. New York: New York University Press.

Afshar, Haleh, and Carolyne Dennis. 1992. *Women and Adjustment Policies in the Third World.* London: Macmillan.

Alizadeh, Parvin, and B. Harper. 2003. "The Feminization of the Labour Force in Iran." In *Iran Encountering Globalization: Problems and Prospects*, edited by Ali Mohammadi, 180. New York: Routledge.

Alloula, Malek. 1986. *Colonial Harem.* Minneapolis: University of Minnesota Press.

Amsden, Alice H. 1985. "The State and Taiwan's Economic Development." In *Bringing the State Back*, edited by Peter B. Evans, Dietrich Rueschemeyer, and Theda Skocpol. Cambridge, UK: Cambridge University Press.

Anderson, C. Leigh, Laura Locker, and Rachel Nugent. 2002. "Microcredit, Social Capital, and Common Pool Resources." *World Development* 30 (1): 95.

Anker, Richard. 2001. "Theories of Occupational Segregation by Sex: An Overview." In *Women, Gender and Work*, edited by Martha Fetherolf Loutfi, 129. Geneva: International Labour Office.

Appelbaum, Richard, and Jeffrey Henderson, eds. 1992. *States and Development in the Asian Pacific Rim.* Newbury Park, CA: Sage.

Ardener, Shirley, and Sandra Burman, eds. 1995. *Money-Go-Rounds: The Importance of Rotating Savings and Credit Associations for Women.* Oxford: Berg.

Arefnia, Khojasteh. 1993. "Eghtesad Girrasmi, Vagheiyah Nashenakhteh dar Tarh Masael Zanan Rostai." *Agricultural Economic Development* (Special Issue) 29: 4–12.

Arenius, Pia, Nan Langowitz, and Maria Minniti. 2005. *2004 Report on Women and Entrepreneurship*. Babson Park, MA: Center for Women's Leadership, Babson College, London Business School.

Armstrong, Karen. 2000. *Islam: A Short History*. New York: Modern Library.

Arrighi, Giovanni. 2007. *Adam Smith in Beijing: Lineages of the Twenty-First Century*. London: Verso.

Azkia, Mostafa. 2002. "Rural Society and Revolution, in Twenty Years of Islamic Revolution." In *Iran in Transition: Twenty Years of Social Change Since 1979*, edited by Eric Hooglund. Syracuse: Syracuse University Press.

Bahramitash, Roksana. 2005. *Liberation from Liberalization: Gender and Globalization in Southeast Asia*. London: Zed Books.

———. 2007. "Female Employment and Globalization during Iran's Reform Era (1997–2005)." *Journal of Middle East Women's Studies* 3 (2): 86.

———. 2011. "Female-Headed Households in Iran." In *Veiled Employment: Islamism and the Political Economy of Women's Employment in Iran*, edited by Roksana Bahramitash and Salehi-Esfahani. Syracuse: Syracuse University Press.

———. 2013a. "Women and Children Pay the Price of Smart Sanctions: What Is Next?" *Turkish Review* 3 (2): 148–52.

———. 2013b. "Women's Entrepreneurship." In *The Oxford Encyclopedia of Islam and Women*, edited by Natana DeLong-Bas. New York: Oxford University Press.

———. Forthcoming. *Social Economy and the Role of Low Income Religious Women in Iran*.

Bahramitash, Roksana, and Shahla Kazemipour. 2011. "Veiled Economy: Gender and the Informal Sector." In *Veiled Employment: Islamism and the Political Economy of Women's Employment in Iran*, edited by Roksana Bahramitash and Hadi Salehi-Esfahani. Syracuse: Syracuse University Press.

Bahramitash, Roksana, and Jennifer Olmsted. 2012a. "Women in the Informal Sector." International Feminist Economics Workshop for Special Issue on Women in the Muslim World, Barcelona, July.

Bahramitash, Roksana, and Jennifer Olmsted. 2012b. "Choice, Constraint and 'Liberating' Employment: Women's Work in Iran." Paper presented at International Feminist Economics Conference, Barcelona, July.

Bahramitash, Roksana, and Hadi Salehi-Esfahani. 2011. *Veiled Employment: Islamism and the Political Economy of Women's Employment in Iran*. Syracuse: Syracuse University Press.

Bahramitash, Roksana, Hadi Salehi-Esfahani, and Jennifer Olmsted. Forthcoming. "Gender and Entrepreneurship in Iran." *Critique: Journal of Middle Eastern Studies* Special Issue on Women in Iran.

Batterbury, S. P. J., and J. L. Fernando. 2004. "Amartya Sen." In *Key Thinkers on Space and Place*, edited by P. Hubbard, R. Kitchin, and G. Valentine, 251–57. London: Sage.

Bauer, Péter Tamás, Gerald M. Meier, and Dudley Seers, eds. 1984. *Pioneers in Development*. New York: Published for the World Bank, Oxford University Press.

Bayat, Asef. 1994. "Back-Street Politics: Squatters and the State in the Islamic Republic." *Middle Eastern Reports* 191: 10.

Beall, Jo, and Sean Fox. 2007. "Urban Poverty and Development in the 21st Century: Towards an Inclusive and Sustainable World." Oxfam Research Report, Development Studies Institute, London School of Economics.

Beck, Lois, and Nikki R. Keddie, eds. 1978. *Women in the Muslim World*. Cambridge, MA: Harvard University Press.

Beck, Lois, and Guity Nashat, eds. 2004. *Women in Iran from 1800 to the Islamic Republic*. Urbana: University of Illinois Press.

Becker, Kristina Flodman. 2004. "The Informal Economy: Fact Finding Study." Swedish International Development Cooperation Agency, Stockholm.

Behiels, M. D. 1985. *Prelude to Quebec's Quiet Revolution*. Montreal: McGill-Queen's University Press.

Benería, Lourdes. 1992. "Accounting for Women's Work: The Progress of Two Decades." *World Development* 20 (November): 1547.

Benería, Lourdes, and Maria S. Floro. 2004. "Labor Market Informalization and Social Policy: Distributional Links and the Case of Homebased Workers." Vassar College Economics Paper #60, Poughkeepsie, New York.

Benería, Lourdes, and Gita Sen. 1981. "Accumulation, Reproduction and Women's Role in Economic Development: Boserup Revisited." *Sign: Journal of Women in Culture and Society* 7: 279.

Bhowmik, Sharit K. 2005. "Street Vendors in Asia: A Review." *Economic and Political Weekly*, May 28–June 4.

Bidet, Éric. 1997. *L'Économie Sociale*. Paris: Le Monde-Editions.

Blumberg, Rae Lesser. 1998. "Income under Female versus Male Control: Hypotheses from a Theory of Gender Stratification and Data from the Third World." *Journal of Family Issues* 9 (1): 51–84.

Blumin, Stuart. 1989. *The Emergence of the Middle Class: Social Experience in the American City*. Cambridge, UK: Cambridge University Press.

Boserup, Ester. 1970. *Woman's Role in Economic Development*. London: Earthscan.

Bouchard, Marie, Giles L. Bouroue, and Benoît Lévesque. 2000. "L'évaluation De L'économie Sociale dans la Perspective des Nouvelles Formes De Régulation Socio-Économique ee L'intérêt Général." In *Cahiers du CRISES* 10.

Bourdieu, Pierre. 1977. *Outline of a Theory of Practice, Cambridge Studies in Social Anthropology*. Cambridge, UK: Cambridge University Press.

———. 1986. "The Forms of Capital." In *Handbook of Theory and Research for the Sociology of Education*, edited by J. Richardson, 241. New York: Greenwood.

Braudel, Fernand. 1975. *Capitalism and Material Life, 1400–1800*. New York: Harper and Row.

Braunstein, E. 2002. "Gender, FDI, and Women's Autonomy: A Research Note on Empirical Analysis." Working Paper (49) for the Political Economy Research Institute, University of Massachusetts, Amherst.

Brydon, Lynne, and Sylvia Chant. 1989. *Women in the Third World: Gender Issues in Rural and Urban Areas.* New Brunswick, NJ: Rutgers University Press.

Bulutay, Tuncer, and Enver Tasti. 2004. "Informal Sector in the Turkish Labour Market." Discussion paper, Turkish Economic Association, Ankara.

Çağatay, N., D. Elson, and C. Grown. 1995. "Gender, Adjustment and Macroeconomics." *World Development* 23 (11).

Calderon, Fernando, Alejandro Piscitelli, and Jose Luis Reyna. 1992. "Social Movements: Actors, Theories, Expectation." In *The Making of Social Movements in Latin America: Identity, Strategy and Democracy*, edited by Arturo Escobar and Sonia E. Alverez. Boulder: Westview Press.

Castells, Manuel. 1992. "Four Asian Tigers with a Dragon Head: A Comparative Analysis of the State, Economy, and Society in the Asian Pacific Rim." In *States and Development in the Asian Pacific Rim*, edited by Richard Appelbaum and Jeffery Henderson. Newbury Park, CA: Sage.

Castells, Manuel, and Alejandro Portes. 1989. "World Underneath: The Origins, Dynamics, and Effects of the Informal Economy." In *The Informal Economy: Studies in Advanced and Less Advanced Developed Countries*, edited by Alejandro Portes, Manuel Castells, and Lauren A. Benton, 11. Baltimore: Johns Hopkins University Press.

Chambers, R. 1994. "The Origins and Practice of Rural Appraisal." *World Development* 22 (7): 953.

Chant, Sylvia, and Matthew Gutmann. 2001. "Mainstreaming Men into Gender and Development: Debates, Reflections, and Experiences." *Oxfam Working Papers.*

Chant, Sylvia, and Cathy McIlwaine. 2008. *Geographies of Development in the 21st Century: An Introduction to the Global South.* Cheltenham, UK: Edward Elgar.

Chen, Martha. 1983. *A Quiet Revolution: Women in Transition in Rural Bangladesh.* Dhaka: Schenkman.

———. 2001. "Women in the Informal Sector: A Global Picture, the Global Movement." *SAIS Review* 21: 71.

Chen, Martha, Ralf Hussmanns, and Joann Vanek. 2012. "Measuring the Informal Economy: Concepts and Definitions." WIEGO Working Paper (Statistics) No. 2. http://wiego.org/informal-economy/concepts-definitions-methods.

Chen, Martha, Joann Vanek, and Marilyn Carr. 2004. *Mainstreaming Informal Employment and Gender in Poverty Reduction: A Handbook for Policymakers and Other Stakeholders, New Gender Mainstreaming Series on Development Issues.* Ottawa: International Development Research Centre.

Chen, Martha, Joann Vanek, and James Heintz. 2006. "Informality, Gender and Poverty: A Global Picture." *Economic and Political Weekly* 41 (21): 2131.

Clift, Jeremy. 2003. "Hearing the Dogs Bark: Jeremy Clift Interviews Development Guru Hernando De Soto." *Finance & Development*, December.

Cunningham, Robert B. 1992. "Fostering Community: A Significant Role for the Medina Souq." *Arab Studies Quarterly* 14 (Winter): 61.

Davutyan, Nurhan. 2008. "Estimating the Size of Turkey's Informal Sector: An Expenditure-Based Approach." *Journal of Economic Policy Reform* 11 (4): 261. doi:10.1080/17487870802598393.

Defourny, Jacques, and Patrick Develtere. 1999. "The Social Economy: The Worldwide Making of a Third Sector." In *L'economie Sociale au Nord et au Sud*, edited by Jacques Defourny, Patrick Develtere, and Bénédicte Fronteneau, 25. Bruxelles: De Boeck Universite.

Demoustier, Daniéle, and Damien Rousseliere. 2006. "Social Economy as Social Science and Practice: Historical Perspectives on France." In *Ethics and the Market: Insights from Social Economics*, edited by Besty Jane Clary, Wilfred Dolfsma, and Dehorah M. Figart. New York: Routledge.

De Soto, Hernando. 1989. *The Other Path: The Invisible Revolution in the Third World.* Scarborough: HarperCollins.

Dignard, Louise, and José Havet. 1995. *Women in Micro- and Small-Scale Enterprise Development.* Boulder: Westview Press.

The Economist. 2010. "Seeing the World Differently: The Poor World Has Changed Fundamentally. Others Are Barely Coming to Grips with the Implications." June 10.

Edelman, Marc, and Angelique Haugerud, eds. 2005. *The Anthropology of Development and Globalization: From Classical Political Economy to Contemporary Neoliberalism.* Oxford: Wiley-Blackwell.

Edwards, Bob, and Michael W. Foley. 1998. "Civil Society and Social Capital beyond Putnam." *American Behavioral Scientist* 42 (1): 124.

Elgeziri, Moushira. 2010. "Wading through Treacle: Female Commercial School Graduates (CSGs) in Egypt's Informal Economy." *Feminist Formations* 22 (3): 10.

Elson, Diane. 1993. "Gender Aware Analysis and Development Economics." *Journal of International Development* 5 (2): 176.

Elson, Diane, and Nilufer Çağatay. 2000. "The Social Content of Macroeconomic Policies." *World Development* 28 (7): 1347.

Escobar, A. 1995. *Encountering Development: The Making and Unmaking of the Third World, Princeton Studies in Culture/Power/History.* Princeton, NJ: Princeton University Press.

Escobar, A., and S. Alvarez, eds. *The Making of Social Movements in Latin America.* Oxford: Westford.

Escobar Latapi, A. 1998. "Los hombres y sus historias: Reestructuracion y masculinidad en Mexcio." *La Ventana* 5: 122–73.

Esim, Simel. 2000. "Solidarity in Isolation: Urban Informal Sector Women's Economic Organizations in Turkey." *Middle Eastern Studies* 36 (1): 140.

Evans, Peter B. 1995. *Embedding Autonomy*. Princeton, NJ: Princeton University Press.

Evans, Peter B., Dietrich Rueschemeyer, and Theda Skocpol, eds. 1985. *Bringing the State Back*. Cambridge, UK: Cambridge University Press.

Fairbanks, S. C. 2005. "Iran." *Countries at the Crossroads 2005*. Washington, DC: Freedom House.

Feige, Edgar. 1990. "Defining and Estimating Underground and Informal Economies: The New Institutional Approach." *World Development* 18 (7): 989–1002.

Ferguson, James. 1999. *Expectations of Modernity: Myths and Meanings of Urban Life on the Zambian Copperbelt*. Berkeley: University of California Press.

Finlay, Barbara. 2006. *George W. Bush and the War on Women: Turning Back the Clock on Progress*. London: Zed Books.

Food and Agriculture Organisation (FAO). 2003. *The State of Food Insecurity in the World 2003*. Rome: FAO.

Fox, Alan. 1974. *Beyond Contact: Work Power and Trust Relations*. London: Faber and Faber.

Frank, Andre Gunder. 1971. *Capitalism and Underdevelopment in Latin America: Historical Studies of Chile and Brazil*. New York: Monthly Review Press.

Friedl, Erika. 1997. *Children of Deh Koh: Young Life in an Iranian Village*. 1st ed. Syracuse: Syracuse University Press.

Fukuyama, Francis. 1995. *Trust: Social Virtues and the Creation of Prosperity*. New York: Free Press.

Gaiger, L. I. 2000. "Solidary Popular Economy in Third-Sector Horizon." Paper presented at the International Society for Third Sector Research (ISTR) Fourth International Conference, Dublin.

Gallaway, Julia H., and Alexandra Bernasek. 2002. "Gender and Informal Sector Employment in Indonesia." *Journal of Economic Issues* 36 (2): 313–21.

Gamari-Tabrizi, Behrooz. 2009. "When Life Will No Longer Barter Itself: In Defense of Foucault on the Iranian Revolution." In *A Foucault for the 21st Century: Governmentality, Biopolitics and Discipline in the New Millennium*, edited by Sam Binkley. New Castle, UK: Cambridge Scholars Publishing.

Geertz, Clifford. 1956. *The Rotating Credit Association: A "Middle Rung" in Development*. Cambridge, MA: MIT, Center for International Studies.

Goetz, Anne-Maria, and Rina Sen Gupta. 1996. "Who Takes the Credit? Gender, Power, Control over Loan Use in Rural Credit Program in Bangladesh." *World Development* 24 (1): 45.

Goldin, C. 1994. "The U-Shaped Female Labour Force Function in Economic Development and Economic History." Working Paper No. 4707, National Bureau of Economic Research, Cambridge, Massachusetts.

Grant, William J., and Hugh Allen. 2002. "Care's Mata Matsu Dubara (Women on the Move) Program in Niger." *Journal of Microfinance* (Brigham Young School of Business) (Fall).

Greve, Arent, and Janet W. Salaff. 2003. "Social Networks and Entrepreneurship." *Entrepreneurship: Theory and Practice* 28 (1): 1.

Grootaert, Christiaan, and Thierry van Bastelaer. 2001. "Measuring Social Capital: A Synthesis of Findings and Recommendations from Social Capital Initiative." *Social Capital Initiative Working Papers*, World Bank.

Güendel, Ludwig, and Mauricio González. 1998. "Integration, Human Rights and Social Policy in the Context of Human Poverty." In *Adolescence, Child Rights and Urban Policy in Costa Rica*, edited by UNICEF. San Jose: UNICEF/HABITAT.

Gugerty, Mary Kay. 2005. "You Can't Save Alone: Commitment in Rotating Savings and Credit Associations in Kenya." Daniel J. Evans School of Public Affairs, University of Washington.

Gurevich, Michael. 1961. *The Social Structure of Acquaintanceship Networks*. Boston: MIT Press.

Gutberlet, Jutta. 2005. "Co-Management of Urban Solid Waste Resources: Experiences and Challenges from Sao Paulo, Brazil." Paper read at Impacts environnementaux et socio-économiques des options de valorisation des déchets solides municipaux pour les collectivités de petite et moyenne taille, Séminaire regional, Rabat, Morocco, June 1–2.

Haghighat-Sordellini, Elhum. 2011. "Iran within a Regional Context: Socio-Demographic Transformation and Effects on Women's Status." In *Gender in Contemporary Iran: Pushing the Boundaries*, edited by Roksana Bahramitash and Eric Hooglund. New York: Routledge.

Hakim, Catherine. 2000. *Research Design: Successful Designs for Social and Economic Research*. 2nd ed. Social Research Today Series. London: Routledge.

———. 2003. "Competing Family Models: Competing Social Policies." *Family Matters* 64 (Autumn): 52.

———. 2006. *Work-Lifestyle Choices in the 21st Century: Preference Theory*. Oxford: Oxford University Press.

Hall, Stuart. 1996. *Modernity: An Introduction to Modern Societies*, edited by Stuart Hall, David Held, Don Huber and Kenneth Thompson. Malden, MA: The Open University.

Halliday, Fred. 1979. *Iran, Dictatorship and Development*. Harmondsworth, UK: Penguin.

Halper, Louise. 2005. "Law and Women's Agency in Post-Revolutionary Iran." *Harvard Journal of Law and Gender* 28, no. 1 (Winter): 85.

Haraway, Donna Jeanne. 1991. *Simians, Cyborgs, and Women: The Reinvention of Nature*. London: Routledge.

Harding, Sandra G. 1986. *Is Science Multicultural?: Postcolonialisms, Feminisms, and Epistemologies*. Bloomington: Indiana University Press.

Hasso, F. S. 2005. "Problems and Promise in Middle East and North Africa Gender Research." *Feminist Studies* 31 (3): 653.

Hearn, Jeff. 1998a. "Troubled Masculinities in Social Policy Discourses: Young Men." In *Men, Gender Divisions and Welfare*, edited by J. Edwards, J. Hearn, and J. Popay. London: Routledge.

———. 1998b. *The Violence of Men*. London: Sage.

Hobsbawm, Eric. 1999. *The Age of Revolution: Europe 1789–1848*. New York: New American Library.

Hoodfar, Homa. 1997. *Between Marriage and the Market: Intimate Politics and Survival in Cairo*. Berkeley: University of California Press.

Hoodfar, Homa, and Diane Singerman, eds. 1996. *Development, Change, and Gender in Cairo: A View from the Household*. Bloomington: Indiana University Press.

Hooglund, Eric. 1982. *Land and Revolution in Iran, 1960–1980*. Austin: University of Texas Press.

———. 1989. "Iran." In *Intervention in the 1980s: U.S. Foreign Policy in the Third World*, edited by Peter Schraeder. Boulder: Lynne Rienner.

———. 2002. *Iran in Transition: Twenty Years of Social Change since 1979*. Syracuse: Syracuse University Press.

Horn, Zoë. 2010. "No Cushion to Fall Back On: Global Recession and the Informally Employed Women in the Global South." *Women's Policy Journal of Harvard* 7: 23.

Husseini, Randa. 1997. "Promoting Women Entrepreneurs in Lebanon: The Experience of Unifem." *Gender and Development* 5 (1): 49–53.

Inkeles, Alex. 1969. "Making Men Modern: On the Causes and Consequences of Individual Change in Six Developing Countries." *American Journal of Sociology* 75 (2): 208–25.

International Institute for Sustainable Development. 2013. *Six S (Se Servir De La Saison Sèche En Savane Et Au Sahel)*. Winnipeg: International Institute for Sustainable Development.

International Labour Office (ILO). 2002a. "Decent Work and the Informal Economy." International Labour Conference, Geneva.

———. 2002b. "Women and Men in the Informal Economy: A Statistical Picture." International Labour Conference, Geneva.

———. 2011. "Statistical Update on Employment in the Informal Economy." Geneva: ILO.

Jackson, Cecile. 2001. *Men at Work: Labour, Masculinities, Development*. London: Routledge.

JahanNews. 2010. "Ministry of Co-Operative Self-Employment Loans to Women Entrepreneur's Households." http://www.jahannews.com/vdcgwt9q7ak9wz4.rpra.html.

Jamal, Firozeh, Mirsatar Saddr Mosavi, and Parvin Dokht Libarjani. 2009. "Barresi Vigeghihayeh Ejemai-Eghtesadi Shaghela Ghirrasmi dar Madarshahr Tabriz (Nemoneh Moredi Sabzeh Meydan)." *Geography and Planning Publication* (Tabriz University Press) 29: 78–115.

Joekes, Susan P. 1987. *Women in the World Economy: An Instraw Study*. New York: Oxford University Press.

Jomehpoor, Mahmood. 2001. "Mashagel Gherey Rasmi Be Onvan Yek Masaeh Shahri Va Abad Ejtemai Va Eghtesadi Aan." *Social Science Quarterly* 15 (16): 69–97.

Kabeer, Naila. 1994. *Reversed Realities: Gender Hierarchies in Development Thought*. London: Verso.

Kalaycıoğlu, Sibel. 2006. "Dynamics of Poverty in Turkey: From a Specific Focus on Welfare System and Social Inclusion in Turkey, to Combat Rural/Urban Poverty, and the Significance of Social Networks and Reciprocal Survival Strategies." *Internet Journal for Cultural Sciences* 16 (June): http://www.inst.at/trans/16Nr/01_3/kalaycioglu16.htm.

Kandiyoti, Deniz. 1988. "Bargaining with Patriarchy." *Gender and Society* 2 (3): 274.

Kapoor, A. 2007. "The Sewa Way: Shaping Another Future for Informal Labour." *Futures* 39: 554.

Kapoor, I. 2004. "Hyper-Self-Reflexive Development? Spivak on Representing the Third World 'Other.'" *Third World Quarterly* 25 (4): 627.

Karimi, Zahra. 2011. "The Effects of International Trade on Gender Inequality in Iran: The Case of Women Carpet Weavers." In *Veiled Employment: Islamism and the Political Economy of Women's Employment in Iran*, edited by Roksana Bahramitash, Hadi Salehi-Esfahani. Syracuse: Syracuse University Press.

Kazemipour Sabet, Shahla. 2007. *Ezdeag and Talagh Javanan Keshvar 1385*. Tehran: Regional Centre for Population Studies and Research on Asian and the Pacific.

Keddie, Nikki R. 2007. *Women in the Middle East: Past and Present*. Princeton, NJ: Princeton University Press.

Keshavarzian, Arang. 2007. *Bazaar and State in Iran: The Politics of the Tehran Marketplace*. Cambridge, UK: Cambridge University Press.

Khosrokhavar, Farhad. 2011. "Post-Revolutionary Iranian Youth: The Case of Qom and the New Culture of Ambivalence." In *Gender in Contemporary Iran: Pushing the Boundaries*, edited by Roksana Bahramitash and Eric Hooglund. New York: Routledge.

Kian, Azadeh. 1995. "Gendered Occupation and Women's Status in Post-Revolutionary Iran." *Middle Eastern Studies* 31, no. 3 (July): 407.

———. 2002. *Les Femmes Iraniennes Entre Islam, Etat Et Famille*. Paris: Maisonneuve et Larose.

King, Richard, and Caroline Sweetman. 2010. "Gender Perspectives on the Global Economic Crisis." *Gender and Development: Oxfam Discussion Papers* (February): 18.

Klein, Emilio, and Victor Tokman. 1988. "Sector informal: Una forma de utilizar el trabajo como consequencia de la manera de producir y no viceversa." *Estudios Sociologicos* 6: 205.

Krishna, Anirudh, Norman Thomas Uphoff, and Milton Jacob Esman, eds. 1997. *Reasons for Hope: Instructive Experience in Rural Development*. West Hartford, CT: Kumarian.

Krueger, Anne O. 1974. "The Political Economy of the Rent-Seeking Society." *American Economic Review* 64: 302.

Kümbetoğlu, Belkıs, İnci User, and Aylin Akpınar. 2010. "Unregistered Women Workers in the Globalized Economy: A Qualitative Study in Turkey." *Feminist Formations* 22 (3): 96.

Lecomte, Bernard J. 1986. *Project Aid: Limitations and Alternatives.* Paris: Development Centre for Economic Cooperation and Development.

Lehsayi-Zadeh, Abdolai, and Afsaneh Omidi. 2001. "Baresy Jayghah Zanan Dar Eghtesad Ghireh Rasmi." In *Women in Development and Politics.* Tehran: Center for Research on Women.

Lévesque, Benoît, Marie-Claire Malo, and Jean-Pierre Girard. 1999. "L'ancienne et la Nouvelle Économie Sociale: Le Cas du QuéBec." In *L'économie sociale au Nord et au Sud*, edited by Jacques Defourny, Patrick Develtere, and Bénédicte Defourny, 195–216. Bruxelles: De Boeck Supérieur.

Levy, Marion J., Jr. 1972. . New York: Basic Books.

Lewis, Reina. 1996. *Gendering Orientalism: Race, Femininity, and Representation.* New York: Routledge.

Lewis, Reina, and Sara Mills. 2003. *Feminist Postcolonial Theory: A Reader.* Edinburgh: Edinburgh University Press.

Leyshon, Andrew, Roger Lee, and Colin C. Williams, eds. 2003. *Alternative Economic Spaces.* London: Sage.

Lila Rajai, Parvin Dokhit. 2008. *Baresy Vigeghihayeh Mashaghel Bakhsh Ghyre Rasmi Dar Madar Shahr Tabriz.* Tabriz: Tabriz University.

Linteau, P. A. 1983. *Quebec: A History, 1867–1929.* Toronto: James Lormier.

Longino, Helen. 1986. "Can There Be a Feminist Science?" *Hypatia* 2 (3): 51.

———. 1990. "Gender Politics and Theoretical Virtues." *Synthese* 104: 383–97.

———. 1995a. "Moral Agency and the Sciences of Mind." In *Minds and Morals*, edited by Larry May, Marilyn Friedman, and Andy Clark. Cambridge, MA: MIT Press.

———. 1995b. "To See Feelingly: Reason, Passion and Dialogue in Feminist Philosophy." In *Feminisms in the Academy: Rethinking the Disciplines*, edited by Donna Stanton and Abigail Stewart. Ann Arbor: University of Michigan Press.

———. 1997. "Feminist Epistemology as a Local Epistemology." *Aristotelian Society Supplementary* 71 (1): 19.

Longino, Helen, and Evelyn Keller Fox. 1996. *Feminism and Science.* Oxford Readings in Feminism Series. Oxford: Oxford University Press.

Losby, J., J. F. Else, M. E. Kingslow, E. L. Edgcomb, E. T. Malm, and V. Kao. 2002. *Informal Economy Literature Review.* Washington, DC: Aspen Institute.

Loutfi, Martha Fetherolf. 2001. *Women, Gender and Work: What Is Equality and How Do We Get There?* Geneva: International Labour Office.

Lovell, Catherine H. 1992. *Breaking the Cycle of Poverty: The Brac Strategy.* West Hartford, CT: Kumarian.

Loxley, John, and Dan Simpson. 2007. "Government Policies Towards Community Economic Development and the Social Economy in Quebec and Manitoba." Report prepared for the Northern Ontario, Manitoba, and Saskatchewan Regional Node of the Social Economy Suite.

Mair, J., and I. Marti. 2006. "Social Entrepreneurship Research: A Source of Explanation, Prediction and Delight." *Journal of World Business* 41: 36.

Mansoor, Ali M. 1999. "The Informal Sector: What Is It Worth?" *Waterlines* 17 (3): 10.

Mason, Andrew, and Elizabeth King. 2001. "Engendering Development through Gender Equality in Rights, Resource, and Voice." In *A World Bank Policy Research Report.* Washington, DC: World Bank.

Mayoux, Linda. 1995. "Alternative Development or Utopian Fantasy: Women and Cooperative Development in India." *Journal of International Development* 7 (2): 211.

———. 2001. "Tackling the Down Side: Social Capital, Women's Empowerment and Micro-Finance, in Cameroon." *Development and Change* 32 (3): 435.

McMurtry, John-Justin. 2009. *Living Economics: Canadian Perspectives on the Social Economy, Co-Operatives, and Community Economic Development.* Toronto: Edmond Montgomery Publications.

Medina, Martin. 1997. *Informal Recycling and Collection of Solid Wastes in Developing Countries: Issues and Opportunities.* Tokyo: United Nations University, Institute of Advanced Studies.

———. 2003. *Serving the Unserved: Informal Refuse Collection in Mexican Cities.* Collaborative Working Group on Solid Waste Management.

Mehran, Golnar. 2003. "The Paradox of Tradition and Modernity in Female Education in the Islamic Republic of Iran." *Comparative Education Review* 4 (3): 269.

Melluci, Alberto. 1988. "Getting Involved: Identity and Mobilization in Social Movements." In *From Structure to Action: Comparing Social Movement Research across Cultures,* edited by Bert Klandermans, Hanspeter Kriesi, and Sidney Tarrow, 329. Greenwich: International Social Movement Research, JAI.

Mendell, M. 2002. "The Social Economy in Quebec: Discourses and Strategies." In *Critical Political Studies: Debates and Dialogues from the Left; Essays from a Conference Held in Honour of Colin Leys,* edited by C. Leys, A. Bakan and E. MacDonald. Montreal: McGill-Queen's University Press.

Milgram, Stanley. 1967. "The Small World Problem." *Psychology Today* 2: 60.

Minh-Ha, Trinh T. 1989. *Woman, Native, Other: Writing Postcoloniality and Feminism.* Indianapolis: Indiana University Press.

Moallam, Minoo. 2005. *Between Warrior Brother and Veiled Sister: Islamic Fundamentalism and the Politics of Patriarchy.* Berkeley: University of California Press.

Moghadam, Fatemeh Etemad. 2004. "Women and Labour in the Islamic Republic of Iran." In *Women in Iran*, edited by Lois Beck and Guity Nashat, 136. Chicago: University of Illinois Press.

———. 2007. "Women, Gender and Informal Sector: Iran." In *Encyclopedia of Women and Islamic Cultures.* Leiden: Brill Academic Publishers.

———. 2009. "Undercounting Women's Work in Iran." *Iranian Studies* 42 (1): 16.

———. 2011. "Iran's Missing Working Women." In *Veiled Employment: Islamism and the Political Economy of Women's Employment in Iran*, edited by Roksana Bahramitash and Hadi Salehi-Esfahani. Syracuse: Syracuse University Press.

Moghadam, Valentine. 1988. "Women, Work, and Ideology in the Islamic Republic." *International Journal of Middle East Studies* 20 (2): 221.

———. 1995. "Women's Employment Issues in Contemporary Iran: Problems and Prospects in the 1990s." *Iranian Studies* 28 (3–4): 175.

Mohanty, Chandra T. 2003. *Feminism without Borders: Decolonizing Theory, Practicing Solidarity.* Durham, NC: Duke University Press.

Mohseni, Manuchehr. 2000. *Study of Awareness, Attitudes, and Socio-Cultural Behavior in Iran.* Tehran: Secretariat of Public Culture of Iran.

Molyneux, Maxine. 2002. "Gender and the Silences of Social Capital: Lessons from Latin America." *Development and Change* 33: 167.

Moore, Henrietta. 1994. "Is There a Crisis in the Family?" In *World Summit of Social Development*, edited by O. P. Geneva: UNRISD.

Moreno-Sanchez, Rocio Del Pilar, and Jorge Higinio Maldonado. 2006. "Surviving from Garbage: The Role of Informal Waste-Pickers in a Dynamic Model of Solid-Waste Management in Developing Countries." *Environment and Development Economics* 11: 371.

Moser, Caroline O. 1989. "The Impact of Recession and Adjustment at the Micro Level: Low Income Women and Their Households in Guayaguil, Ecuador." In *The Invisible Adjustment: Poor Women and the Economic Crisis.* New York: UNICEF.

———. 1993. *Gender Planning and Development: Theory, Practice, and Training.* London: Routledge.

Moslem, Mehdi. 2002. *Factional Politics in Post-Khomeini Iran.* 1st ed. Modern Intellectual and Political History of the Middle East Series. Syracuse: Syracuse University Press.

Moss, Laurence S., and Andrew Savchenko. 2006. *Talcott Parsons: Economist Sociologist of the 20th Century.* Malden, MA: Blackwell.

Moulaert, Frank, and Oana Ailenei. 2005. "Social Economy, Third Sector and Solidarity Relations: A Conceptual Synthesis from History to Present." *Urban Studies* 42 (11): 2037.

Nahavandi, M., and S. Ajavarlo. 2009. "*Motaleh Vaziateh Zanan Sarparast Khanevar Ba Takid Bar Zanan-E Dast Forosh-E Metro*: Research on Metro

Vendor Female Heads of Households." Paper read at Empowerment and Capacity Building of Female Heads of Households, Tehran.

Nayeb, Said. 2001. "Baresi Sakhtar Bazar Dar Ghyr Rasmi Iran." Paper read at Iranian Economy, Tehran, University of Tarbeyat Moalem.

Neamtan, Nancy. 2005. "The Social Economy: Finding a Way between the Market and the State." *Policy Options* (July-August): 71–76.

Nguyen, Van V. 1949. *Saving and Mutual Banking Societies.* New Haven, CT: Yale University, South East Asian Studies.

Niger-Thomas, Margaret. 1995. "Women's Access to and the Control of Credit through ROSCAs in Cameroon: The Manfe Case." In *Money-Go-Rounds: The Importance of Rotating Savings and Credit Associations for Women*, edited by Shirley Ardener and Sandra Burman. Oxford: Berg.

Nomani, Farhad, and Sohrab Behdad. 2006. *Class and Labor in Iran: Did the Revolution Matter?* 1st ed. Modern Intellectual and Political History of the Middle East Series. Syracuse: Syracuse University Press.

OECD Yearbook 2012: Better Policies for Better Lives. Paris: OECD.

Olmsted, Jennifer. 2005. "Is Paid Work the (Only) Answer? Women's Well-Being, Neoliberalism and the Social Contract in Southwest Asia and North Africa." *Journal of Middle East Women's Studies* 2 (1): 112.

———. 2011. "Gender and Globalization: The Iranian Experience." In *Veiled Employment: Islamism and the Political Economy of Women's Employment in Iran*, edited by Roksana Bahramitash and Hadi Salehi-Esfahani. Syracuse: Syracuse University Press.

Oppenheimer, Valarie Kincade. 1970. *The Female Labour Force in the United States: Demographic and Economic Factors Governing Its Growth and Changing Composition.* Population Monograph Series. Berkeley: Institute of International Studies of the University of California.

Paguntalan, Aileen May C. 2002. *Nimble Fingers, Clenched Fists: Dynamics of Structure Agency and Women's Spaces in a Manufacturing Company.* Quezon City: UP-Center for Women's Studies and the University of Michigan.

Paidar, Parvin. 1995. *Women and the Political Process in Twentieth-Century Iran.* Cambridge Middle East Studies Series. Cambridge, UK: Cambridge University Press.

Palmer, I. 1992. "Gender, Equity and Economic Efficiency in Adjustment Models." In *Women and Adjustment Policies in the Third World*, edited by Haleh Afshar and Carolyne Dennis, 69. London: Macmillan.

Pantaleo, Katie. 2006. "Gendered Violence: Murder in the Maquiladoras." *Sociological Viewpoint* 13 (Fall): 13–23.

Pearce, J. 1999. *Epose Regional Report—Community Business Scotland Network.* Edinburgh: CBS.

Pearson, Ruth. 1997. "Renegotiating the Reproductive Bargain: Gender Analysis and Economic Transition in Cuba in the 1990s." *Development and Change* 28 (4): 671.

Peet, Richard, and Elaine Hartwick. 1999. *Theories of Development.* 1st ed. New York: Guilford Press.

Peredo, Ana Maria, and James J. Chrisman. 2006. "Toward a Theory of Community-Based Enterprise." *Academy of Management Review* 31 (2): 309.

Polanyi, Karl. 1957. *The Great Transformation: The Political and Economic Origins of Our Time.* Boston: Beacon Press.

Portes, Alejandro. 1998. "Social Capital: Its Origins and Applications in Modern Sociology." *Annual Review of Sociology* 24: 1.

Portes, Alejandro, and William Haller. 2005. "The Informal Economy." In *The Handbook of Economic Sociology*, edited by Neil J. Smelser and Richard Swedberg. Princeton, NJ: Princeton University Press.

Portes, Alejandro, and Julia Sensenbrenner. 1993. "Embeddedness and Immigration: Notes on the Social Determinants of Economic Action." *American Journal of Sociology* 98: 1320.

Povey, Elaheh Rostami. 2001. "Feminist Contestations of Institutional Domains in Iran." *Feminist Review* 69: 44.

———. 2005. "Women and Work in Iran (Part 1)." Stateofnature.org. http://www.stateofnature.org/?p=5243.

Poya, Maryam. 1999. *Women, Work and Islamism: Ideology and Resistance in Iran.* London: Zed Books.

Putnam, Robert. 1993. *Making Democracy Work: Civic Tradition in Modern Italy.* Princeton, NJ: Princeton University Press.

———. 1995. "Tuning In, Tuning Out: The Strange Disappearance of Social Capital in America." *Political Science and Politics* 28 (4): 664.

Quarter, J. 1992. *Canada's Social Economy: Co-operatives, Non-profits, and Other Community Enterprises.* Toronto: James Lorimer.

Quarter, J., L. Mook, and A. Armstrong. 2009. *Understanding the Social Economy: A Canadian Perspective.* Toronto: University of Toronto Press.

Rahnema, Said. 1996. *Rebirth of Social Democracy in the Iranian Left Movement.* Stockholm: Baran Book Ferlag.

Ranani, Mohsen. 2001a. "Tarh Nizsanji Niroyeh Motekases va Sisatgozari Toseeh Manbeh Ensani Keshvar." Research paper for Center for Research and High Education Policy, Tehran, Iran.

———. 2001b. "Sakhtar Eshteghal dar Baekhsh Ghireh Rasmi Keshvar" *Economic Journal* 49–50: 21.

Rankin, Katharine N. 2002. "Social Capital, Microfinance and the Politics of Development." *Feminist Economics* 8 (1): 1.

Reynolds, Paul D., William D. Bygrave, and Erkko Autio. 2004. *Gem 2003 Global Report.* Babson Park, MA: Global Entrepreneurship Monitor, Babson College, London Business School.

Rifkin, Jeremy. 1995. *The End of Work: The Decline of the Global Labor Force and the Dawn of the Post-Market Era.* New York: G. P. Putnam's Sons.

Roldan, M. 1988. "Renegotiating the Marital Contract: Intra-Household Patterns of Money Allocation and Women's Subordination among Domestic

Outworkers in Mexico City." In *In a House Divided: Women and Income in the Third World*, edited by D. Dwyer and J. Bruce, 229. Stanford, CA: Stanford University Press.

Roy, O. 1994. *The Failure of Political Islam.* Cambridge, MA: Harvard University Press.

Ruwanpura, K. N. 2008. "Separating Spaces? Ethno-Gendering Social Networks" *Contemporary South Asia* 16 (4): 413.

Safa, Helen I. 2005. *The Myth of the Male Breadwinner: Women and Industrialization in the Caribbean.* Boulder: Westview Press.

Said, Edward W. 1979. *Orientalism.* 1st Vintage Books ed. New York: Vintage Books.

Salamon, Lester M., and Helmut K. Anheier. 1995. *The Emerging Nonprofit Sector: The Nonprofit Sector in Comparative Perspective: An Overview.* Baltimore: Johns Hopkins University Press.

Salehi-Isfahani, Djavad. 2005. *Labor Force Participation of Women in Iran: 1987–2001.* Blacksburg: Virginia Tech Department of Economics.

Sanders, Jimy, Victor Nee, and Scott Sernau. 2002. "Asian Immigrants' Reliance on Social Ties in a Multiethnic Labor Market." *Social Forces* 81 (1): 281.

Sassen, Saskia. 1997. "Informalization in Advanced Market Economies." In *Issues in Development Discussion Paper.* Geneva: International Labour Office.

Schuler, Sidney Ruth, Syed M. Hashemi, and Shamsul Huda Badal. 1998. "Men's Violence against Women in Rural Bangladesh: Undermined or Exacerbated by Microcredit Programmes?" *Development in Practice* 8 (2): 148.

Schuurman, Frans J. 2003. "Social Capital: The Politico-Emancipatory Potential of a Disputed Concept." *Third World Quarterly* 24 (6): 991.

Sekhavati, M. 2004. "Women's Poverty in Iran." *Defenders' Newsletter.*

Seljak, David. 2006. "Resisting the 'No Man's Land' of Private Religion: The Catholic Church and Public Politics in Quebec." *Religion and Canadian Society: Traditions, Transitions, and Innovations*, edited by L. G. Beaman. Toronto: Canadian Scholar's Press.

Sen, Amartya. 1990. "Gender and Cooperative Conflicts." In *Persistent Inequalities: Women and World Development*, edited by Irene Tinker, 123. Oxford: Oxford University Press.

Sen, Gita, and Caren Grown. 1987. *Development, Crises, and Alternative Visions: Third World Women's Perspectives.* New Feminist Library Series. New York: Monthly Review Press.

Sethuraman, S. V., ed. 1981. *The Urban Informal Sector in Developing Countries: Employment, Poverty and Environment.* Geneva: International Labour Office.

———. 1995. *The Rural Informal Sector in Asia: Policies and Strategies.* Geneva: International Labour Office.

Shaditalab, Jaleh. 2005. "Iranian Women: Rising Expectation." *Critical Journal of Middle Eastern Studies* 14 (1): 35.

Singerman, Diane. 2006. "Restoring the Family to Civil Society: Lessons from Egypt." *Journal of Middle East Women's Studies* 2 (1): 1.

Skocpol, Theda. 1985. "Bringing the State Back In: Strategies of Analysis in Current Research." In *Bringing the State Back*, edited by Peter B. Evans, Dietrich Rueschemeyer, and Theda Skocpol, 33. Cambridge, UK: Cambridge University Press.

Smelser, Neil J., and Richard Swedberg, eds. 2005. *The Handbook of Sociology.* Princeton, NJ: Princeton University Press.

Sparr, Pam, ed. 1994. *Mortgaging Women's Lives: Feminist Critiques of Structural Adjustment.* London: Zed Books.

Spidla, Vladimir. 2012. "Empowering Women in Turkey: A Priority in the Pre-Accession Progress." European Stability Initiative. http://www.esiweb.org/pdf/esi_turkey_tpq_id_83.pdf.

Spivak, Gayatri Chakravorty. 1988. "Can the Sub-Altern Speak?" In *Marxism and the Interpretation of Culture*, edited by Cary Nelson and Lawrence Grossberg. Urbana: University of Illinois Press.

St. Martin, Kevin. 2009. "Toward a Cartography of the Commons: Constituting the Political and Economic Possibilities of Place." *Professional Geographer* 61 (4): 493–507.

Streenivasan, Jyotsna. 2000. *Ela Bhatt: Uniting Women in India.* New York: Feminist Press at the City University of New York.

Sullivan, Zoreh T. 2000. "Eluding the Feminist, Overthrowing the Modern? Transformations in Twentieth-Century Iran." In *Global Feminisms since 1945: A Survey of Issues and Controversies*, edited by Bonnie G. Smith, 215. London: Routledge.

Sweetman, Caroline. 1997. *Men and Masculinity.* Edited by C. Sweetman. Oxford: Oxfam.

Tansel, Aysit. 2000. "Wage Earners, Self-Employment and Gender in the Informal Sector in Turkey." *Gender and Development* 24: 1–46.

Tendlar, Judith. 1989. *Power in the Movement: Whatever Happened to Poverty Alleviation?* New York: Ford Foundation.

Timberg, Thomas. 1995. "Review Article: The Poor versus the Disfranchised: Welfare versus Empowerment." *Economic Development and Cultural Change* 43 (3): 651.

Tinker, Irene. 1997. "The Making of the Field: Advocate, Practitioners and Scholars." In *The Women, Gender and Development Reader*, edited by Duggan Lynn, Lauri Nisonoff, and Van Wiegersma, 33. London: Zed Books.

Tipple, Graham. 2005. "The Place of Home-Based Enterprises in the Informal Sector: Evidence from Cochambamba, New Delhi, Surabaya and Pretoria." *Urban Studies* 42 (4): 611–32.

Tohidi, Nayereh. 2007. "Muslim Feminism and Islamic Reformation: The Case of Iran." In *Feminist Theologies: Legacy and Prospect*, edited by Rosemary Radford Ruether, 93. Minneapolis, MN: Fortress Press.

Topalov, Christian. 1999. "Les 'Réformateurs' Et Leurs Réseaux: Enjeux D'un Objet De Recherche." In *Laboratoires Du Nouveau Siécle: La*

Nébuleuse Réformatrice Et Ses Réseaux En France, 1880–1914, edited by C. Topalov, 11. Paris: Editions de l'école des Hautes Études en Sciences Sociales.

Tremblay, Crystal. 2009. "Advancing the Social Economy for Socio-Economic Development: International Perspectives." *Public Policy Paper Series* 1 (September): http://dc.msvu.ca:8080/fr/bitstream/handle/10587/570/paperfinal.pdf?sequence=1.

Truman, Harry. 1949. Inaugural Address. Trumanlibrary.org. http://www.trumanlibrary.org/educ/inaug.htm.

Tsikata, Dzodzi, and Joanna Kerr. 2001. Introduction to *Demanding Dignity: Women Confronting Economic Reforms in Africa*, edited by Dzodzi Tsikata and Joanna Kerr. Ottawa: North-South Institute.

Tucker, Judith E. 1976. *Egyptian Women in the Work Force: An Historical Survey*. Middle East Research & Information Project.

———. 1985. *Women in Nineteenth-Century Egypt*. Cambridge: Press Syndicate of the University of Cambridge.

———. 1993. *Arab Women: Old Boundaries, New Frontiers*. Indiana Series in Arab and Islamic Studies. Bloomington: Indiana University Press.

Uemura, Takehiko. 2000. *Sustainable Rural Development in Western Africa: The Naam Movement in the Six S*. Sustainable Development Department (SD), Food and Agriculture Organization of the United Nations (FAO). http://www.fao.org/sd/rodirect/roan0006.htm.

United Nations (UN). 2003. *United Nations Common Country Assessment of the Islamic Republic of Iran*. Tehran: United Nations.

United Nations Development Programme (UNDP). 2006. "Towards the Rise of Women in the Arab World." In the *Arab Human Development Report*. New York: Regional Bureau for Arab States.

US State Department. 2006. *Country Reports on Human Rights for 2005: Iran*. Washington, DC: State Department.

Vuorinen, P. et al. 1999. "Elargir le Marché du Travail pour une Cohesion Sociale. Une recherche d'initiatives pour la création d'emplois." Final report for the Council of Europe, Office of the European Committee for Social Cohesion, 2nd meeting, Strasbourg, June.

Wade, Robert. 1988. *Village Republics: Economic Conditions for Collective Action in South India*. Cambridge, UK: Cambridge University Press.

———. 1990. *Governing the Market: Economic Theory and the Role of Government in East Asian Industrialization*. Princeton, NJ: Princeton University Press.

Wallerstein, E. 1974. *The Modern World System: Capitalist Agriculture and the Origins of the European World Economy in the Sixteenth Century*. New York: Academic Press.

Walras, Léon. 1868. *Recherche De L'idéal Social: Leçons Publics À Faites*. Paris: Guillaumin.

Waring, Marilyn. 1990. *If Women Counted*. San Francisco: HarperCollins Publishers.

———. 1999. *Counting for Nothing: What Men Value and What Women Are Worth.* Toronto: University of Toronto Press.

Westlund, Hans. 2003. "Social Economy and Employment—The Case of Sweden." *Review of Social Economy* 61 (2): 163.

Williams, Colin C. 2006. *The Hidden Enterprise Culture: Entrepreneurship in the Underground Economy.* Northampton, MA: Edward Elgar.

Williams, Fiona. 1998. "Troubled Masculinities in Social Policy Discourses: Fatherhood." In *Men, Gender Divisions and Welfare*, edited by J. Edwards, J. Hearn, and J. Popay. London: Routledge.

Women Manager Entrepreneurs Association. 2004. Proceedings of the First Conference on Social Entrepreneurship, Tehran.

Woolcock, Michael. 1998. "Social Capital and Economic Development: Toward a Theoretical Synthesis and Policy Framework." *Theory and Society* 27 (2): 151.

World Bank Group. 2007. *Genderstats.*

Yegenoglu, Meyda. 1998. *Colonial Fantasies: Towards a Feminist Reading of Orientalism, Cambridge Cultural Social Studies.* Cambridge, UK: Cambridge University Press

Index

Beneria, Lourdes, 25, 73
Bourdieu, Pierre, 23–24, 28, 69

Chambers, Robert, 18
Chen, Martha, 55

development and development theory, 4, 13
  associative movements, 38
  center/core-periphery, 6
  community-based, 34, 39
  community-development programs, 26
  community economic development, 38
  community social capital, 26
  democratic participation, 36
  economic development, 3, 5, 9, 12, 23, 25, 30, 36, 38, 39, 47, 78
  economic empowerment, 22, 48, 131–32, 171, 187–88
  empowerment, 22, 32, 34, 36, 48, 58, 131–33, 171, 187–88
  ethnocentric, 9
  Global South, 17, 50, 52, 56
  Grameen Bank, 29, 31, 34, 41
  habitus, 23–24, 28
  international development, 3, 8, 33, 44
  Keynesian model, 7
  market-led, 21–22, 26, 30–31
  market-led growth, 22, 31
  minimalist state, 12, 25
  modernization, 6–9, 11, 14–15, 19, 25, 47, 73–75, 78, 86
  modernization theory, 6, 47
  neoclassical economics, 28
  neoliberalism, 7, 25, 28, 30, 39
  poverty-alleviation, 40, 178
  poverty-relief, 26
  social safety net, 3–4, 22, 34–35, 40, 70, 103, 142, 171–72, 186
  Third World, 3, 9, 10, 12, 15, 17, 18, 19, 52, 73, 76
  underdeveloped, 5–8
  Westernization, 8–9, 12, 78, 88

economy, 3, 5, 7, 9, 15, 20–23, 25, 28, 29, 30, 32, 34–40, 42–58, 60–64, 66, 68–70, 73–74, 76–78, 80, 82, 85–86, 88–90, 99, 103, 106, 113, 117, 130, 149, 150, 163, 171–73, 177–78, 186–87
  cooperatives, 33, 37, 39, 172, 179, 181
  female labor market/ force, 46, 77, 85–88, 91, 163
  gross domestic product (GDP), 8, 49
  gross national product (GNP), 5
  Human Development Index (HDI), 85

economy (*continued*)
International Monetary Fund, 9, 197
labor market, 13, 37, 46, 50, 55, 62, 65, 69, 82
Newly Industrialized Countries (NICs), 7
OPEC, 7
public-sector, 37, 39, 78, 96–98
unemployment, 4, 17, 32–33, 48, 50, 52, 62–63, 82, 88, 89, 92, 94, 99–100, 103, 105, 113, 121, 156, 171, 188
unemployment benefit, 113
unions, 5, 37, 39
World Bank, 9, 19, 22, 27, 58, 86
entrepreneurship, 4, 13, 21, 29, 40, 42–45, 48–49, 53–54, 66–67, 95, 102, 171, 173, 186
female entrepreneurship, 13, 44
small and medium enterprises (SMEs), 44, 102
social enterprises, 39
Escobar, Arturo, 9
Esim, Simel, 59–60

feminist theory, 15
Haraway, Donna, 14, 19
Harding, Sandra, 13
Longino, Helen, 13, 30
See also postcolonialism: postcolonial feminist theory
Foucault, Michel, 11

informal economy, 3, 20, 22, 29, 34, 40, 42–58, 60–64, 68–70, 73, 77, 113, 130, 149
casual labor, 45–46, 49, 58
De Soto, Hernando, 47
dualist school, 48
formal economy, 21, 45–49, 58, 60, 73, 76–78
Hart, Keith, 46
informal market, 44–45, 47–48, 57–58, 60, 62, 66, 69
informal networks, 24, 28
invisible economy, 3
legalist school, 47
low-paid jobs, 54, 148, 152, 157, 181
modernization school, 47
own-account workers, 45, 55, 66
parallel economy/market, 3, 69
seasonal labor, 58
self-employment, 32, 33, 45, 49, 180
shadow economy, 3
structuralist school, 48
underemployment, 58
international organizations, 48, 162, 164
Bangladesh Rural Advancement Committee (BRAC), 30, 40–41
Global Entrepreneurship Monitor (GEM), 44
Green Belt Movement (GBM), 40–41
International Labour Organization (ILO), 46
Organization for Economic Co-operation and Development (OECD), 44
Self-Employed Women of Ahmadabad (SEWA), 40
Swedish International Development Agency (SIDA), 44
United Nations Development Fund for Women (UNIFEM), 57
Women in the Informal Economy: Globalizing and Organizing (WIEGO), 48, 54, 70, 73

Kabeer, Naila, 15, 29

masculinity, 161, 163
masculinity crisis, 163

Mayoux, Linda, 29, 34
microfinance, 21, 29, 42–43, 59
  microcredit, 4, 13, 22, 28–35, 94
  microenterprise, 28–29, 42–44, 48, 54–56, 59, 62, 64, 67, 94, 99, 148, 172, 185, 186, 188
  rotating credit and saving associations (ROSCAs), 26, 33, 38, 65, 70, 103, 127, 134, 166
  social collateral, 29
Moalem, Minoo, 17
Mohanty, Chandra, 15, 17

nongovernmental organizations (NGOs), 14, 29–30, 32, 38, 42, 60, 84, 94, 178, 183, 187

Orientalism, 3–5, 10–11, 19
Other/Othering/the Other, 11, 19, 21–22, 24–25, 34, 47, 69, 121–22

Paidar, Parvin, 15–16, 85
Portes, Alejandro, 22–23, 44
postcolonialism, 14, 16, 19, 20, 79
  colonialism, 5, 11, 14 (*see also* development and development theory)
  postcolonial feminist theory, 13, 15
Putnam, Robert, 22, 24

Said, Edward, 10–11
Sen, Amaryta, 8
social economy and social entrepreneurship, 1, 21–22, 28, 35, 36–40, 42–43, 171–73, 177, 186–87
  Ashoka, 40
  mutual help, 3
  people's economy, 38
  reciprocity, 22–23, 38
  reciprocity transactionism, 23
  social capital, 20, 22
  social entrepreneurship, 42–43
  social network, 1, 4, 20–23, 25–27, 33, 39, 58–59, 68–70, 101, 103, 114, 125–29, 133, 148, 166–67, 171, 175, 186, 188
  social transformation, 4, 18, 22, 31, 35, 40
  third sector, 22, 28, 35, 37–39, 42, 69
  voluntary self-help, 26
  See also development and development theory
Spivak, Gayatri, 14
subaltern studies, 13, 16–19, 21
  See also Orientalism; Other/Othering/the Other

Weber, Max, 6, 19
women/gender, 3–4, 11–13, 21, 31, 34, 42, 43–45, 48, 53–57, 59–61, 64–66, 74, 77, 86–87, 89–91, 95–98, 102, 116–17, 133, 149, 158, 162–64, 167, 173, 182–83, 189, 191, 194
  agency, 16, 19, 21, 44, 79
  female entrepreneurship, 13, 44
  female-headed households (FHH), 92
  gender-rights advocacy, 84
  gender segregation, 34, 59, 65, 86–87, 89, 91, 116–17, 167
  subaltern women, 21
Women Managers and Entrepreneurs Association (WMEA), 186
Woolcock, Michael, 22

CPSIA information can be obtained at www.ICGtesting.com
Printed in the USA
LVOW10*2037221013

358121LV00002B/2/P

9 781137 342867